SOCIODRAMA

SOCIODRAMA

Who's In Your Shoes?

PATRICIA STERNBERG
&
ANTONINA GARCIA

Foreword by
ZERKA T. MORENO

PRAEGER

New York
Westport, Connecticut
London

Library of Congress Cataloging-in-Publication Data

Sternberg, Patricia.
    Sociodrama : who's in your shoes? / Patricia Sternberg and
Antonina Garcia ; foreword by Zerka T. Moreno.
      p. cm.
    Bibliography: p.
    Includes index.
    ISBN 0-275-93053-X (alk. paper)
    1. Sociodrama. I. Garcia, Antonina. II. Title.
HM254.S74   1990
302'.15–dc20   89-33970

Library of Congress Catalog Card Number: 89-33970
ISBN: 0-275-93053-X

First published in 1989

Praeger Publishers, One Madison Avenue, New York, NY 10010
An imprint of Greenwood Publishing Group, Inc.

Printed in the United States of America

The paper used in this book complies with the Permanent
Paper Standard issued by the National Information Standards Organization (Z39.48—1984).

10 9 8 7 6 5 4 3 2

Copyright Acknowledgment

Grateful acknowledgment is made to Beacon House, Inc. for permission to modify and reprint
The Canon of Creativity by J. L. Moreno, from *Who Shall Survive?* 3rd ed., 1978, p. 46.

This book is dedicated to Jacob Levy Moreno, the visionary,
and to the dream of what sociodrama can accomplish in
connecting the world community.

CONTENTS

FOREWORD *by Zerka T. Moreno* xi

ACKNOWLEDGMENTS xiii

INTRODUCTION xv

PART ONE

1 Warming Up to Sociodrama 3

 Defining Sociodrama 3

 Similarities and Differences: Sociodrama and Psychodrama 5

 Sociodrama, Creative Drama, and Role Play 7

 Historical-Theoretical Background: Foundations and Origins 8

 Moving Forward 12

 Summary 12

2 Examining Sociodrama Structure 15

 Sociodrama Components 15

 Sociodrama Goals 21

 Holistic Benefits 24

 Summary 24

3   Getting Started   25
     Discovering Common Denominators and Central Issues   25
     Designing a Warm-Up to Suit Your Group   26
     Warm-Ups and Ice Breakers   28
     Warm-Ups for Cohesive Groups   31
     Warm-Ups for Terminating Groups   33
     Summary   34

4   Moving from Warm-Up to Action   37
     Translating Individual Issues to Group Action   37
     Enlisting Enactors   43
     Interviewing the Enactors   44
     Setting the Scene   45
     Summary   46

5   Exploring Roles, Expanding Roles   47
     Examining Old Roles and Trying Out New Ones   47
     Exploring Differences Between Individuals and Groups   52
     Summary   53

6   Structuring the Action   55
     Often-Used Techniques: What They Are, When to Use Them   55
     Summary   68

7   Assessing Needs and Meeting Goals   71
     Reviewing Themes   71
     Facilitating the Goal of Catharsis   71
     Facilitating Action Insight   73
     Facilitating Role Training   74
     Going with Resistance   75
     Finding the Balance Between Letting Go and Self-Control   77
     Closing the Action   78
     Summary   79

8   Taking Stock and Moving Forward   81
     Setting the Tone for Sharing   81
     Sharing Experiences   82

De-Roling   84

Reaching Closure   84

Trying Out Alternative Solutions   85

Summary   86

9   Mastering Directing Skills   89

Warming Up for Directing   89

Warming Up with the Group   91

Creating a Safe, Nonjudgmental Environment   93

Facilitating Group Process   98

Summary   100

10   Examining Sociodrama Underpinnings   101

Surveying Moreno's Theories   101

Examining Moreno's Role Theory   101

Exploring Spontaneity Theory   107

Exploring Sociometric Theory   112

Summary   116

PART TWO

11   Sociodrama in Theatre   119

Defining Theatrical Areas   119

Using Sociodrama in Theatre   120

Creating Plays Through Sociodrama   120

Using Sociodrama in Theatre Education   123

Using Sociodrama in Theatre in Education   126

Summary   126

12   Sociodrama in Education   127

Giving Background   127

Using Sociodrama in Teaching History and Social Studies   128

*Using Sociodrama in Understanding Cultural Issues and in
Teaching Languages*   129

Using Sociodrama in Teaching Literature   132

Using Sociodrama in Teaching Psychology and Nursing Skills   133

Using Sociodrama in Adult Education   134

	Using Sociodrama in Religious Education	135
	Summary	135
13	Sociodrama in the Workplace	137
	Using Sociodrama in Business and the Professions	137
	Using Sociodrama to Train Personnel	138
	Using Sociodrama for Team Building and Networking	142
	Using Sociodrama to Unlock Creativity and Generate New Choices	144
	Summary	146
14	Sociodrama in the Community	147
	Focusing on Origins	147
	Exploring Social Issues, Resolving Community Problems	148
	Exploring Prejudice Through Sociodrama	150
	Summary	153
15	Sociodrama in Psychotherapy	155
	Giving an Overview	155
	Developing Social Skills	156
	Reducing Isolation	157
	Restoring Spontaneity	158
	Expanding Role Repertoire	159
	Enhancing Self-Esteem	160
	Learning New Behavior	161
	Summary	163
16	Pulling It All Together	165
	Hearing What Experienced Leaders Say with contributions by G. Max Clayton, Linda Gregoric Cook, Ken Sprague and Marcia Karp, Dale Richard Buchanan, Madeleine Byrnes and Barry Stevens, David F. Swink, Ann E. Hale, Warren Parry, Abel K. Fink, Adam Blatner and Allee Blatner, and Rosalie Minkin	165
	Summary: Drawing Conclusions, Beginning Anew	179
	APPENDIX	181
	BIBLIOGRAPHY	189
	INDEX	195
	ABOUT THE AUTHORS AND CONTRIBUTORS	199

FOREWORD

The subtitle of this book is a reformulation of a wise Native American's resolution: "Let me not judge a man till I have walked a mile in his moccasins."

There are many ways to speak of sociodrama or role playing, as it is now generally called, but the point I wish to make here is that genius resides in seeing the obvious and simple in a new way. Jacob Levy Moreno, as an educator, dramaturge, and healer of the mind, besides being a poet and philosopher, was responding to the voice of an inner muse that pointed out to him that man's mind is not a closed system. He did not believe that, however important individual psychotherapy may be, it would or could respond satisfactorily to the many ills of mankind.

When facing another human being in a battle of wits and mind, how often do we say to our opponent: "Put yourself in my position. What would you have done?" Moreno made that question into an answer. Indeed, he said for us to experience each other truly, we must *both* reverse our positions and enter into the subjectivity of the other mutually, not unilaterally. But the only way to do this is in action. Thus he began to look for a medium that could carry this burden and found it in improvisational theatre, later called by him the Theatre of Spontaneity.

The cataclysmic aftermaths of World War I inspired him to take his idea before the public and, according to his story, which may be apocryphal, he held a session on April Fool's Day, 1921, in a theatre in Vienna to test some of the audience for their ability to become the new world leader and to bring it to peace. Apocryphal or not, his intent was clear—namely, that a new kind of leader was needed. The hidden, subtler message was that leaders are often there in front of us, and we fail to recognize them. Moreno surely had some such idea in mind as well, and he hoped to become a more visible one, with positive energies.

Regrettably, no such leader emerged from his very first sociodrama; instead, there emerged fanatic nationalism with its twin, fascism, and communism—all of them apparently bent upon bringing the world to the precipice. The leaders of these movements, the negative ones, were allowed to lead us into World War II, which brought its own, even greater horrors. That war made us once again part of a larger universe, highlighting our intertwined destinies with others.

Thus it may not be too surprising, in retrospect, that Moreno once again turned his attention to the concerns of the collective elements in human endeavor and how they can turn destructive. In 1943 he wrote his chapter "The Concept of Sociodrama," later incorporated into the first *Psychodrama* volume. That year, 1943, was a watershed in the history not only of the world at large, but in the United States. We were not faring too well militarily; we were facing dangerous and implacable barriers to world peace, in the West and the East. Eventually, together, some delicate balance was restored. It is still delicate though the protagonists have shifted positions.

This is the larger background against which the idea of sociodrama emerged. Moreno directed a number of sociodramas throughout his lifetime, including one exploring the events of the 1948 Harlem riots, the Henry Wallace disturbances in 1949, the Eichmann trial, the John Kennedy assassination, to mention but a few. During World War II there were sessions on the black-white problems, the Japanese-American confrontation, the difficulties facing returning soldiers after the war who had married former so-called enemies, and so on.

While Moreno's work has not yet become an instrument for universal peace as he, the utopian, had hoped, we must not overlook the possibility of helping peaceful interaction on a small scale, hoping that this effort will become a cornerstone in a much larger edifice. Moreno thought we might learn more from small group interaction than from the anonymous monolithic forms, as medical science began to throw light upon disease by dealing with its microscopic elements.

The authors of this book are making a meaningful and carefully thought-out contribution toward using sociodrama for mediation in many settings. Their work must be applauded and may well be one of the rivulets that will eventually lead into a larger confluence toward greater peace in the world. Peace, like charity, should begin at home. In these pages the reader will find excellent guideposts for their own work in this field.

Zerka T. Moreno

ACKNOWLEDGMENTS

The authors wish to acknowledge the support and assistance of many people in the preparation of this book:

Eduardo Garcia for his unstinting contributions to the book. He has provided both editorial and technical assistance. He has also given Antonina Garcia limitless emotional support and patience throughout the process.

Dollie Beechman Schnall for her very astute editing and her unerring eye for the misspelled word and misused grammatical construction.

Richard Sternberg and Alexandra Garcia for their understanding, support, sense of humor and, best of all, good hugs.

Cathy Blackburn for her careful reading and comments, Yvonne De Carolis for her word processing assistance, and Linda Albert for her assistance with Chapter 13, "Sociodrama in the Workplace."

Natalie Winters, Bill Woodruff, and Dale Buchanan, great cheerleaders all, for their encouragement and discussions about sociodrama and this book.

Dr. Robert Siroka and Jacqueline Dubbs-Siroka for introducing Antonina Garcia to sociodrama, for training her and supervising her early work in the field.

The support of the Department of Theatre and Film at Hunter College and the Speech/Theatre Team at Brookdale Community College.

The Huntington Hospital staff, the Psychology Department of Eastern State School and Hospital, for their enthusiasm about Patricia Sternberg's use of sociodrama.

Our clients and students, past and present, who have enriched our experience of sociodrama through their spontaneity.

INTRODUCTION

Sociodrama is a group learning process focused on providing practice in solving problems of human relations. It also helps group members to clarify values and feelings and gives them an opportunity to practice new behaviors. The group is the subject. The focus is theme- and situation-oriented. Sociodrama unlocks the common threads of human experience for everyone. It illuminates the thoughts, feelings, and hopes of all who participate. It offers the chance for those participants to learn about themselves, the world, and their place in it. People can try on new ways to encounter each other and experience the power of group support. They can enjoy the feelings of being in another person's shoes—playing another role—as well as learning the liberating experience of expanding their own primary roles in life. Those who have participated in sociodrama with an experienced leader are overwhelmingly enthusiastic about the experience. It is a nonthreatening, nonjudgmental method of exploring and experiencing problem solving.

Although sociodrama is used throughout the world, it is still not practiced as widely in the United States as it is elsewhere. The reason is obvious. There is no book on sociodrama to guide would-be practitioners in the field. Even though there are articles and short sections in a few publications and one text written in 1949 (Haas), a book such as this is long overdue. There are courses in sociodrama offered in various parts of the country (both authors teach such courses), but even for such course work, there is no textbook or definitive "how-to" work written in this field.

Sociodrama: Who's In Your Shoes? will offer that guidance both theoretically and practically. It is meant to serve business people; educators on a variety of levels; psychotherapists; sociologists; psychologists; psychodramatists and drama therapists; guidance and career counselors; political activists; recreational specialists and other group leaders of special populations, such as substance abusers, psychiatric patients, and incarcerated groups.

Even though skilled practitioners in the field of sociodrama are relatively few in number, both of the authors, Professor Patricia Sternberg of Hunter College in New York City and Professor Antonina Garcia of Brookdale Community College in Lincroft, New Jersey, have not only taught courses in sociodrama but have also conducted a variety of workshops and demonstrations throughout the country. In addition, they have extensive experience in conducting sociodrama groups with a variety of populations. They share years of experience, knowledge, understanding, and unlimited enthusiasm about the power of sociodrama.

Sociodrama: Who's In Your Shoes? is designed to help the reader understand how and why sociodrama works so powerfully. It also provides practical advice on how to conduct sociodrama sessions. Part One will explore the historical and theoretical foundations of sociodrama. Most importantly, though, in this section of the book you will learn how to structure a sociodrama session, how to move toward accomplishing group goals through enactment, and how to avoid some of the pitfalls of sociodrama directing. Part Two will focus on how to use sociodrama in various fields: education, business, therapy, social action, and theatre. It will also contain essays written by other sociodramatists who discuss how they use this vibrant modality.

Jacob Levy Moreno believed deeply in spontaneity and creativity and the importance of using these to transform the world around us and within us. It is in this spirit that the authors wrote this book. Having learned and read about sociodrama, having observed others direct, we have developed our sense of the art of sociodrama direction. If our reader is new to sociodrama, we encourage you to use this book as a jumping-off place from which to develop your own spontaneity and creativity as a sociodrama director. If the reader is already well-versed in sociodrama, we warmly share with you our experience, knowledge, and deep satisfaction of using the modality.

Sociodrama can literally transform your life by changing the way you look at problem solving. It can teach you the excitement of exploring *the new* as well as discovering unexplored facets of *the old*. The authors invite you to join them in exploring the many aspects of sociodrama and to discover new directions in problem solving. May you share as much joy and enthusiasm in reading this book and experimenting with its contents as the authors did in writing it.

Part One

Part One details how to conduct a sociodrama session from warm-up, through enactment, to sharing. It provides the historical and theoretical foundations for sociodrama. It gives the rudiments of sociodrama practice to anyone drawn to directing.

1

WARMING UP TO SOCIODRAMA

DEFINING SOCIODRAMA

Police receive a call that a husband is beating his wife on South Main Street. As they approach the door, they hear shouts and threats. They burst into the apartment to find a woman brandishing a meat cleaver. She and the man facing her are threatening each other. What will the police do?

A man is having a great time on the planet Venus. He is at a party meeting the planet's dignitaries. One is telling him about a super resort he really shouldn't miss while he is visiting. A multicolored creature with six eyes offers to teach him the latest dances while another hands him a plate of what he figures must be Venutian food. What should he do?

A newly divorced woman is going out on her first date in fifteen years. As her escort arrives to pick her up, she is trying to calm herself down, telling herself that he is a nice man and not the serial murderer who has eluded the police for months. Her oldest child teases her about her nervousness, and her younger child is so furious she is dating he won't speak to her at all. What should she do?

People argue heatedly at a town meeting as to whether or not a boarding home for deinstitutionalized adults should be built in their neighborhood. Some fear that their property values will go down. Others fear their children will be molested. Still others point out that the proposed inhabitants are harmless and have a right to live in the community. What should the town council decide?

All the vignettes mentioned above are scenes from sociodramas. They are performed by members of groups, everyday people, not actors. They represent some of the enjoyment, excitement, and intensity that draw people to socio-drama. Sociodrama is a group action method in which participants act out agreed-upon social situations spontaneously. Sociodrama helps people to ex-press their thoughts and feelings, solve problems, and clarify their values. Rather than simply discussing social issues, sociodrama gets people out of their chairs and exploring *in action* topics of interest to them. As they explore various issues, they put themselves in other people's shoes in order to understand themselves and others better. One of the reasons that sociodrama works so well is that it taps into the truth about humanity that we are each more alike than we are different.

Sociodrama concerns itself with those aspects of roles that we share with others. For example, all students study—at least occasionally; all emergency room nurses will encounter dying patients in the course of their careers; all police officers intervene in domestic disputes at one time or another; all em-ployees have bosses with whom they must deal.

Basing itself on the premise of shared experience, a sociodrama group might seek to define a problem members would like to solve: if they are social work-ers, they might want to be better able to deal with a situation in which parents deny a child's misbehavior at school. Additionally, the members may find a situation in which they would like to gain greater understanding: if they are police trainees, they may want to learn to understand a rape victim's feelings. The members might also define a decision they would like to be able to make—for example, students wanting to decide whether or not to go away to school rather than live at home and commute to school. Members may want to clarify their values regarding an ethical/moral issue: a community group may explore the ramifications of racism in their school system. Members may seek to train themselves in certain role aspects about which they feel uncomfortable: a group of the hard-core unemployed may want to role-train interview decorum. Fi-nally, members may want to become more spontaneous and playful: a group of tired executives may want to recharge their emotional batteries and restore their creativity so they can take pleasure in their jobs instead of simply putting in time until retirement.

Because sociodrama gives the experience of sharing concerns and roles with others, it most often occurs in groups. In a typical sociodrama session, a *warm-up* period takes place in which participants decide what topic the sociodrama *enactment* will explore. The participants volunteer or occasionally are assigned roles by the director of the sociodrama. The drama itself is never scripted but arises instead from spontaneous interactions among the *enactors*. After every enactment there is a *sharing* in which group members discuss the enactment, the solution or ideas it presented, and sometimes generate new materials for future sociodramatic clarifications. The sharing is a time to begin to process and integrate what has taken place moments before in action. With its action/reflection components, sociodrama speaks to both sides of the brain. It is a kinesthetic, intuitive, affective, and cognitive educational technique.

In leading a sociodrama session, the director listens for the various issues of concern to group members. These are called *open tension systems*. Out of the group interactions and statements of specific members, one major issue seems to excite the group's interest most. This is the *shared central issue*. It is the shared central issue that provides the focus for the sociodrama exploration: fear of success, for example. The director also begins to notice that members seem to be experiencing strong drives to fulfill some needs or desires, such as to act playfully, or assert one's independence. These drives are called *act hungers*. The goals of each sociodrama are achieved as the director helps participants to fulfill the act hungers. Sociodrama has as its goals *catharsis* (expression of feelings), *insight* (new perception) and *role training* (behavioral practice). Whatever the issue, sociodrama sessions provide an opportunity for people to express a whole range of emotions, from tears to laughter, from agitation to serenity.

Throughout our lives, we consider how to solve problems, clarify values, and change our behavior. These concerns are objects of discussions in groups. The problem is that talking isn't always enough to enable us to change our thoughts, feelings, and behavior. What we need is a holistic action approach in order to effect a thoroughgoing change. Sociodrama is one of the most efficient yet safe methods available for obtaining information in the area of psychic emotional experience without undergoing the actual experience.

SIMILARITIES AND DIFFERENCES: SOCIODRAMA AND PSYCHODRAMA

Jacob Levy Moreno, the originator of sociodrama, viewed each person as a composite of the roles he or she plays. When Moreno discussed role, he referred to a culturally recognized and agreed upon cluster of behaviors.[1] What Moreno also noticed is that each role has both collective (shared) and private (individual) components.

The collective components are those role aspects that people share in common. For example, we can take the role of police officer. Police officers fill out parking tickets; they arrest suspects; they attend to crime victims. These are role aspects police share. However, while all police learn to perform these common skills attendant to their role, each officer has unique styles of performing these functions. Thus one officer may first attend to a rape victim's physical and emotional state, while another will move quickly to collect information to apprehend the rapist.

Moreno devised two modalities to facilitate exploration of role: sociodrama for collective components and psychodrama for private components. Sociodrama, then, concerns itself with the collective role aspects. In a group for newly divorced people, for example, the sociodrama might explore how difficult it is to resume dating, or how to relate to former spouses in matters involving the children. Participants would volunteer to play roles the group wants to explore. Perhaps one would volunteer to play a potential date, and another the role of a newly divorced person. The group would decide on the setting and perhaps a role characteristic or two: "The first scene will take place at the restaurant where the daters have gone to dine. The woman is afraid her date will act like her former husband and isn't sure how she'll respond if he does." After the setting and any pertinent role characteristics have been established, the participants spontaneously enact the situation. *At no time in a sociodrama session would the group act out a specific member's problem or real-life situation. Rather, the group chooses a hypothetical situation to explore its shared underlying issues.*

Psychodrama, on the other hand, focuses on private role aspects and on the individual's personal problems. In a psychodrama group, Doris might act out a custody struggle she is having with her former husband, Mel. She would choose a member of the group to play her ex-spouse and would coach that person in how to play the role appropriately. Throughout the psychodrama, the focus would be on Doris, her thoughts and feelings about Mel. The group would assist in examining her life situation and finding appropriate and satisfying ways for her to deal with it.

Like psychodrama, sociodrama deals with thoughts and feelings. As such, participants often express deep emotions—laughter, anger, tears. Unlike psychodrama, sociodrama focuses at all times on the way participants tap into the collective issue and not the private, personal problem. Thus sociodrama is less self-revelatory than psychodrama. It attends to shared, rather than individual role aspects. Sociodrama creates "for instance" situations. Psychodrama recreates real situations or scenes from the individual's personal dreams or fantasies. Finally, sociodrama is primarily an educational modality, while psychodrama is a therapeutic modality.

There are many similarities that should be noted between psychotherapy and education. Each is concerned with human development. Both the educator and the psychotherapist want the people who work with them to grow and change, to have greater understanding of themselves and the world. Both help people to build proficiencies, to become more skillful in specific areas. Both are involved with the enhancement of self-esteem. As people feel more competent, they feel better about themselves. When viewed as a whole, education, as well as therapy, provides opportunities for people to interact and express thoughts and feelings. Language arts courses come to mind, in which students express their emotional and aesthetic response to literature, or social studies courses in which students interact about their opinions and values. Both education and psychotherapy have the ultimate aim of the evolution of the whole person.

Education and psychotherapy are different in that psychotherapy focuses directly on the ways in which a person has somehow become split off from himself and the rest of the world. Therapy helps a person to restore and reintegrate all aspects of the personality. For example, if a person is suffering from panic attacks, he withdraws from those around him. He is not aware of his own personal strengths and further may be unaware of some wounded parts of himself that need tending and nurturing. The educator, on the other hand, is not focused on a person's intrapsychic and interactional wounds. Nor is the educator engaged, as the therapist is, in the working through of these problems. The educator rather aids in human development in a global way through communication, inspiration, and the transmission of information.

Sociodrama, as an educational modality, directs its attention to human growth and interaction by attending to collective role aspects. It also promotes human development in a global manner. Further, like the most exciting educational experiences, sociodrama actively immerses the participant in the process. In the same way that a person can be moved by reading and discussing a novel and how one identifies with it, a sociodrama participant is involved, activated, and impacted by the group process as it creates enactments of importance to all.

SOCIODRAMA, CREATIVE DRAMA, AND ROLE PLAY

In considering sociodrama, creative drama, and role play, there are obviously more similarities than differences. In all three modalities, the techniques draw on a person's innate need and ability to learn with the whole body, mind, and intuition. However, whereas creative drama has spontaneity and creativity as its basic goals, and role play has sociological problem solving as its basic goal, sociodrama gives equal importance to the three. In addition it focuses on role exploration, role rehearsal, and role expansion.

Sociodrama, creative drama, and role play are sometimes confused with each other. Since the previous two sections dealt with sociodrama definitions, only a comment is needed here. Moreno's work focused on the "here and now," a term he coined. He saw clearly the psychological and sociological nature of the dramatic experience. His dreams for sociodrama went so far that he hoped to change the world into a more responsive, humane, and compassionate society through the use of sociodrama techniques.

Creative drama, on the other hand, concentrates on the individual rather than the group or society. Winifred Ward, an American and the founder of creative drama, was concerned with the "individuality of the individual" and helping each participant unlock his or her own particular creativity. To Ward, creative dramatics was "an inclusive expression designating all forms of improvised drama, dramatic play, story dramatization, impromptu work in pantomime, shadow and puppet plays and all other extemporaneous drama" (Ward, 3). She also believed that informal drama, like sociodrama, is created by the players themselves. It may be original as to idea, plot, and character, or it may be based on a known story.

Here is another definition of creative drama offered by the Children's Theatre Association of America:

Creative drama is an improvisational, nonexhibitional, process centered form of drama in which the participants are guided by a leader to imagine, enact, and reflect upon the human experience. Although creative drama has been thought of in relation to children and young people, the process is appropriate to all ages (McCaslin, 8).

Thus creative drama focuses on the creativity in every person. While sociodrama also follows principles of spontaneity and creativity, its focus is primarily on the group and on using spontaneity and creativity in problem solving and exploring social behavior.

Role play is the most commonly used group action modality. In it participants act out situations and discuss them afterward. Role play, which spun off from sociodrama and creative drama, is putting yourself in the role of another person or playing yourself acting or behaving in a way different from the usual role you play in life. The focus of the action is sociological.

In both sociodrama and role play, group members enact situations to rehearse behavior, solve problems, explore current or historical events, and develop sensitivity to other peoples' feelings. The major differences between sociodrama and role play can be discerned during the enactment segment of the session. Although both involve portrayals, sociodrama employs many specific techniques to deepen and broaden the scope of the enactment. Some of these which will be discussed in detail in Chapter 6 are: *role reversal, the aside, doubling, soliloquy, mirroring, the empty chair, future projection, freeze frame, sculpting, and walk and talk*. These techniques help participants to "shift perspectives, develop empathy in action, express a wide range of thoughts and/or emotions which would remain underdeveloped and unstated in a straight role play" (Garcia, 35).

It is important to mention that theatrical training and/or interest in theatre are unnecessary for sociodrama. The modality is not meant to train actors but rather draws on a person's innate need and ability to learn with one's whole body, mind, and intuition.

HISTORICAL-THEORETICAL BACKGROUND: FOUNDATIONS AND ORIGINS

Moreno

Jacob L. Moreno (1889–1974) is the originator of sociodrama. He developed it, coined the term, and gave it its original shape and substance. Sociodrama grew out of Moreno's love of the theatre, his interest in the dynamics of human encounter,[2] and his commitment to social action.

As early as 1909, when Moreno was a philosophy student at the University of Vienna, he began experimenting with theatre and dramatic play. He would gather children together in the Augarten and other Viennese parks and enact with them, first, well-known fairy tales and plays and, later, improvisational works from their imaginations and his own. Working with the children until 1911, Moreno began developing ideas about how basic the mimetic urge is. As he observed the children, he began to hypothesize about roles and the therapeutic and educational value of role-taking.

In 1913, while a medical student at the University of Vienna, Moreno began to explore the sociodynamics of adults. This came about in a rather unusual way. It seems that Moreno encountered a pretty young woman one day while strolling through the Praterstrasse. The woman was dressed in a red skirt and white blouse bedecked with red ribbons. No sooner had they begun to chat when a police officer appeared and carted off the woman. Moreno followed the two to the police station. At last, when the woman emerged, Moreno discovered that she was a prostitute who had been arrested for advertising her wares in broad daylight, and out of the red-light district. It seems that her gaily colored garment was viewed as an advertisement in Victorian Vienna. He also discovered that prostitutes had no rights under the law at that time and they were not permitted admission to hospitals.

How could it happen that prostitutes had no legal rights? Well, if sex didn't really exist in Victorian Vienna, then prostitutes certainly couldn't exist. And if they didn't exist, they didn't need hospitals or legal rights. Moreno could see the dangers arising from this level of denial. Although Viennese society claimed prostitutes didn't exist, there was no denying the venereal disease they transmitted. Furthermore, Moreno felt that these women should be accorded the same legal rights as every other Viennese citizen and clearly had a right to their human dignity. So the young activist obtained medial treatment for them, interested a newspaper publisher in the women's plight, and found them legal aid as well.

Most important, though, Moreno set up groups of eight to ten women, meeting two or three times a week. In these sessions, the prostitutes had an opportunity to air their concerns and provide help and support for each other. As Moreno observed the phases through which these groups journeyed, he began to develop ideas about how groups work and how collective role aspects bind people together and provide focus for group process. He also began to hypothesize about collective and private role aspects.

Between the years 1915 and 1917, Moreno was a medical officer at a Tyrolean refugee camp that the Austrian government had set up near Mittendorf to house those who fled the Tyrol before the oncoming Italian army. While working with this large group of people Moreno observed how they adjusted to their new surroundings and to each other. He was interested in how the refugees aligned themselves—socially, emotionally, and politically. He developed a plan for creating a community that was sensitive to people's choices—unlike the refugee community where people were thrown together regardless of their wishes. Although he was unable to implement his plan, the seeds of sociometry were clearly sown in Moreno's mind. (Sociometry is the measurement of interpersonal and intergroup choices. Through it one can explore people's at-

tractions, repulsions, and feelings of neutrality. The very fabric of the sociodrama session is based on sociometry: how group members interact, what issues
people choose to explore, and how they choose to explore them.)

After beginning to develop his theories through work with children, prostitutes, and refugees, Moreno turned his attention to the general population. As
a young physician and lover of theatre, Moreno had grown disenchanted with
the theatre of his youth; he felt it was no longer vital. It needed the active
participation of the audience and the spontaneity of the actors responding to
audience challenges to rejuvenate it. Moreno experimented with ways to make
theatrical experience more meaningful and communal through his development of the Theatre of Spontaneity (*Das Stegreiftheater*), 1921–1923. Moreno's
ultimate goal was not good theatre but rather community participation in community issues. Spontaneity was of paramount importance. The actors were to
be unrehearsed. There would be no scripts, but rather spontaneous interaction
among actors and between actors and audience. Process, not product, was what
counted.

Dr. Moreno gathered together professional actors and trained them in his
method of spontaneity work and as social researchers.[3] As social researchers,
the actors, and their director Moreno, immersed themselves in the news events
of the day. Audiences were invited to suggest current issues for spontaneous
dramatization. The actors would improvise the events and respond to suggestions from the audience for viewing the issues from various perspectives. Together, actors and audience created what Moreno later called the Living Newspaper.[4] It focused on sociocultural issues. Out of these early experimentations,
sociodrama arose.

Moreno also noticed that, in doing spontaneity work, occasionally private,
personal material emerged from his actors. He and his audience and actors
seemed as much moved by these spontaneous productions as by those engen-
dered by social issues. Out of this experimentation with actors' personal issues,
psychodrama emerged.

Moreno came to the United States in 1925. Between the years 1929 and
1931 he continued to experiment with actors and audiences in the Living
Newspaper format. He opened the Impromptu Theatre in Carnegie Hall, providing three sessions weekly. These sessions were open to the public, bringing
his ideas and practice to a wide range of people. Here again, as in Vienna,
Moreno trained professionals to enact situations spontaneously, which were
suggested by the audience or the events of the day. Audience members could
actively participate by becoming part of the enactment with the trained auxiliaries or they could simply observe the action. Later, as sociodrama developed
as a modality used in many settings, some sociodramatists continued to work
with a group of trained auxiliaries. The reader will see reports from some of
these in Chapter 16. Other sociodramatists directed groups in which the participants themselves volunteered to play all the roles in the enactments. It is

the latter type of sociodrama group to which this book directs it major emphasis.

Moreno worked with all segments of the population—infants, children, adults, and the elderly. He worked with business people, military people, and prisoners. He worked with the general public as well as psychiatric populations. Moreno saw sociodrama as being useful to all people wherever they congregate.

Stanislavski

In *As You Like It*, act 2, Shakespeare wrote:

> All the world's a stage
> And all the men and women merely players:
> They have their exits and their entrances;
> And one man in his time plays many parts. . . .

Acting is a basic ingredient of the theatre, but it is equally indispensable to human behavior. The means by which ordinary people convey their needs—words, gestures, body language, tone of voice—all of these elements are the same tools actors use on the stage to create a character and/or emotion. The basic difference between a person in real life and an actor on stage is that the stage actor is always conscious of a theatrical performance. Oftentimes this stage reenactment appears more truthful than situations we encounter in real life. This was not always true in the theatre, however. At one time all stage acting was much larger than life.

Stage realism came to the forefront of theatrical style in the late nineteenth century with three playwrights: Henrik Ibsen (1828–1906) of Norway, August Strindberg (1849–1912) of Sweden, and Anton Chekhov (1860–1904) of Russia. Each of these men wrote strongly realistic plays, which demanded a new style of acting, one that was equally realistic.

The man most responsible for creating this new technique for realistic acting was Konstantin Stanislavski (1863–1938). He developed a system, known as "The Method," which is the basis for virtually every approach to realistic acting. In *An Actor's Handbook*, Stanislavski (126) said, "The actor must first of all believe in everything that takes place on stage, and most of all—he must believe what he himself is doing—And one can only believe in the truth."

It is not clear if Moreno knew directly of Stanislavski's work, but it was available in the European and American culture at the time. Stanislavski had many ideas about imagination and flexibility that were mirrored in Moreno's work. Perhaps the most obvious was what Stanislavski called "The Magic If." We can imagine ourselves in almost any situation simply by applying the "Magic If":

"What if we have to save the children from . . ."
"What if we were alone and threatened by . . ."
"What if you were the director of the hospital and we wanted . . ."

Stanislavski urged actors to use this power of fantasy and imagination as a tool to induce reality on stage. He believed the goal of art was spiritual communication with people. Stanislavski saw the theatre as group process. He said, "The art of the theatre is collective work, it is essential that everyone in the group work for the benefit of the whole performance and not solely for himself" (in Moore, *The Stanislavski System,* 21). Moreno, of course, developed his Theatre of Spontaneity along the same lines. The basic difference between the two theorists is that Stanislavski chose art as the end to achieve his goal, while Moreno concentrated on process and actively involving the audience in that process to achieve his.

When "The Method" is examined, still more similarities appear. Stanislavski felt his system prepared the actor for an ensemble—the logical, truthful, purposeful, mutual behavior of all characters. Just as human behavior in life depends on relationships with other people, in an ensemble each role is conditioned by all the other roles. The same can be said for sociodrama in which the co-action of participants is of paramount importance. Although Moreno and Stanislavski had different objectives in their work, they both understood and respected the power of drama. Each of them worked throughout his life to help others discover that power and how to use it as a great equalizer for all people.

MOVING FORWARD

You don't need to be a sociologist or an actor to do sociodrama. Because it is based on the role aspects that we have in common, sociodrama can serve a wide variety of groups and is effective with all ages. Some of the settings where sociodrama can be used with great success are in schools, churches, businesses, psychotherapy sessions, social action groups, and theatre. The authors encourage the readers to find still more settings where sociodrama can flourish.

SUMMARY

Sociodrama is a group action method that deals with roles we share with others. It taps into the truth about humanity that we are more alike than we are different. Sociodrama helps people to *clarify values, problem solve, make decisions, gain greater understanding, learn to play roles in more satisfying ways, practice new roles, and become more spontaneous and playful.* Moreno devised two modalities to facilitate exploration of roles: sociodrama for collective components and psychodrama for private components. Sociodrama, then, concerns itself with collective role aspects and is primarily sociological and educational in nature.

NOTES

1. Moreno is not referring to "playing a role," a slang phrase for acting in a phony way.

2. Moreno first wrote about the concept of encounter in 1914 with his "Invitation to an Encounter."

3. An actor whom Moreno trained in this way is Peter Lorre.

4. The March of Time and the Works Progress Administration living newspaper project in the 1930s loosely fashioned their format on Moreno's Living Newspaper. However, they deviated in a significant way in that professional writers wrote scripts.

2

EXAMINING SOCIODRAMA STRUCTURE

SOCIODRAMA COMPONENTS

Moreno was a great believer in the "here and now," a phrase he coined. He felt that we could have the most meaningful encounters with each other if we were living in the present, open to interact with the people who are with us rather than thinking about the TV show we watched last night or about what we were going to wear Saturday on a date. He developed sociodrama as a way to help people encounter each other in the present moment. In creating sociodrama, Moreno defined three essential components to every session: the warm-up, the enactment, and the sharing. Without the presence of all three, the session ranges from less effective to ineffective.

The Warm-Up

The warm-up comprises the first portion of every sociodrama session. It is a time when group members withdraw attention from things happening outside the group and direct their attention to what is happening in the group at the present moment. When a person comes to a group session of any type, he is coming from someplace else. He may have just had an argument with his girlfriend; he may have just received a promotion at work; he may have overslept and rushed over.

Whatever he has been doing, he has had thoughts and feelings about the activity. He may walk into the room where the group is taking place, still running over the argument in his mind. Although his body is in the room where the sociodrama group will meet, his mind is in his girlfriend's apartment. The task of the group leader is to assist the members to cool down from the roles in which they were engaged prior to the group meeting so that they will not be distracted. He also warms them up to the role of group member and to the interactions taking place among members in the present.

The warm-up is the time when members get comfortable with each other, when the themes of the group emerge, and when members get ready for an enactment. Imagine if you walked into a session, and the director immediately said, "Okay, Mary, you'll play John's girlfriend. John, you'll tell Mary you have AIDS." PANIC! You'd probably be terrified, unwilling, embarrassed to portray this scene in front of the group, worried you would make a fool of yourself, furious with the director for putting you on the spot. Most likely, you would feel unready, not warmed up to the issues or to the idea of portraying them.

On the other hand, if the director gives group members time to interact with each other, discuss issues that are on their minds, choose what it is they want to explore, when the time comes for the enactment, people are eager to participate in the action and, lo and behold, don't feel a bit foolish or out of their depths.

One of the reasons that sociodrama is so much fun, so involving, and so relevant to group members is that the sociodramatic enactments are developed, decided upon, and created by group members. The director's job is to facilitate the group's exploration of issues it wants to explore, not issues the director wants to explore. The well-directed warm-up provides the director with the information needed to help the group get what it wants and needs.

The warm-up may be either cognitive or affective and may be either initiated by the director or by group members. Cognitive warm-ups provide information and speak to our intellect. Examples of cognitive warm-ups include lectures or discussions in which either the director or group members give the group information on a particular topic. For instance, the director may give information to personnel officers about methods of interviewing potential employees. Or, in a group of hotel desk clerks, one member may explain the procedure for crediting guest accounts when the hotel has made an error. Or a group of high school students may be discussing the requirements for writing personal essays for college applications.

Although the cognitive warm-up begins by presenting information, the information warms group members up to feelings they have in relation to it. When a high school student thinks about writing a personal essay, she is not merely concerned with her grammar and sentence construction. She is also concerned about how to present herself. She may feel insecure and worried. A lot is riding on what she writes, and she may be putting off writing the essay because of her fears. Thus, although the group has begun its work in a cognitive frame, the warm-up readies the members to deal with affective issues in the enactment.

An affective warm-up speaks directly to our emotions and our bodies. It is often interactional and physically active. It gets us moving and adds liveliness to seemingly lifeless groups. Every group leader has at one time or another had the experience of looking out at a group and seeing what seems to be a bunch of wax figures, silent with eyes glazed over. There used to be people in there, but who knows where they have gone. An affective warm-up often jostles and jollies a group into waking up and participating. In a group of teachers learning to deal with difficult students, the director might ask the teachers to take the role of students with behavior problems; imagine they are all in the school hallway; stand, mill around, and interact with each other as difficult students. Or in another group, the director may ask people to separate into pairs; imagine that a long-lost aunt has left each pair $1 million in her will. The only stipulation is that the partners must agree on how it will be spent. The pairs will have five minutes to decide how they will spend the money.

A warm-up may be either structured, like the two described immediately above, or unstructured. An unstructured warm-up is one that emerges from spontaneous interactions among group members and director. For example, as the members are filing into the room, one may be telling the others about unfair treatment he feels he has received from a fellow worker. Other members may begin to share similar experiences, recounting their own feelings of dismay, frustration, and annoyance. Out of this sharing of common issues, the enactment springs.

Whether affective or cognitive, structured or unstructured, the warm-up is essential in readying the participants to come together and develop the enactment. The warm-up allows the shared central issues of the group to crystallize and become apparent. The shared central issues are the tensions and uncertainties, the main emotional concerns that group members share at a particular time. Jerry felt hurt when his co-worker had called him lazy to their boss. Eleanor is upset that a co-worker accepted praise for some work Eleanor had done. Bart is frustrated that one of his team members isn't doing her share of the tasks and has indicated to others that it is Bart who is behind in his work. All three group members have told different stories, but the feelings and issues underlying the facts are similar: hurt at being misunderstood; disbelief that such a thing could happen; feeling let down; rage at unfairness; co-worker rivalry; desire to set the record straight. The common concerns beneath the stories are the central issues.

As the group warms up and when the shared central issue has emerged, the director facilitates the transition from warm-up to action by restating the issue and soliciting ideas for enactment from the group. The director might say, "We seem to be talking a lot about feeling let down and wanting to set the record straight. Other than these instances that have really occurred, in what situations might a person find himself where he would feel similarly?" Up to this point group members may have been sharing personal experiences. Now, the director is asking them to step back from their own specific experience and generate examples of similar but nonpersonal experiences. They may suggest the following situations: your roommate messes up the apartment right before people arrive for dinner. Your boyfriend arrives an hour late to take you to a concert, and you still have to pick up another friend who is going with the two of you. You had a major presentation due today, and your colleague left out a portion of the segment for which he was responsible.

After brainstorming different situations, the group votes on which one to explore in a sociodrama. Whichever they choose to enact, the scenes are tied to the shared central issue of the group. Remember, the members generated those situations based on the question the director asked relative to their main issues. Thus, even though Jerry, Eleanor, Bart, and the other members are not enacting scenes from their own lives, they are nevertheless dealing with the concerns underlying the scenes.

Warm-ups are frequently personal in that members are speaking about things that interest them and about which they have feelings. Nevertheless, sociodrama sessions are not psychotherapy sessions. "The enactments represent group issues in which the members explore societal roles they share. . . . The enactments are *not* efforts to solve a specific individual's emotional problem" (Garcia, 9).

The Enactment

The enactment is the second portion of the sociodrama session. It is the time when group members spontaneously act out a scene or scenes of their choice. After all, without the drama, where is sociodrama? The enactment seeks to address the shared central issue directly and to help participants express feelings about that concern in action, to understand it better, or to find and practice new ways to deal with it. If that group of teachers mentioned above wanted to learn to improve their skills in handling difficult students, they might enact a situation in which a student causes a serious disturbance in study hall. The member playing the teacher would represent the group in trying to solve the problem. Several group members may want to take turns playing the teacher, trying a variety of ways of handling the situation. Still others may be eager to play the student to gain a better understanding of what the student thinks and feels.

The values of enactment over simply discussing an issue are manifold. In a discussion, we often talk about our feelings, whereas, through enactment, we have the opportunity to directly express feelings we may have about a particular situation. Perhaps in similar situations in life we would not be at liberty to express our feelings fully. The frame of sociodrama provides a safe environment for the expression of emotions without reprisals.

In our everyday lives we sometimes feel that to make a mistake may be dangerous, costly, or emotionally devastating. Yet we have no place where we can practice how to behave and learn from our mistakes as well as our triumphs. Sociodrama provides that safety net for trying out new behaviors. Away from actual crime scenes, police trainees can practice how to intervene in domestic disputes, to negotiate for hostages, and so on. Away from bosses, employees can learn to ask for raises assertively; away from employees, bosses can learn to discuss employees' performance without alienating workers or discouraging their improvement. Teenagers can practice encountering parents regarding greater freedom. Newly transplanted workers can practice meeting new people.

When we discuss matters, it is easy to hide behind intellectualizing statements, to dream about what we would do in a particular situation without ever having to test out our thoughts and imaginings. When we are in action, we open ourselves to more possibilities. Because others are interacting with us in ways that we have not planned, our feelings, thoughts, and how we would handle a situation emerge spontaneously and honestly. This happens because our intellect and emotions are tied to our actions and interactions with others in role. For example, if I were a member of a group discussing ethical matters, I might espouse certain ideas about abortion. In an enactment, if I were to play a woman impregnated as a result of a rape and considering abortion, feelings I had not considered might arise. The issue may feel more complex than it did when I was simply discussing it. I might reassess and readjust my thinking. Conversely, my enacting a pregnant woman may confirm my opinions and reaffirm the values I stated originally. The enactment, then, is the heart of the sociodrama session. It is the action that provides us with the core of material to draw from in the sharing.

The Sharing

The sharing is the segment of the sociodrama session that occurs at the conclusion of the enactment. It serves to bond the group and to begin the reflection necessary to integrate what was learned through the drama. It is the time when members of the group have the opportunity to let each other know how they connected with what they just saw in the enactment. They may share feelings, insights, ways in which the action paralleled experiences in their own lives. Often, what one member shares will touch off new feelings and insights for other members.

During the sharing, the director asks participants to share their own feelings and experiences and discourages analysis of the acting or judgments about the feelings expressed by the enactors. He or she models acceptance of all viewpoints. It is important for the director to remember and remind the group that sociodrama is not a theatrical endeavor, thus the quality of the acting is unimportant. Process, not product, is paramount in sociodrama. It is interesting to note, however, that once a group becomes cohesive, enactors take roles with great believability. The reason is that once a person has assumed a societal role in relation to others, the coactions within the role relationships occur spontaneously and with feeling. Frequently, after an enactment, enactors will report being surprised to find how much anger, sadness, joy, and so on they experienced during the action.

The sharing is a time when those who actively participated in the enactment are reintegrated into the group. Part of this reintegration occurs because the members who viewed the action are actively connecting with those who enacted. They do this by sharing the thoughts and feelings the enactment activated.

One of the greatest values of sharing is that through the process individuals become less isolated. They come to see that others have similar experiences, respond similarly, feel as they do. This realization often comes as a great relief, especially when members are expressing feelings of anxiety or low self-esteem. In a session led by one of the authors, the group chose to enact a sociodrama in which an elderly man had married a very young girl. The author was surprised that the group chose this issue, since none of the prior group material indicated interest in this topic. The group explored the issues of familial and social acceptance of the match, explored how the couple dealt with social obligations to friends they had had before the marriage. The audience was deadly still during the action. In the sharing, first one, shyly, then more and more members revealed that they were either the older or younger member of a May/December couple. They also shared the relief and acceptance they felt at being able to speak openly as they never had before about their experiences and concerns.

The sharing is also a time for generating alternate solutions to the problems explored in the enactment. These solutions may be tried out in future enactments. Members frequently realize that there are many appropriate ways of solving problems. They also come to see that our criteria for choosing the solution we will use are dependent upon our personality characteristics and interpersonal styles. This realization helps participants become more tolerant of the differences among people.

Finally, during the sharing the group reaches closure on the issues explored. Group members share feelings, ask questions, discuss the action, and plan new behaviors. Through this process, they cool down from the enactment, move to a cognitive frame, and ready themselves for the end of the session.

In the warm-up, group members often share personal feelings and experiences and warm up to central issues that are then expressed in the enactment. In the sharing, group members again speak about their own experiences, this time in relation to what they have experienced through the enactment. The warm-up, enactment, and cool-down process is cyclical. An enactment and its sharing warm us up to issues in life, which in turn warm us up to other sociodramas.

Periphery/Center/Periphery

In sociodrama the intensity of the work moves from the periphery to the center and back to the periphery again. During the warm-up, the group is allowing its themes to emerge. The central concerns of the group are dealt with peripherally. The enactment moves the group to the center of the issue with which it is dealing. The sharing allows the group to return again to the periphery of its concerns.

Within each enactment, too, this model occurs. The first scene, which is more peripheral, warms up the participants to greater involvement in the action. As the sociodrama continues and the action moves to the center of the issue, the attention and work intensify. Finally, as the sociodrama nears its end, the director facilitates typing up loose ends, helping the enactors to return to the periphery of the issue and reach closure.

SOCIODRAMA GOALS

A sociodrama may have any or all of the following goals: catharsis, insight, and role training. The director assesses the need for these during the warm-up and facilitates the group's reaching them in the enactment and sharing.

Catharsis

Catharsis is a term Moreno borrowed from ancient Greek theatre. Aristotle used it in his *Poetics* to denote the purging of the emotions of fear and pity the audience feels when watching the fall of a great man in a Greek tragedy. When Moreno discusses catharsis in relation to sociodrama in his article "The Concept of Sociodrama" (1943a), he is referring to the deep expressions of emotions that take place in sociodrama enactments. He points out that this purging of emotions, unlike in theatre, takes place in the enactors as well as in the audience.

Catharsis is helpful to participants in that they may acknowledge and express feelings that were hidden either from themselves or others. They have an opportunity to vent pent-up emotions. This venting gives immediate relief, and it has an even greater value. When one's emotions go unexpressed, a person frequently finds it difficult to deal with a particular situation. It is as if those dammed up feelings stand as a barrier to one's full understanding of the matter and to one's spontaneity in responding to the people involved. Therefore, when one expresses one's emotions fully through catharsis, the barrier is removed, providing a starting point for viewing difficult situations in alternate ways.

Occasionally in life we find ourselves in situations where it is either inappropriate or unwise to express our feelings openly. Perhaps a friend has arrived an hour late for an appointment. You are with business associates in a crowded restaurant. It wouldn't be a good idea to shriek and storm out. Nevertheless, you may inwardly feel furious. If you were not in a restaurant but were instead enacting a similar scene in a sociodrama, you would have a chance to express the angry feelings and learn to deal with them.

It is important to note that although catharsis is one of the goals of sociodrama, personal attacks and confrontations are to be avoided. One of the positive legacies of the Encounter Movement is that people are more willing to share feelings in groups. One of the negative legacies is an abuse of the expression of feelings: people came to feel it was O.K. to say anything, no matter how hurtful, to each other. Such aggressive and confrontational behavior is in fact counterproductive to good communication. If Sue says to Mary, "You're a rotten person. You never act the way you're supposed to. Why don't you straighten up?" What is Mary supposed to say and feel? Should she defend herself, attack back, or what? Sue has not clearly expressed feelings, but has rather expressed opinions and judgments, although probably in an emotional manner. These judgments stand in the way of Sue owning what she herself feels and of her actually communicating her real feelings to Mary. For example, instead of telling Mary she feels disappointed that Mary can't come to dinner with her as she'd hoped, she angrily attacks her.

When the ground rules for the group are laid, it is a good idea for the director to spend some time explaining the difference between aggressive and assertive statements. It is also helpful to clarify what is meant by expressing feelings.

Insight

Another sociodramatic goal is insight. We experience insight when we recognize the true nature of something that we had been unaware of before. Insight is an "Aha!" experience. In cartoons, when a character achieves an insight into what is going on, a light bulb appears over her head.

We have all experienced insight. The value of insight is that it allows us to view a particular problem in a new and different way. For example, Jack suddenly realizes the reason he gets so frustrated when he speaks to Camille is that the tone of Camille's voice is similar to his sister's, with whom he always feels inferior. Recognizing that similarity, yet also that Camille and his sister are two different people, Jack may find he is now able to respond to Camille without frustration.

Insight has long been a goal of personal growth. Usually when we think of insight, however, we think of a person sitting and contemplating a problem and suddenly having a leap of understanding that helps to solve the problem in a new way. In sociodrama, the insight occurs in action. The enactor experiences the shock of recognition through expressing role relationships. Action insight is kinesthetically based. In a group of people whose goal is to develop socialization skills, members might enact a situation in which a person new in town is attempting to meet others at the community pool. The enactor playing the new person may realize in action that the reason he is having so much difficulty is that he is giving one-word answers to questions and staring down at the ground. He may also realize that the people speaking to him are trying to be friendly, unlike what he had anticipated. Finally, he may realize that his response to them doesn't match their input. As a result of these insights gained in action, he becomes more relaxed and takes the risk of being friendly to the people with whom he is speaking. Achieving an insight in action is often a powerful impetus for change.

Role Training

Lecture and advice are seldom enough to help us know how to act in an unfamiliar situation. We need to experiment and practice what to do and say. However, learning by plunging right into the life experience may be costly, embarrassing, possibly even dangerous. For example, when faced with an unruly prisoner, a new prison guard better be able to do something to handle the situation effectively. If he can't remember what he was told to do and isn't great at thinking on his feet, he may be in trouble. Experience can sometimes be a costly teacher.

Recognizing the potential problems and emotional duress involved in on-the-job learning, Moreno advocated role training as a way of providing an opportunity for people to try on new roles and situations in a safe environment. Role training, simply put, is behavioral rehearsal. Rather than face an actual prisoner, a guard in training could experiment with handling prisoners sociodramatically. He and other trainees could take turns acting as guard or prisoner in a variety of situations they will be likely to encounter. Thus, when he and the others are faced with difficult situations with prisoners, their bodies and minds will have had some experience in doing so.

In role training we may be trying out a new role or may be experimenting with better ways to play a role we are already playing in life. A group of angry teenagers may want to practice better ways to communicate with their parents. Whenever they try to talk to their parents at home, they get into fights. They can't seem to find a way to behave differently although they want to do so. In a sociodramatic enactment, there is no fear of reprisals for trying something new. Their parents aren't there to cry, swat them, or throw them out. They can practice as many options as their spontaneity and time allow. They can get feedback from their peers and try still more approaches if they wish.

Blatner (79) points out, "The function of behavioral practice is to experiment with a variety of new behaviors (1) in a fail-safe context, (2) with feedback regarding the effectiveness of these trial behaviors, and (3) with opportunities for repeated attempts until some degree of satisfaction is achieved."

On rare occasions, the authors have heard trainees say before trying role training, "What's the use of this stuff? It's not for real." They find out very quickly when they are in role and staring down the barrel of a gun or having to deal with someone playing an irate customer that they feel frightened, angry, frustrated, brave, or whatever else they would experience in life. The reason is that our feelings are connected to our coactions with others, and sociodrama recreates those role relationships.

HOLISTIC BENEFITS

Sociodrama is a kinesthetic modality that engages our emotions, minds, and bodies. Because it uses the whole person, it is appropriate for its goals to address that. Catharsis speaks primarily to the emotions, insight to the mind, and role training to the body. We know from life experience that any one of these goals may help us to change. Having a good cry helps us to feel better. Realizing that you dislike Jean because she looks like your "rotten" mother helps you to try to get to know Jean instead of assuming she is "rotten." Practicing speaking up for yourself helps you to tell the gas station attendant he overcharged you for gas.

However, it is equally possible that any one of these goals, taken alone, will be insufficient to insure change. Most of us have probably had the experience of ranting and raving at someone and still walking away unsatisfied. A person might also know that he eats more when he gets depressed, yet that insight may not stop him from reaching for his third piece of chocolate cake. Regarding behavior change, someone may stop drinking and still engage in alcoholic behavior. Recognizing that any one goal might be insufficient in a particular situation, in an effort to use anything and everything that works, and again because sociodrama engages the whole person, Moreno slated all three goals for sociodrama, to be utilized in any combination the group needs at a given time.

SUMMARY

We have seen that every sociodrama session has three components: the *warm-up*, when people prepare for action; the *enactment*, when members of the group participate in spontaneous dramatic action; and the *sharing*, when members let each other know how they have identified with the action, what they have learned from the action or how they might want to handle the situation themselves.

The goals of sociodrama are *catharsis, insight,* and *role training.* A given enactment may address any or all of these goals. Briefly, *catharsis* is a deep, releasing expression of emotion. In sociodrama, *insight* is a new realization occurring in and through action. *Role training* is practicing in an enactment new behaviors to use elsewhere in life.

3

GETTING STARTED

DISCOVERING COMMON DENOMINATORS AND CENTRAL ISSUES

Now that you understand the structure of sociodrama, its goals, and the benefits derived from the procedure, you are ready to start. As you know, an effective warm-up speaks directly to our emotions and our bodies. It is often interactional and physically active. Whether affective or cognitive, structured or unstructured, the warm-up is essential in preparing the participants to come together and develop the enactment. The importance of the warm-up cannot be stressed enough. It is the foundation upon which your sociodrama enactment is built.

The warm-up prepares your participants to work together and focus on the here and now. In this part of the session you discover the group's concerns and hypothesize what the group needs. You will help group members discover the many common threads of human experience. For some sessions you will structure the whole warm-up yourself, and with others you will guide the participants to create a warm-up according to their needs. With still others, the direction of the warm-up will emerge from the group itself. Whether you choose to structure a warm-up or prefer to go with the group's process spontaneously, it is useful to have a warm-up in mind in case the group is dry of ideas at a given time.

DESIGNING A WARM-UP TO SUIT YOUR GROUP

Where do you begin in planning your warm-up? The first question to ask yourself is, "How can I create a warm-up to match this group?" There are several significant considerations to keep in mind: size of group, age and/or experience level, physical well-being, emotional maturity or stability, and setting for the session. These are all points to consider before the group meets for the first time.

It is a good idea to check the above considerations ahead of time and incorporate your findings in the warm-up design. However, the more difficult problems are the intangibles inherent in every group, such as: Where is the group in terms of cohesion? How well do they know and respect each other and the leader? What is the trust level of the group? What are the goals and/or purposes of the group? It is up to the leader to help the participants discover what feelings and concerns the group has in common. Keep in mind that these discoveries take time and patience, but that they build group trust.

Most important, you as the leader must convey in your manner and presence that this will be a "safe environment" in which to work. That safety includes your assurance to the group that there is no "right" or "wrong" in this work or any possibility of failure, that confidentiality is to be maintained. Creating a comfortable, friendly, nonjudgmental, and nonthreatening environment for your participants is all-important. You can continually reinforce this atmosphere by your manner and behavior in a variety of ways. For example, seat the group in a circle if possible, and include yourself. This helps your members feel equal and be able to see each other. Also, it keeps your focus on them as a whole. In the beginning stages, be careful not to spotlight any one individual. Throw questions open to the whole group. It is important for the individuals to be comfortable with each other as well as with the leader.

One of the ways to assist groups in developing central issues and priming the communications pump is to design a structured warm-up to fit the needs and goals of the group. When designing a successful warm-up, the most important thing to remember is to pay attention to the group's needs. For instance, your warm-up with prisoners ready to be paroled will be different from one with housewives dealing with child-rearing issues. The warm-up for an ongoing group will be different from the first meeting of a new gathering.

If you find the group ready to move in a specific direction and to create its own warm-up, simply put yours aside for another time. For example, with an elderly population, the death of one of the members may occur the morning of the sociodrama session. Participants will most likely be more warmed up to the crisis than to whatever else was planned. You can use the opportunity to help group members begin to cope with the loss of one of their own.

What is standard procedure in one group could be totally inappropriate in another. For example, don't go into a psychiatric setting and begin with a discussion of today's news story of a sensational murder-suicide. Needless to say, initiating that kind of "today's news" warm-up could be too anxiety arousing for the population. However, if you are working with young women living in a dormitory on campus who are concerned with safety issues, starting such a discussion could be appropriate. (It should be noted that were the members of the psychiatric group to bring up the news of the murder-suicide themselves, it would be both appropriate and wise to attend to their warming-up process regarding the issue.) Keep in mind that your warm-up fulfills several purposes. Primarily, you are trying to facilitate that proper balance between being too excited and too lethargic. The warm-up design should serve as a readying process.

Many leaders use physical activities as warm-ups. Some include deep breathing exercises or guided physical relaxation. Others use sensory awareness exercises to warm up the imagination. Still others go further and utilize body warm-ups in much the same way as in actor training. These leaders feel that the enactor's instrument is composed of his body, voice, emotions, and imagination. They say that every individual can benefit from such physicalization. Just as the actor's instrument is tuned up in readiness to "play," sociodrama group members can benefit from this tuning up process as well. The format for these warm-ups will include physical exercises, body work, vocal exercises, and sensory work to flex the imagination and the emotions. Physical warm-ups are great for getting participants up and moving, engaging in activities all together with no focus on any individual. They are especially good with groups like the elderly who get very little exercise.

Once again, the group size and physical space are important in determining what body warm-ups you choose. If you do physical warm-ups, you want everyone to work together at the same time so that they ready themselves simultaneously. Therefore, scale the action to the space. A word of warning here! Many leaders who come from an acting/theatre background must remind themselves continually that they are not training actors with these activities but merely helping their participants to warm up for the enactment phase of sociodrama.

In fact, there are many ways to get people up and moving. Ask your group to move around the room and stop when they meet someone wearing the same color they are wearing. Direct them to share a happy childhood memory with that person. Or ask people to select partners and share a childhood ambition. Or ask people to take the role of their favorite animal and move around the room and vocalize accordingly. As you can see, the varieties of this type of warm-up are endless.

Whether you decide to use physical warm-ups or stick with discussion, all warm-ups in a new group or a group with new members should include learning names. It is always better to say, "I agree with what John is saying," instead of referring to him as "the guy in the red striped shirt." Even if all or some group members already know each other, if the leader doesn't know them, it is important to learn their names as soon as possible. Don't be surprised by some groups who live in the same place over a period of time and still don't know each other's names.

When your participants are ready to move on to the enactment, you'll know it. They will be at ease with you and each other, eager to proceed to the next level of work. Keep in mind that all warm-up activities have a dual purpose: to relax everyone involved and put each person at ease but at the same time to whet the appetite for further work. Don't rush the warm-up phase; it is too important to the entire process of sociodrama.

No matter what structured warm-up you use for any group, after each one, guide the group members to share their feelings about it. How did they feel? What happened? What did they want to happen? When many similar thoughts and feelings emerge, you will see that your group is ready for action. Ask yourself: What concerns are coming through? Are these central to the group? Shall we focus on specific examples for enactment? Are we ready for enactment?

WARM-UPS AND ICE BREAKERS

Warm-ups and ice breakers are essential to any group but most especially for new groups meeting for the first time. Each time someone walks into a new group, he or she experiences apprehension, fear, and suspicion in varying degrees. One may have thoughts like, "What if people don't like me?" or "I don't want to make a fool of myself," or "I won't know how to act." Similarly, most leaders know the occasional ordeal of walking into a new group and meeting verbal resistance or a hostile stare that challenges with the unspoken words, "Show me how this nonsense can benefit me!" Here is where a good warm-up can help members ease their way into group participation in a gentle, nonthreatening manner. A good rule to keep in mind for beginning groups is: the more structure involved in the activity, the easier it is for the participants.

Name Games

First things first. As mentioned previously, in any group, you want to recognize everyone by name. No one likes to be called, "Hey, you!"—not even the leader. It is best to start by going around the circle with everyone saying his or her name. One of the easier games to start with is the initial game. The leader says his or her name and one thing that describes himself that starts with the same first letter as his first name. For example, "My name is Pat and I'm Perky" or "My name is Nina and I'm Nimble." With certain groups, especially those with low self-esteem, you may want to add that the describing word must be something positive (keep it light-hearted; we are not looking for in depth self-disclosure here). After everyone has given his or her name and a word to describe himself, ask if someone remembers all the names. Encourage volunteers, and let anyone who wants to, try to repeat everyone's name.

If you prefer some action in the process and if members have at least heard each other's names, use a ball or bean bag for a kind of "name" tag. The idea here is to toss the ball to someone in the circle as you say his or her name. Let's say Harry throws the ball to Marge. As he tosses it, he says, "Hello, Marge." Marge in turn must say Harry's name as she catches the ball. Therefore, Marge would answer, "Hello, Harry," as she catches it. Marge now throws the ball to anyone else in the circle whose name she knows. The process continues until all people's names have been restated. If the process runs aground in that the member with the ball doesn't remember anyone else's name, ask him or her to choose someone whose name he would like to know and toss the ball to that person. The receiver repeats his or her own name as well as the name of the tosser. The tosser repeats the receiver's name before the receiver throws to someone else. (A variation on this, if you are sure someone will know the name of the receiver, is to have another member say the receiver's name when the ball is in the air.)

There are numerous name games, two of which are listed in the Appendix. Select the ones that you feel are appropriate for your group. Don't forget, sometimes name games bear repeating for several sessions and even to open each session if there is a significant time lapse between meetings or if new members have joined.

Ice Breakers for New Groups

Here are two warm-ups that work well with beginning groups to "break the ice" and create a relaxed environment. The third warm-up, the Headline Game, is equally suitable for new or already cohesive groups and is based on Moreno's Living Newspaper.

Getting-to-Know-You Circle

This is one of those rarities, an especially good ice breaker for large groups. Have a whistle handy. Divide your group into two equal circles, one inside the other. Direct the circles to face each other. At the sound of the whistle, the two circles rotate in opposite directions. At the next whistle, members stop and face the persons directly opposite them. Each participant introduces him- or herself and proceeds to find out as much as possible about the other within the time allotted (about one minute).

Blow the whistle again and repeat the procedure as many times as you like. Make sure you stop your circles in a different place each time so that different people talk to each other. You can add your own variations. It is helpful to prime the conversational pump by asking specific questions such as, "Find out something funny that happened to your partner as a child," or "Ask your partner about her favorite TV program and why she likes it." This simple activity is guaranteed to get people talking and generating interest in each other.

If your group seems relatively relaxed and comfortable, move into one large circle and ask for volunteers to tell what they remember about any one person they spoke to in the group. Next, ask if anyone talked to another who shared one of his or her own interests or concerns. You may notice some common issues come to light at this point. As people share what they discovered, you will notice certain themes emerging. Perhaps it will happen that several people were born outside the United States, or some had a pet who gave joy to their childhood. Maybe several admit to feeling nervous about meeting new people. In any group you are bound to discover commonalities, issues of mutual concern to the group. These are the issues you will explore sociodramatically when the group members are ready.

Common Denominator Game

Here is one of our favorite ice breakers for any size group. Direct your participants to count off by threes: 1-2-3, 1-2-3, and so on. If the group is very small, use pairs, mixing them up from different areas of the circle. Ask that people work with someone they don't know if possible. When the pairs or trios are established, ask them to take a few minutes and discuss three things they have in common. These commonalities are not to be anything obvious or observable, such as "We're all three wearing glasses." Instead, they must choose something nonobservable. For example, they may all three be great cooks, or studying karate. They may hate wrestling on TV or are allergic to long-haired cats. The point is, it takes a lot of conversation to find out what they do have in common. Not only are interesting similarities and differences uncovered, but also a sense of camaraderie develops during their search for what they have in common. Give them a few minutes for discussion. When each of the pairs or trios has completed the task of discovering three things in common, ask one person to act as spokesperson for the group and share their discoveries. You can play several rounds of this game, changing your threesome each time, or you can add others to the group. The more people in the group, the more difficult the exercise becomes.

After you have completed the Common Denominator Game as described, you might try some of these variations:

1. Discover a problem (or problems) you have in common.
2. Discover three concerns you share about your family, the environment, your country, your community, school, hospital, or whatever.
3. What current personal or work issues do you share with each other (your specific group in this location)?

Headline Warm-Up

Moreno originated the famous Living Newspaper format, where group members would create sociodramas based on the day's headlines. It works as well today as it did in 1921. Try it for yourself. This activity keeps your work focused on the group and not on any one person.

Bring in a newspaper. Members can read several headlines first and decide which ones they want to enact. Ask them which headlines appeal or repel. Give them some options such as acting out the situation that created the headline, acting the headline itself, or even acting out what might happen next. Let your players make their choices with a partner or in a small group. Advise them to discuss it first, then play it for themselves. When they are ready, each pair or group can share their enactment with everyone. If you want to add a little spice to the headlines, select some from the tabloids in the supermarket, like "Alien Abducts Housewife" or "70 Year Old Woman Marries Her Dead Brother and Gives Birth to Twins." Those add a sense of playfulness as well as fantasy. After everyone has shared their improvisations, the group may choose one headline to explore in greater depth through sociodrama.

If there is insufficient time for small groups to enact headlines, the leader may simply read headlines to the larger group and elicit those of greatest concern or interest for more discussion. The action can emerge from that discussion.

WARM-UPS FOR COHESIVE GROUPS

Cohesive groups demand a different kind of challenge. The warm-ups and discussion materials here must provide variety, high interest level, and enough difficulty to stimulate the group. When a group reaches the cohesive state, they are ready to confront problem issues and explore them fully. In addition, the tightly structured activities for beginners are no longer necessary. Open discussion usually prompts participants to come forth with several issues or concerns and/or problems for sociodrama exploration.

It is the leader's responsibility to evaluate the group's current stage of development. Have the norms of the group been set? Do people feel free to express their ideas and opinions? Do members value each other's concerns? Do they work together as a group rather than as individuals, each with his or her own agenda? If your answer to these questions is "Yes," then in all probability your group has reached cohesion. You are ready to design a warm-up accordingly. As always, listen to members' needs. Perhaps something was not completed from your last session, or the group may demonstrate a need to experience a warm-up geared to what happened to them recently. For example, say you are working with a group of nurses who had a suicide on their service during the week. They require a sociodrama to help them vent their feelings about the incident. Their warm-up may be discussing their feelings or where they were when it happened. All you have to do is listen to discover the direction in which to begin.

On the other hand, if your participants are business executives who are facing personnel cutbacks, their concerns are on future action. In other words, they are preoccupied with decisions yet to come. Who will they let go? How can they minimize the unpleasantness? How will they handle the added burden for themselves of more work? These issues and their personal concerns surrounding them are ripe for exploration.

You may discover, however, that there are times even with cohesive groups when you must prime the pump—give them a push to get started with meaningful discussion or a structured warm-up. When that happens, here is a "quick start" activity that promotes personal feelings and emotional reactions. It is a short open-ended dialogue that affords a transition for a variety of situations. You may be surprised at the feelings it will evoke and the drama that occurs even though the script offers only the simplest conflict with no indication of character. What happens is each participant reads into the situation, the characters, and their relationships according to what he or she is feeling. Two players read the scene until it stops. Then they improvise the situation from there. The leader can stop the action at any point thereafter. As you can see, there is no setting, no character description, not even gender indicated in the script. (Additional scenes are in the Appendix.)

ONE: Where do you think you're going?

TWO: Out!

ONE: Out where?

TWO: Just out.

ONE: Just out where?

TWO: What do you care?

ONE: Who said I care? I just wanted to know where you're going, that's all.

TWO: Well, if you don't care, it doesn't matter, does it?

ONE: No! You can go to hell for all I care!

If your players need help in getting started when the script ends, ask the following questions:

1. Who are the people in the scene?
2. What is their relationship?
3. Where is Two going?
4. Does One care?
5. What happens next?

You'll see how drastically the drama changes with each pair of players. Everyone identifies quickly and inserts his or her own *persona* into the scenes without even realizing it. Frequent comments are, "That's exactly how my husband talks to me!" or "That's my mother. That's just the way she is." Oftentimes people allow their own feelings to surface; however, when you are ready to move from the warm-up to the sociodrama enactment, you shift the action away from the personal, and to the group theme.

Another good energizer for cohesive groups is the physical warm-up. Usually, cohesive groups find it much easier to work in close proximity to one another. Physical contact and touching are a natural part of these activities. Here is a nonverbal exercise that will promote insightful discussion afterward. To begin, ask group members to stand up and form a circle with arms linked and both feet firmly on the floor. Direct your players to create a sound and movement in which the whole group participates as one. (They may not discuss it but are to let it occur spontaneously.) Try it again. Direct the group to move forward and back this time. Repeat the exercise on the right foot only. Repeat on the left foot, and move the body from side to side.

Of course, the important part comes next. Ask members to discuss their feelings. Did they feel support from each other? Did they feel they supported others? Did they want to? Did they feel like being one part of the whole? You will hear feedback like, "I felt totally secure" or "I was too tense to move easily," and even, "It was like being a link in a strong chain." You begin to hear similarities in what people say. Certain themes surface from which a sociodrama ultimately emerges.

You may never need any of these energizer activities, but if you do, they work well to stimulate feelings and discussion. When your group reaches a truly cohesive level, its energy is self-perpetuating. The group support inspires inventiveness and creativity. The sense of security gained from this cohesive state promotes a feeling of safety and a willingness to dig deeply into shared central issues.

WARM-UPS FOR TERMINATING GROUPS

Transitions are extremely important and stressful times. As it was essential to help individuals become comfortable being group members at the group's inception, it is equally important to devote your time and sensitivity to helping the group reach closure at its termination. If the group has been together for several months or longer, two–four sessions should be devoted to the leave-taking process. Many groups resist dealing with termination (as they resist becoming more intimate), but the leader must be firm and gentle in facilitating closure nevertheless.

There are several areas to address in helping terminating groups reach closure. It is important to provide a climate where people can express what they liked as well as what they didn't like. Group experience being imperfect like the rest of life, no matter how wonderful the group, people will have both negative and positive feelings about it. You may deal with these directly by asking members the following questions about their experiences in this group: What did you enjoy most or feel worked best? What regrets or disappointments do you have? What did you learn here that you will use in your life after the group is over? As a further warm-up, you might ask a group how they usually end relationships—in anger, in friendship, ignore them, what?

The warm-up for terminating groups is physically closer and emotionally deeper than for others. It must offer a feeling of sharing. Ask members what the group has meant to them and what they want to take away with them. As always, listen to the needs of the group and be aware of any unfinished business. One warm-up we have found to be both fun and enriching is to say to members, "If our group experience were a book you had written, what would be its title?" You might also ask members to title the first chapter, which is about the first session, and the last chapter, which is about the last session. Ask them also to choose one session in between the first and last which they found especially important and entitle that. After they have completed this process, they share their titles and experiences and create their final sociodrama.

Oftentimes, the last warm-up becomes a kind of ritual, giving a sense not only of the ending but also of a new beginning: Alpha and Omega, so to speak. Your goal here is to stress the continuity of what has gone before and what will come after. The greatest gift you can give any group is helping them realize they are not alone. Now they understand the process of sharing feelings and problem solving. Hopefully, they gain the insight to appreciate the possibility of finding alternatives in the situations they meet in life.

As a matter of fact, one young man returned several weeks after completing his work in a sociodrama group and confided to the leader, "You saved my marriage! There I was yelling at my wife in the same old way, when I remembered how we discussed feelings in our warm-ups and tried various alternatives in our enactments. It was almost like I heard a voice saying, 'There's always an alternative!' So I stopped yelling and said, 'Tell me how you feel about it, honey. Maybe there's an alternative!' "

Just as babies learn to crawl before they walk, so must sociodrama participants warm up to action before they can begin their work in problem solving, feelings expression, and values clarification.

Finally, remember that warm-ups are "warm-up to action" procedures. In order to get started, you must create the proper environment for your participants to be comfortable with themselves, each other, and the leader. Only then are they ready to discover their common denominators and shared central issues. Once these concerns burst forth, the commonality of the group is reinforced. Remember the purpose of the warm-up: to whet their appetites, pique their curiosity, and stimulate their desire for sociodrama enactment.

SUMMARY

The effective warm-up is the foundation for sociodramatic enactment. Therefore, in *designing a warm-up* it is essential to take into consideration the following: *population, size of group, setting, age and developmental stage of mem-*

bers, physical well-being, goals and purpose, level of emotional stability, and stage of group development.

All warm-ups have a dual purpose: to relax everyone involved and put them at ease but at the same time to motivate them for further work. After each warm-up, the leader guides group members to share their feelings about it. Are there any concerns coming through? Is the main shared issue emerging? The leader labels these, assuring the group that the work to follow is connected to their needs.

4

MOVING FROM WARM-UP
TO ACTION

TRANSLATING INDIVIDUAL ISSUES TO
GROUP ACTION

There are a variety of ways to tell when a group is ready for action. Members may be speaking eagerly about their experiences. Someone may say something that the others respond to with energy and spontaneity where earlier the conversation seemed to limp along. Several people may literally be sitting at the edge of their seats or expressing strong emotion when they speak. Once you have determined that the group is ready for action, as the director ask yourself, "What will the action be?" and "How do I enlist members to participate in it?"

In order to answer these questions, the director must listen closely and attend to the group interactions as they evolve. The group's dynamics are intensely important to the director, since the action emerges directly from the group's process. She must discover what common themes are emerging from the discussion that can be explored sociodramatically. As she listens to people tell their individual stories (plots), she listens for the themes (universal ideas and issues) that tie the stories together. Among these themes are unresolved issues shared by group members, for instance trusting a friend. They are called *open tension systems*. The director also listens for what specific needs people have that can be satisfied through the action of the sociodrama, for instance the need to assert independence. These are called *act hungers*. Out of the open tension systems and act hungers, one main issue crystallizes—for instance, setting limits with friends. This issue, with which all group members seem to be concerned, is called the *shared central issue*.

It should be noted that this may seem a complex process at first. It takes time and practice to master the ability to conceptualize group themes. However, once the director understands how to view a group in this way, the sociodrama flows effortlessly from the wellsprings of understanding group needs and interests.

Open Tension Systems

As group members interact during the warm-up, people share from their own life experience. The details of those experiences may be vastly different. Sometimes hearing so many different stories is confusing to a director, who will wonder how to determine what kind of sociodrama to do.

Although the stories are dissimilar, the director, by listening, will be able to pick up a variety of themes that underlie the individual plots. These themes represent feelings and issues that are unresolved, thus open. They are called *open tension systems*. The word *system* is used because these tensions are interactional, either externally or internally. Where the systems are internal, a person struggles within himself about an issue, for instance the person who says, "I really ought to exercise more. I'm out of shape and gaining weight. But I'm so tired when I get home at the end of the day, I can't seem to drag myself to work out. I don't know what to do."

Where the systems are external, the person is in a struggle with someone else. For example, at one sociodrama session Joe and Mark may be scrapping because Mark had agreed to pick up Joe for the meeting, but he was fifteen minutes late in arriving. Ellen, Jane, and Bob are expressing concern about what attire is appropriate for the lawn party their boss is hosting this weekend. Marie says she seldom gets asked to parties. Susie is very upset because she received a C for a paper on which she worked very hard. Jack can't figure out what the big deal is with Susie. She usually gets good grades and succeeds in other ways, and he has never been able to keep a job for more than a year.

Some of the tensions that underlie these varying stories are:

feeling misunderstood	feeling envy
feeling unimportant to others	feeling annoyed
worrying about being judged	feeling misjudged
feeling inadequate	feeling excluded

These upsets that have not yet been resolved make up the open tension systems. They are called systems because they are interpersonal as well as intrapsychic. The open tension systems are stated in abstractions and are the themes that underlie members' personal, individual stories and their interactions with each other in the moment: greed, rage, fear of intimacy, dependency/independence, trust/mistrust, and so on (D. R. Buchanan, private interview).

Act Hungers

While the open tension systems deal with the dynamics of the group and the group themes, people feel the need or impulse to take action in relation to those themes. If the theme is inadequacy, the group may have a collective urge to declare to the world, "Accept me as I am, and tell me I'm worthwhile!"

As people speak, the director begins to become aware of their strong impulses to say, to do, to hear, or to receive something. This urge to act or to receive is called an act hunger. With regard to saying something, some members may want to express how awful it feels to be excluded. Others, needing to do something, might want to express their anger by stomping out of a room during an enactment. On the other hand, members may desperately want to know what people do that gets them negative attention. Their need to hear this information is strong. Or members may need to receive hugs and reassurance.

Through the process of the warm-up, it becomes clear that group members share some act hungers. In the course of the sociodrama, the director performs interventions that give participants the opportunity to satisfy them. It is important to note, however, that in sociodrama the act hungers are resolved through the medium of hypothetical situations, not the members' personal situations.

When Moreno refers to act hunger in *Psychodrama—First Volume* (66–67), he discusses the infant's basic needs. He finds that the infant is engaged constantly in fulfilling, or engaging others to fulfill, his hungers, whether they are for food, drink, comfort, or whatever else. The infant is not cognizant of past or future. The only time he is aware of is the present, and he wants his needs met *now*.

To extend Moreno's ideas, it seems that as we grow and become more independent physiologically, socially, and cognitively, we become more able to fulfill many of our basic needs ourselves. Nevertheless, throughout life, we experience the need to complete certain actions. We have the strong urge to embrace someone or shout at them or the urgent desire to be included. Sometimes we even feel it in our bodies—for example, in our throats if we need to say something others have told us not to say; in our stomachs if we need to receive some emotional nurturance. Often it is too threatening to attempt to satisfy act hungers in life. Sociodrama provides the opportunity for a person to satisfy the act hunger in a safe setting and to practice how to go about satisfying it in life more comfortably. For example, if a storekeeper finds it intimidating to insist that teenagers not loiter in the store, he or she might want to practice assertively encountering youths in a sociodrama.

Determining the act hungers is invaluable for the director, since it is the satisfaction of the act hungers in the enactment that accomplishes the goals of sociodrama. The goals are catharsis, insight, and role training. Every sociodrama should satisfy at least one of them and more if necessary to meet the group's needs. When group members have expressed in the warm-up that they are tired of saying "Yes" to everyone, there is an audible and palpable sigh of relief from the whole group as one of the enactors, playing a secretary, refuses the office manager's demand that she stay late.

As an example from the group we have discussed throughout the chapter, members had several act hungers: to be accepted and included, to stand up for oneself, to feel more adequate, to express anger and disappointment. The chosen sociodrama may be a situation in which a person, who knows no one else but her date, goes to a yacht party. The date disappears, talking to his friends and acquaintances. It seems to the main enactor that all the others at the party have known each other for years and, unlike the newcomer, are boaters. During the sociodrama, the enactor meets someone and confesses that she knows nothing about boating and feels inadequate. The person she is speaking to assures her that there are many other things to discuss besides boating and says that he too felt insecure recently when he attended a small party where everyone else discussed bridge, a game he doesn't play. The enactor, and the audience identifying with her, experience relief when she is accepted and validated and the act hunger is satisfied. In a scene that takes place after the party, satisfying other act hungers, the enactor expresses anger to her date for drifting away without introducing her to anyone. She acknowledges that she felt anxious about approaching people she didn't know. Now she feels proud of herself that she was assertive in meeting people and that she could carry on even though she had felt afraid. The act hungers, then, emerge in the warm-up and are satisfied in the enactment.

Shared Central Issue

During the warm-up, the director listens for the various open tension systems and act hungers and seeks out those that are similar or recurrent among members. The theme to which most group members are warmed up, we call the shared central issue. In the group mentioned above, the shared central issue that emerged is, "What may one do when feeling inadequate?" If the director restates that dominant theme for the group, it helps them to further focus their thinking and clarify their feelings regarding the issue: "We seem to be asking ourselves what we should do when we feel inadequate."

It is essential for the director to keep the shared central issue in mind so that the action in the enactment addresses that issue, thus satisfying group needs and desires. In sociodrama the director is led by the group and performs interventions that help the group to meet its needs. It is through addressing the shared central issue that the act hungers are fulfilled and some of the open tension systems are resolved. If, during the enactment, the participants go off on a tangent or begin to work on a side issue, the director can do a variety of things. She or he can freeze the action and ask the group if this is the area of the problem they wanted to explore. If it is not, group members can suggest ways to refocus the action. If instead they say this is an area they now want to explore, they can resume the action. Further, the action can be refocused by freezing it, bringing one of the enactors out, asking him what he thinks is going on in the situation and what he wants to do about it. After he has determined what he wants to do, the director can return him to the setting and resume the action.

At St. Elizabeth's Hospital in Washington, D.C., practitioners, headed by James Enneis, developed a central concern model for psychodrama. The central concern is closely related to the shared central issue in sociodrama. It differs only in that those who developed the central concern feel that (1) it is possible to direct a psychodrama session without attending to a central concern, and (2) if a director brings in a prepared warm-up, a central concern does not necessarily develop, and, more than likely, the group warms up to the director's personal issue rather than to its own. It is our belief, however, that whether the director does or doesn't structure a warm-up, the group's shared central issue emerges. It is the director's responsibility to watch for its inevitable appearance. He may need to facilitate this. For instance, if the director has prepared a warm-up but the group clearly is already warmed up to different issues, the director should discard the warm-up in the interest of the group. This is also true if the director starts a specific warm-up and the group warms up to a different issue. For example, if the director hears group members worriedly talking about management shifts in their departments as they enter the room, it is best to table, or at least modify, his prepared warm-up regarding creativity in the workplace. Or if the members, who are usually talkative and willing to participate, can't seem to find a partner for the structured warm-up, perhaps the members are not being resistant, but rather have other things on their minds. They may be dealing with their own internal process more than their social process. The director may abandon the planned exercise and ask group members where they are, what is on their minds. It is never a disgrace to discontinue an exercise in the service of the group. In fact, members will appreciate your sensitivity to their needs. Whether the director structures a warm-up or relies on group process to warm members up to their issues, it is essential that the director pay attention to the group's concerns rather than to his or her own.

Sociodrama emphasizes shared problems and role aspects. Therefore, the whole action rests on the base of, emerges from, and is resolved through treatment of the shared central issue. It is for these reasons that the director listens so carefully for it.

Helping the Group Choose the Action Frame

In sociodrama the group, not the leader, determines what the sociodramatic action will be. In other words, a leader seldom decides ahead of time what the group will enact. On the rare occasion when this happens, the leader needs to check out with the group if members want to do the enactment suggested. It is also a good idea for the leader to ask him- or herself why he or she wants the group to perform a specific enactment. If there is an unspoken agenda to set the group straight about something, the group will probably pick it up and rebel. For example, the director, a third grade teacher, is annoyed because one child stole a quarter from another. She wants to teach the children that stealing is wrong and that the person who did it should be ashamed. She is probably going to encounter quite a bit of resistance, since she wants to use sociodrama to scold the children, not to allow them to explore their own values.

While the leader may design and structure a warm-up, it is the group that decides what the action will be. How, then, can a director facilitate the shift from the warm-up to the enactment? During a warm-up, the director listens for the open tension systems and act hungers and for what central issue emerges from these. Once you have determined the shared central issue, it is often helpful to restate it for the group so that members may begin to brainstorm what situation they would like to enact. For example, let's go back to our group that dealt with feelings of inadequacy. There the leader might say, "We seem to be talking a lot about feeling inadequate. What situation can you think of where a person may feel inadequate?" Or for a group of salespeople, "We seem to be wondering how to cope with a difficult customer. Who can give an example of a situation in which a customer may be difficult to handle?"

As group members begin to suggest situations, it is useful to write them on a blackboard, flip chart, or piece of paper. One you have written down all the suggestions, reread them for the group, asking them to vote for the one they'd most like to see enacted. Depending on the purpose of the group, you may want to ask them to choose the situation from which they feel they'll learn the most seeing enacted or the one to which they feel most connected.

It is not always necessary to brainstorm suggestions and have the group vote, although that is certainly a simple way to start an enactment. Sometimes the consensus of the group is clear without engaging in this process. At other times the group and director may choose a general setting for a sociodrama and may wish to trust to the enactors' spontaneity to see where the action goes. For example, members agree that they want the scene to take place in a school playground at recess. As enactors volunteer to participate, the rest of the enactment begins to flesh itself out. In whatever way the group members choose the enactment situation, once they have done so, you are ready to go.

ENLISTING ENACTORS

The chosen situation will often indicate the number of participants needed: a couple is deciding whether or not to move because one of them has a wonderful job offer across the country. Rather than choose the participants, it furthers the group warm-up and spontaneity to ask for volunteers for the available roles. Also, group members feel and, in fact, are more in charge of their own group process if members volunteer for roles.

After some initial hesitancy in the first session, members are usually eager to take roles, sometimes even vying for particular ones they suspect will be fun to enact. Since the sociodrama situation is one they chose and which addresses their concerns, members *want* to participate and don't need to be dragged into the action kicking and screaming. Also, after the first session, they realize that they can learn a lot by playing roles that are different from the ones they play most comfortably in life. A worker in a donut store might want to play a manager. Someone else, who considers himself clumsy, could take the role of a dancer.

Over a period of time, if you notice that the same few people volunteer most of the time, ask for volunteers who haven't enacted yet. If the group is composed of many timid people, you may want to intersperse new with more experienced enactors to help the new ones feel more comfortable. You can also design warm-ups to be done in dyads or small groups in which members have to act something out—for example, their favorite comic strip character. In this way, they can get more practice taking roles in a less threatening setting than before the large group.

If no one volunteers when you ask for someone to play the wife who has the job offer, simply ask for someone to play the husband. Often, group members may be more willing to play the reciprocal role. Once someone has volunteered for that, ask again for someone to play the wife. It is to be noted that in sociodrama males can play females, and females can play males. Mentioning this to a group is often liberating. There is always someone who is eager to become more cognizant of the thoughts and feelings of the opposite sex.

Often in a new group, and occasionally in an ongoing group, there will be a dead silence when you call for participants. Some good-natured coaxing may help, but don't feel that you have to break the silence. After a few moments, a member who can't stand the suspense will most likely offer to take part.

For the times when the chosen situation doesn't dictate the number of participants and their relationships, the director can ask the group, "Who is in this scene? What are their relationships?" These questions further warm up the group to the action and a willingness to volunteer for a role. Another way to proceed is to ask, "Who'd like to participate in the sociodrama?" Once members volunteer, the director asks who they are in this drama and what his or her relationship is to the others. This latter technique is often fun and sparks group spontaneity. Let's say the group has decided to do a sociodrama exploring what happens when a person tells his friends he is gay. The director may say, "Who'd like to be in this sociodrama?" leaving open the number of enactors. Four members volunteer. Bob says he will play the gay person. John says he'll play his best friend since childhood. Sally says she'll be a woman Bob dated for a year, but is now simply his friend. Beth says she'll play someone who doesn't know Bob very well, but is present because she's dating John. Sometimes at this point someone else will volunteer, warmed up by the role descriptions of the other enactors—Vic says he wants to play Bob's lover.

Another thing to consider when enlisting enactors is how many you can work with without the scene becoming unmanageable or chaotic. If you are inexperienced at sociodrama, two or three participants are probably plenty. No need to be heroic. The group will learn just as much with fewer participants, certainly more than if it is chaotic. If, however, you have a new group and ten people have offered to be in the enactment, you may not want to discourage them. If you do choose to use a large number, remember that you can freeze portions of the action at any time and focus on just one segment.

INTERVIEWING THE ENACTORS

Once members have volunteered to participate in the action, it is important to ready them further to assume their roles and build the audience's interest in seeing enacted the sociodrama they chose. This is done by interviewing the enactors. The director asks questions that help everyone to have more details about the characters and their relationships. In an effective management training group, if the sociodramatic situation is one in which a manager needs to mediate a dispute between two employees, you may start by asking the "manager" how long he has been in his job. You may ask how he feels about mediating; how he feels about each of the workers; if he has any ideas about who is wrong and who is right. These questions are asked and answered aloud before the whole group. The other enactors are instructed to ignore what would normally not be said to them directly, although clearly they can hear every word. The reason for this tack is that in the rest of life, we often gain information and learn how others feel about us indirectly. Either we hear things via the grapevine or we use our listening skills to read the vocal tones and nonverbal messages of others. Having the enactors overhear each other gives them added information about the others' attitudes and feelings. The director interviews all the enactors, and continues to probe the dynamics of the situation. He may ask Employee One how he gets along with his manager and if this is the first such dispute he has had with Employee Two. The director may ask one or all of the enactors what the dispute is about or may ask the audience to determine it. In some sociodramas the group is interested in exploring the difficulties that occur in a given situation. They are equally interested in all of the parties. This is called a *group-centered sociodrama*. For example, say the sociodrama is to be about how a family reacts when the parents announce they are going to separate. People may be as interested in the individual children's responses as in the reactions of the parents. When such a sociodrama occurs, it is helpful to give equal time to interviewing each enactor.

On the other hand, there are times when a group has primary interest in one of the roles. This is called a *protagonist-centered sociodrama*. Take, for instance, a sociodrama where a student is struggling to balance the pressures of school, work, family, friends, and a boyfriend. In this sociodrama, it is best to spend the most time interviewing the enactor playing the student.

Regarding interviewing, the entire process should take only a few minutes. You are trying to warm up the participants, the audience, and yourself. This is also the time when you can discover further how you may help the group through the sociodrama. Is their act hunger for catharsis, insight, and/or role training? Has it changed, intensified, or diminished since earlier in the session?

SETTING THE SCENE

The last thing you do before beginning the enactment is scene setting. Some of this may have emerged naturally in the group's choice of situation: four people are in an office when a person comes in and takes them hostage. We know the setting is an office. We have only to find out from the participants where their desks are in the office and the places of any other important furnishings. For this sociodrama, it would also be useful to find out the placement of windows and doors. It is a good idea to have a few extra chairs on hand so that group members don't have to give up their seats. Groups are amazingly creative in finding available objects that may represent other objects—for example, several chairs put together make a bed, and an empty cup becomes a telephone receiver.

If the scene is not implicit in the choice of situation, you may either ask the group to say where the first scene is set or ask the enactors to assist in choosing where the action will take place and how the environment looks. In a sex education course, students enact a scene in which two teenages are alone in a house. They have been going steady for six months. They have never made love and are discussing whether or not to do so now. You might ask them where they are having this discussion. After they define the place, ask them what the room looks like and where the furniture is. Ask them to take chairs and arrange the room accordingly.

It helps to anchor the action, create the mood and further ready the group for the enactment to follow, when you set the scene. Humans have limitless imaginations. As Coleridge pointed out when discussing theatre, people can willingly suspend their disbelief whenever they choose. The space below a table can become a shelter to hide in; three chairs put together may represent a couch; someone's scarf may double for a sling; a lipstick for a vial of poison. Incredibly, when a group has set a scene and the important objects in it, members begin to see and experience them. Often you'll hear mention of the setting in later sessions as if it had been as fleshed out as a movie locale.

SUMMARY

During the warm-up, members begin to reveal their *act hungers,* their strong need for completion: to say, do, hear, or receive something. The *open tension systems* also emerge. These unresolved stress systems are sometimes interpersonal, regarding encounters among group members. They may also be intrapsychic, regarding internal struggles. The *shared central issue* grows out of the open tension systems and act hungers. It is the main concern held by the group in a given session. Rather than focus on individual problems, the director helps the group to choose a hypothetical situation that embodies the shared central issue.

After members choose a situation, the director *enlists enactors* from the group to play the necessary roles. Next the director *interviews the participants* and helps them to *set the scene* so that the action of the sociodrama may have some physical frame of reference and may proceed.

5

EXPLORING ROLES, EXPANDING ROLES

EXAMINING OLD ROLES AND TRYING OUT NEW ONES

Moreno said *"man is a roleplayer, . . .* every individual is characterized by a certain range of roles which dominate his behavior, and . . . every culture is characterized by a certain set of roles which it imposes with a variety of degrees of success upon its members" (*Who Shall Survive?*, 88).

Whether baker or farmer, lover or landlord, we are engaged in role behavior continually. Sometimes we are quite pleased with how we play a role. For instance, we see ourselves as good friends or excellent administrators. On other occasions we are dissatisfied with how we act in particular situations, or we get the urge to try on a new role: "I've always wanted to be a white water rafter!" Sociodrama provides a safe setting for exploring old roles and experimenting with new ones.

Exploring Past and Current Roles and Role Relationships

In our current lives, each of us plays roles that we find satisfying. We may enjoy being a parent, a friend, or an astrophysicist. However, even our most satisfying roles evolve and transform over a period of time. The role relationships are dynamic, not static and can't be static if we are to continue enjoying them. As parents, when our children grow and change, so does our relationship to them shift. We relate differently to our twenty-year old than we did to our infant. If we don't, we are in for some rocky times. Also, by playing the role of parent, we become more adept at portraying some aspects than we are at portraying others: we may be a fine confidant or guide to our six-year old, but we may not feel comfortable disciplining her. In other words, we may find a particular role highly satisfying even though we play some aspects of it imperfectly. One of the great joys of being human is that we can continue to grow in roles and modify the roles we play throughout our lives.

Most of us also play some roles in which we feel uncomfortable to a greater or lesser degree. There are a variety of causes for this discomfort. We may feel uncomfortable because we are new at playing the role and are thus unsure of our behavior in the situation, like a computer programmer on her first job, for example. Or maybe we don't particularly like the role in which we participate and experience *role conflict:* Mike doesn't like being a florist, but his family, which owns the business, puts pressure on him to keep doing it. On the other hand, perhaps it is the *role relationship* we don't like: Martha gets annoyed when, almost every time she has lunch with her friend Betty, Betty criticizes her, and Martha feels guilty and angry. Instead, we may have *role fatigue:* Doreen is tired of working as a short-order cook, but no other jobs seem to be available to her. On the other hand, we may have difficulty with a role because we suffer from *role confusion:* "What am I supposed to do? How am I supposed to play this role?" throughout life we grow and change in the roles we play. Each sociodrama session provides a forum for people to explore the roles they play, to praise themselves for the roles they play well, and to practice playing those roles in ways more satisfying to them.

Mary Lou was passed over several times for job promotions. She was not perceived as a take-charge person, nor did she perceive herself that way. Actually, she knew her job very well, oftentimes helped her co-workers without being asked, and even found ways in which to make their work easier. In a sociodrama group, Mary Lou played a variety of roles in which she would take credit for her work and found a new pleasure in doing so. She learned to perceive herself in a new way and behave accordingly. When that happened, others began to see her differently and in a leadership role. Although still helpful, she no longer allowed people to take advantage of her. It wasn't long afterward that Mary Lou received the first of her many promotions.

Jason had the opposite difficulty. He settled most of his problems with a four-letter-word retort, complete with clenched fists and tight jaw. His supervisor and co-workers perceived him as violent and unstable. Whenever his supervisor would criticize his work or suggest ways to do things differently, Jason would fly off the handle. He was warned that he would be fired if he had one more outburst. It wasn't easy for Jason to begin with the staff communications group, but he did. Through the sessions he learned that criticism of one's work is not criticism of oneself. He also discovered that all his feelings were perfectly normal; what he needed to learn was how to deal with those feelings in a new way. Jason learned to relax more and to listen nondefensively, really listen, to what other people said. During an enactment when another player yelled and stormed at him, Jason realized how threatening his angry behavior must seem to others. Slowly, but surely, he learned to vent his feelings in an acceptable way. He learned to play the employee role differently, keeping his body physically relaxed, which helped change the way others perceived him. And, perhaps most importantly, he learned to ask for clear directions on how to do certain things and not be afraid to say, "I don't understand," or "Could you explain that again?" which wasn't easy for him. Over time, Jason found new satisfaction in his work and with his ability to communicate without venom.

Often, people find that they are able to take successful behaviors from one role and apply them to another role they play. For example, Charles pointed out, "As a store manager I have no difficulty dealing assertively with my co-workers. There, I'm the boss, part of the corporate management team—no question about it. But, at home, with my wife and mother-in-law, it's like I'm a different person. There are certain standards I want at home, but, for some reason, it's easier to do it their way. I let them walk all over me." Charles realized he wasn't using his assertiveness at home and changed his behavior there to include some of that skill.

Sometimes group members need to explore a particular role they share and discover what each needs to do to play the role in a more comfortable manner. A group of volunteer AIDS counselors may convene to discuss the stresses of assisting people with so devastating a disease. Specifically, they may choose to explore ways to comfort someone whose family has rejected him. In the course of an enactment, or in several brief vignettes, each counselor may want to practice what to do or say in this kind of situation. Since there is no right or wrong way to proceed, members can begin to develop and become comfortable with their own styles of relating. By the same token, they may modify their styles as a result of the responses they engender in an enactment. For example, if someone realizes that his matter-of-fact style is off-putting to someone else playing an AIDS patient, he may try to practice better listening skills. Dave, a counselor, is gifted with a logical mind. In an enactment, he may say to a "patient" whose parents have rejected him, "Well, Ben, you haven't gotten along with your parents for years. There's no reason to expect them to act nicer now." While Dave's logic is on target, he may be unaware that Ben feels hurt, sad, and abandoned that his parents have let him down once again. If Ben responds with anger in the enactment, Dave may realize that what he meant as a supportive statement wasn't taken as such. Dave may see what Ben needs at the moment is a good listener, someone to recognize how bad he feels and defer logic until later. He may also realize that he chose to be logical since he couldn't acknowledge his own distress about Ben's painful situation. Dave may return to the enactment and try the scene again, adjusting his behavior to fit his new knowledge.

Sociodrama, then, provides excellent opportunities for fine tuning the roles we play. It helps us to acknowledge and demonstrate our competence and provides a safe setting for exploring and practicing new and more satisfying ways to play our current roles.

Expanding Role Repertoire

Role repertoire is a term used to denote the group of developed roles we use
and have used in our lives. They are the roles that are currently available to
us: seamstress, ball player, friend, spouse, PTA member. Sociodrama helps
people explore old roles and practice how to try out new ones. This trying out
serves as a rehearsal for the expected and/or unexpected life situations to come.
The more roles a person plays successfully, the more varied societal experiences
one can have, the more places one can go safely, the more people with whom
one can associate comfortably, and the more opportunity one has for a happy,
invigorating life. Also, trying out new roles can be fun!

In his only encounter with Freud, Moreno reported that he told Freud, "You
analyze people's dreams. I try to give them courage to dream again" (*Psychodrama—First Volume*, 6). The act of helping people expand their role repertoire
helps them expand their dreams as well. The first step is to imagine doing
things differently. Sociodrama offers the structure and milieu for acting out
these dreams before putting them into action in everyday life.

Thousands of amateur theatre groups across the country attest to the interest
and popularity of trying out new roles. Participants spend hundreds of hours to
originate theatre productions. One of the great attractions is that players often
have the opportunity to speak and behave differently than they usually do.
Anyone who has ever participated in this type of activity knows the feeling of
excitement, elation, and sometimes even catharsis that occurs from playing a
role totally outside one's experience. Sociodrama, like theatre, gives a person
permission to behave in a different way, to try out new roles.

In a somewhat less theatrical context, observe the burgeoning popularity of
the Whodunit Mystery Weekends. Not only are the participants asked to play
detective and solve a bogus crime, but quite often they are asked to assume a
particular role, come dressed for the part (sometimes even in period costumes)
and take an active role in the mystery. The general public often pays hundreds
of dollars to take part in this make-believe murder mystery. The appeal of this
type of entertainment in which everyone, public and actors alike, participates,
tells us something about our innate desire to try out new roles.

Whether exploring an old role or preparing to take on a new role, sociodrama builds on the strengths that a person already has, rather than highlighting weaknesses and inadequacies. When we learn, we build on the known to
discover the unknown. During the process, we need to know that we are not
jumping into the abyss. Otherwise, we become discouraged and quit. If a piano
teacher went into a first lesson with a student who had never had a music
lesson, imagine the student's response if the teacher whipped out Ravel's "Tar-
antella" and said, "Play it!" Panic! Clearly the student would need to know a
great deal. The student would have to know the instrument and how to play
it, how to read music, and what notes correspond to each of those white and
black things on the piano before tackling that complicated piece. In reality

the teacher starts with a simple piece, perhaps one whose melody is already known to the student, the familiarity being a bridge, so that learning to play would not seem so difficult. Thus, in a sociodrama group when members try on new roles, we help them to build on roles they already play successfully. They may be able to utilize skills they have in their repertoire and apply them to a new role.

In a group of social work students, member after member confessed knowing the theory, but they were confused and scared about what they'd actually *do* when face to face with an individual or family in need of counseling. What these men and women didn't realize in their anxiety was that they already had in their role repertoire many of the role components they would need in order to be good social workers. They were warm, empathetic people. They were optimistic, had good senses of humor and some ability to analyze systems. In a variety of sociodramas, the students practiced, among other things, interviewing clients, developing rapport, comforting distraught people, and working with clients to develop and implement goals. This spontaneous practice helped them to realize how much they already knew and to take risks to try on new behaviors.

Before we can take on a new role we must first perceive it. If we don't know what a neonatologist is (one who studies the newborn), we can hardly expect or plan to become one. Once we have perceived a role, we can take steps to learn how to play it in life. Say a person wants to become a receptionist. He may need to learn specific skills relative to working office equipment. Someone may teach him how to use the equipment, but he will also need hands-on practice with it to become skilled. He will also have to learn how to field phone calls; to answer calls courteously; to deal with persistent clients who want to see his employer NOW. By placing him in simulated situations, sociodrama can help this future receptionist practice all the interpersonal skills and become proficient before ever seeing a client. This behavioral rehearsal helps a person feel more confident and assured in his new role.

Expanding Role Through Fantasy

Have you ever imagined yourself as a great hero or heroine, vanquishing your evil enemies and reveling in the glories of righteous victory? Or imagined yourself as a great explorer of this planet or others far away in a distant galaxy? Have you wished you could scamper around again like a small child or make the mischief that a puppy does? Sociodrama provides ample opportunity for such creative and enjoyable play. It also provides an acceptable framework for people to explore their fantasies freely, act frivolously, and generally shake off the constraints of normal social interaction. Instead of speaking formally, one manager to another, participants can interact, Bugs Bunny to Snow White, or Martian to Saturnian.

Aside from being lots of fun, taking on fantasy roles helps us to spark our spontaneity and creativity. It also gives us a time out from our daily concerns and a chance to deal with them in a metaphorical way. For example, by mid-term our college students are usually at wit's end. They are exhausted, can't imagine how they will complete the work for all their courses, and at the same time manage to juggle work, home, and social obligations. They are a pretty frazzled lot. That is the time when we especially like to use fantasy sociodramas. They give the students a delightful diversion, a time out from their troubles, and at the same time give them the opportunity to explore how they will handle all they have got to do when the sociodrama is over. For example, one group chose to go to an island paradise where they were waited on hand and foot. Those in the sociodrama basked in the sun, breathed in relaxation, enjoyed being catered to, and loved pretending to be the idle rich. One of the participants decided to be host to the others at his island villa. As the sociodrama progressed, the poor, overburdened host realized that everyone else was having a great time, but he was exhausted from trying to keep his guests happy. In the course of the sociodrama, he explored ways to set limits, to give to himself, and to ask others for some of the things he needed. By the time the sociodrama ended, the students were animated and chatty. They had the chance to re-create—the real meaning of recreation. They also had ideas about what they could do to help themselves through the difficult period of midterms: prioritize what must be done, what should be done, and what could be dropped; say "no" to demands that can't be met; be good to themselves each day in a specific way—take a ten-minute nap, watch a half hour of TV, do a crossword puzzle, read a pulp magazine. They also decided to ask others for help—get a study partner, get a baby-sitter the day before a big exam, or ask their roommate to make dinner for both of them.

One of the most important lessons that sociodrama teaches is that learning can be uproarious fun. One of the kinds of role expansion that groups love the most is the enactment of fantasy roles. You can count on hearing the room ring with laughter and feel newly charged group energy whenever you work with fantasy.

EXPLORING DIFFERENCES BETWEEN INDIVIDUALS AND GROUPS

As Moreno pointed out in his chapter on sociodrama, "Every individual lives in a world which looks entirely personal to him, and in which he partakes in a number of private roles. But the millions of private worlds overlap in large portions. The larger portions which overlap are truly collective elements. Only the minor portions are private and personal" (Psychodrama–First Volume, 351). Everyone operates as an individual and as a group member of society as well. Some individuals function more comfortably on a one-to-one basis, while others are more successful in groups. How we deal with ourselves and how we deal with each other are our main issues of concern throughout our lives.

We have all known people who are comfortable as individuals but don't function well as part of a group. "I'm not a joiner," they'll say, or the now infamous TV commercial line, "I'd rather do it myself!" For example, take a singer named Shirley who sings beautiful solos, but cannot bring herself to learn to harmonize with others. Here is an illustration of an individual who is less comfortable as a member of the group. Sociodrama would offer Shirley techniques for learning how to function without losing her individuality. She could learn listening skills, become less threatened by opinions of others, become more able to have her needs met within a group, and to meet other's needs without losing herself.

On the other hand, there are individuals who function at the opposite extreme. They feel most comfortable and safe when they are members of a group. Let's take a group of single mothers. They find their time after work taken up with chauffeuring kids to various activities, cooking, cleaning, and shopping. They allow themselves to become overwhelmed with household responsibilities and children's desires to be driven to friends, soccer, and so on. They can't seem to find time for that exercise class or a walk in the park; in fact, they wonder if they have a right to such nonessentials.

In investigating the differences between individuals and groups, ask members to think about their own dual roles. In what situations do they find themselves that they aren't sure which should take precedence—the individual or the group? This particular dilemma makes for good discussion and sociodrama. When must the individual remember the words of Shakespeare: "This above all. To thine own self be true"? (*Hamlet*, act 1.) And when must he think as a group member the old maxim, "The greatest good for the greatest number"?

As you can see, this dilemma becomes a conflict when the decision of what to do requires the confrontation of the individual versus the group. For example, say an elderly couple has lived in their home for forty-five years and don't want to move. The county wants to buy their property to put in a new road that will benefit the economic life of the entire community. What is to be done? Can both the individuals' and group's needs be met? How? Investigating a hypothetical situation like this sociodramatically gives members an opportunity to explore and clarify their values. It gives them insight into both sides of the question. It also helps them to examine ways to accommodate the needs of both the individual and the group.

SUMMARY

In sociodrama, the director creates opportunities for the participants to try on a variety of roles to gain greater expertise and flexibility in experiencing life situations. When we explore our *role repertoire*, we reaffirm what we like about how we play those roles. We also have the opportunity to examine behaviors we don't find as satisfying and practice changing those behaviors.

Sociodrama also provides the laboratory in which to experiment in trying out *new roles*. Trying on new roles is personally expanding and exhilarating. Sometimes a director will help members to create a new role by examining an old one, by identifying those strengths and building on that foundation.

Everyone operates as an individual but also as a member of a larger entity, the group. A sociodrama provides a culture medium for individuals to learn how to be group members and for those members to learn how to express their individuality, to individuate, as well. Occasionally, we feel conflicted when a decision requires the confrontation of the *individual versus the group*. The leader guides the enactors and audience to greater understanding of the need to support both and the ability to attend to personal needs without disrupting group process.

6

STRUCTURING THE ACTION

OFTEN-USED TECHNIQUES: WHAT THEY ARE, WHEN TO USE THEM

In *Psychodrama–Third Volume* (16), Moreno said "that there are certain invisible dimensions in the reality of living, not fully experienced or expressed, and that is why we have to use surplus operations and surplus instruments to bring them out. . . ." Moreno termed these invisible dimensions *surplus reality* and the operations and instruments to bring them out, surplus reality techniques. Some examples of surplus reality are dreams, daydreams, thought fragments, and unacknowledged feelings. Some examples of surplus reality techniques that Moreno developed are role reversal, doubling, the aside, and walk and talk.

Sociodrama differs from role play and creative drama, primarily because it employs a variety of these techniques that Moreno devised to widen and deepen the scope of the enactment. The director uses them throughout the drama as needed. Let's take a look at some techniques used in sociodrama and the types of situations in which a specific one would provide an enhancement, enrichment, or alternative route to the action.

Role Reversal

The technique of *role reversal* is one of the most profound techniques that Moreno developed. As a young man, he had a deep interest in theology and philosophy. He wanted to better understand God and God's relationship to people. He decided that the best way to do this was to put himself in God's place and to consider creation and the Creator's relationship to humans. The result of this experiment was a body of poems addressed to humanity that Moreno, as God, wrote in 1913. Moreno scribbled these verses on a castle wall near Vienna for all the world to see. (It should be noted that Moreno affectionately referred to himself as a megalomaniac. He appears to have been correct.) Later he published them in a volume entitled *The Words of the Father.*

Although Moreno's first experiment in role reversal was a rather dramatic one, we all do similar reversals with lesser folk routinely. "Put yourself in my place! How would you feel?" How many times have we said this to someone, wishing the person would just understand us, see our point of view? Conversely, most of us frequently try to figure out what the other person is thinking and feeling so that we can be more empathetic and communicate better.

Sociodrama takes this common internal process of role reversal one step further. Through the technique of role reversal, participants literally put themselves in each other's place. In a sociodrama, Hillary and Bill are discussing whether or not to invite Bill's parents over on his birthday. Hillary says she doesn't want to invite them because his mother always criticizes her cooking. Bill says he knows his parents would want to celebrate with him, and he wants to be with them too. Each feels the other is being unreasonable. The director asks the two enactors to reverse roles. Bill moves to where Hillary stood and becomes Hillary. Hillary moves to where Bill stood and becomes Bill. Bill tries to take Hillary's role as fully and honestly as possible. Hillary does the same with Bill's role. They continue their discussion, each in the other's role. In taking Bill's role, Hillary becomes aware that he misses his parents, whom he hasn't seen much since he and Hillary married last fall. She also sees that he has avoided them because of his mother's criticism of Hillary. In taking Hillary's role, Bill realizes that, because of his mother's disapproval, Hillary worries that Bill is sorry he married her. By the time the director has asked Bill and Hillary to return to their own roles, each has a better understanding of the other and is more empathetic of the other's feelings. Rather than battle with each other, they can work together to resolve the difficulty in a way that is satisfying to both.

In an enactment, there are many circumstances that call for role reversal. In the above example, role reversal was used to develop empathy in the enactors.

Use role reversal

to develop empathy

to shift perspective

to develop understanding of the situation

to allow enactors to answer their own questions

to enable enactors to see themselves as their fellow enactors see them

to help enactors have a catharsis

to help enactors get unstuck

Let's discuss the use of role reversal to shift perspective. Sometimes enactors seem to perceive the situation they are dramatizing solely from their own viewpoint. They neither see nor will entertain any other possibilities. The director calls for a role reversal to allow the enactor to look at his or her situation in a new light. Often this momentary shift will help the person to discover a new way to view the circumstances.

Similar and connected to shifting perspective, you also call for role reversal when you feel the enactor doesn't seem to understand the larger context of a situation. Say she needs a cognitive grasp of the dynamics, as with Ellen who is discussing the use of the family car with her mom. When Ellen reverses roles, as Mother, she finds herself beleaguered by several children making demands at the same time and by a husband on the phone, saying he'll be late for dinner. Ellen realizes that with so much happening at once, her mother will hardly be receptive to lending out the car. When she returns to her own role, she decides to approach her mother after dinner when things have calmed down a bit.

Whenever enactors ask a question, reverse roles and let them answer their own question. This is one of the most important uses of the technique, because it reempowers the person. Often when we ask a question of someone else, deep down we know the answer ourselves, even though we don't think we do. Jesse says, "Becky, do you think I can do it?" If you reverse him into Becky's role, he must search himself for Becky's answer to the question.

It is also helpful at times for an enactor to see herself as others see her, as when Rona enacts the role of someone on a first date. When she reverses roles, she sees that she has been mumbling, causing her date to ask her to repeat herself at several points in the conversation. She also sees that she has been keeping her head down. When she returns to her own role, she looks at him, speaks up, and, since he is no longer asking her to repeat herself, she starts to relax and have a good time.

Occasionally, an enactor will play a role in which he cannot express his feelings comfortably. In calling for a role reversal with a character who easily expresses himself, the enactor can often have a catharsis, such as when Sean plays a customer service representative talking to an irate consumer. In his own role he is polite and soft spoken. In the customer's role he can rant and rave to his heart's content. You may find good use of this technique if a timid or intellectualizing person is enacting a scene. In role reversing him into a role where the other person was freely venting, the enactor will be freed up to express also. Because he is in someone else's role, not his own, the person will find it easier and more permissible to express emotions. After the enactment, discuss how it felt to discharge those emotions. You may also want to point out that since the enactor was able to express emotions in the drama, whether in his own role or not, he may now find it easier to show his feelings in other settings.

There are several techniques to use when the action seems to grind to a halt or one or more of the enactors seems stuck. One of these is role reversal. Just the simple act of getting out of our own role for a minute is often enough to quicken spontaneity. All of us know what it feels like to be overwhelmed in a situation. We don't know where to go or what to do. We need a breather so we can get our bearings. Role reversal can provide this.

Now that you know many of the uses of role reversal, let's go over the mechanics of doing it. When it is time for a role reversal, say to two enactors, "Reverse roles."

Instruct them to

• switch places

• take on each other's body posture

• try as much as possible to assume the other character's personality

• be careful not to caricature each other

Be sure to return the enactors to their own roles before the end of the enactment.

Once the two have reversed, ask the enactor to repeat the last thing that was said before the role reversal occurred. In other words, Rob says, "That's silly, Pam. How can you be so childish?" The director tells them to reverse roles. After they do, Pam as Rob says, "That's silly, Pam. How can you be so childish?" The repetition of the last line before the reversal is very important. For one thing, it anchors the dialogue after the momentary break in action caused by the reversal. Also, no one has to try to figure out how to start the action going from new roles. For another, it provides an opportunity for the enactor to hear what he or she has just said from a different perspective or to answer a question if he or she has asked one.

You may call for role reversal between enactors as frequently as necessary. Before you end the sociodrama, however, be sure to reverse them back to their own roles. It is also essential to complete a role reversal between two people before reversing one of them with a third. Otherwise, chaos will ensue. No one will know who is who or what is what. If you reverse Sally and Pat, Sally is in Pat's role, and Pat is in Sally's. It will be confusing if you next reverse Ivan with Pat who is in Sally's role. Now, Sally is in Pat's role, and Pat as Sally is in Ivan's role, and Ivan is in Sally's role. We get confused just writing this. Imagine how you'd feel if you were one of the enactors or the director. The thought of how you would get Pat back in his own role is mind boggling. The way to avoid this mess is to reverse Pat and Sally back to their own roles and then reverse Sally and Ivan.

Despite the somewhat lengthy written directions, people easily learn the mechanics of role reversal. Once mastered, group members are freed to receive the considerable benefits of being able to experience and view a situation from a variety of perspectives.

The Double

When engaged in conversation, we frequently have thoughts or emotions that we never mention to the person with whom we are speaking. In talking with a friend who has a brand new hairdo you hate, you may deliberately keep the subject away from hair styles, rather than insult her. She compliments you on your generosity to a mutual friend, and you feel like a heel for not liking her hairdo. You hope she won't ask how you like it. You wrestle with whether to lie to her and say you like it just to be nice, whether to tell the truth and risk upsetting her, or whether to change the subject.

Many things go through our minds that we don't voice aloud. In exploring social interactions, Moreno believed that it is valuable to hear what people are thinking and feeling. In this way, what is normally hidden in a situation becomes manifest. He invented a special role to bring hidden processes to the surface. That role, *the double,* is played by one or more group members. The double is a mind/feeling reader. He or she is a person whose role it is to tune into the enactor's unexpressed thoughts and feelings and express them. The double is the enactor's hidden voice, one's truest self. The double helps the enactor to realize and acknowledge what she is thinking and feeling. The double positions himself behind and slightly to the side of the person for whom he doubles. The double takes on the posture and gestures of the person so that he may more readily tune in to how the enactor is feeling. Sue has her fists clenched and is speaking sweetly to Ted. Her double, standing by her, clenches his fists and says aloud, "I'm controlling myself, Ted, but, boy, am I annoyed at you." If Sue is feeling as her double has indicated, she repeats what he has said. If she is not feeling that way, she corrects the statement. Ted responds to whatever Sue says to him. He does not respond to the double, since that is Sue's *inner voice.*

The director, as well as the group members, may double. Through doubling, the director may help the group to meet its goals. She or he may facilitate their expressing feelings, problem solving, and gaining insight. As with role reversal, the double can be used in a variety of ways. Some of these are:

to support

to verbalize nonverbal communications

to physicalize one's words

to magnify feelings

to observe and question the self

The double supports with statements that affirm the enactor and validate his or her thoughts, feelings, opinions, and actions. For example, after Milt says, "Hey, Jeff, give me your keys. I'll drive home. I didn't drink tonight, and you did," his double says, "I'm glad I spoke up. I feel safer now." The double reinforces the appropriateness of Milt's actions.

When an enactor demonstrates through body language that she is feeling some things that she is not saying, the double verbalizes those feelings. Jill tells Larry she really enjoys his company. However, she is sitting as far away from him as she can get. She has her arms folded and her legs crossed. Her body is faced away from him. The double says, "I like you, but I'm not ready to get close yet. Don't rush me!"

Sometimes the double physicalizes the words the enactor speaks. The enactor says, "You're a pain in the neck." The double massages his own neck and groans. This kind of doubling often helps a person to realize that he is actually feeling physical tension that he wasn't aware of. Sometimes the double feels that the enactor wants desperately to convince the other person to side with him, though the other is resisting. He may physicalize that struggle by reaching out and tugging on the other person.

The double also can help an enactor by magnifying her feelings. Debbie is softly telling Betty, "I'm a little disappointed that you didn't invite me to your birthday party. All the other kids in the class were invited." Her double says, "A little disappointed? Boy, am I hurt that you don't like me!"

Another way the double can assist the enactor is by questioning the self. This is especially useful if there is a clear dissonance between what the person is saying and with his or her affect. The enactor, giggling, tells his child he really shouldn't track mud in the house. The double may say, "I'm annoyed with that kid. I wonder why I'm giggling." This gives the enactor a cue to examine his or her actions more closely.

There are two other kinds of doubles that are often helpful to use. The first of these is what we call polar doubling. When an enactor is attempting to resolve a moral dilemma or make a difficult choice, assign one double to express one choice and the other to express its polar opposite. For example, in an enactment, Gwen is contemplating an extramarital affair. One of her doubles is her inner voice that says, "Why not do it? No one will ever know." The other is her inner voice that speaks from the opposite pole of feeling: "Am I crazy? I'll know!"

Multiple doubles are a group of people who double for one person. This is useful in a variety of circumstances. When an enactor seems unable to get in touch with what he is feeling, you may ask the group, "Who thinks they may know what Ken is feeling right now?" As people raise their hands or nod, ask them to come and stand with the enactor. Instruct them to make their doubling statement one at a time. When they have finished, ask the enactor to repeat the one that best represents what he feels.

Multiple doubling is also called for when group members are champing at the bit to get involved. They may either jump up spontaneously and double or ask you if they may double. It is wonderful when many members are so identified with the action on stage that they can't sit still. With this kind of spontaneous multiple doubling, several people may be standing behind the enactor at the same time, waiting for the right moment to double. Remind them not to talk at once, nor to speak when the enactor is speaking.

Remember that either the director or group members may double. Here are some directions for doubling. Stand to the side of and slightly behind the person for whom you are doubling. You need to be where you can easily see the person's gestures and facial expressions, yet far enough out of direct vision not to be a distraction. Once you have positioned yourself, take on the person's posture and gesture. This will help you to tune in to how the person is really feeling. When you become aware that the enactor is not expressing some thought or feeling that she apparently has and you feel is germane to the enactment, that is the time to make a doubling statement or action. After you have made the statement, instruct the enactor to repeat the statement if it reflects how she feels or correct it if it doesn't. It is essential that the enactor repeat or correct what has been doubled. In this way, she acknowledges what she is experiencing. Also, since the double represents the inner voice, the other enactors don't respond to it. Although in reality they hear what the double says, they respond only to what the enactor says. Following this convention obviates potential confusion with doubles and enactors all talking at once and at cross-purposes.

When you are doubling, try to tune in to what the person's inner self is saying. When you speak, keep your doubling brief, a couple of sentences, at most. If you do lengthy doubling, the enactor will have forgotten what you have said by the time you have finished and will be unable to repeat it.

At any time you may ask a group member to come to the playing area and double for an enactor. Some directors also like to tell members to get up and double whenever they feel in touch with some feeling an enactor is not expressing. This encourages all to warm up and take an active role in each enactment as they feel moved to do so.

Sometimes the director will ask for a volunteer to double for a particular role throughout the drama. This happens most frequently when the focus of the enactment is on one of the players. In a group of young men and women, the chosen situation is that a woman is trying to get up enough courage to tell her parents that she is moving out of the family home, quitting her current job, taking a new one in another state, and moving in with her boyfriend. The group's interest is in how she will do this and what she is thinking and feeling during the experience. Some directors also like the double to place a hand on the shoulder of the enactor. This helps to tune in to the person's feelings. It also helps the enactor to physically experience the double's support.

The Empty Chair

The empty chair technique is one in which an empty chair is placed before the group. The director asks members to imagine that someone or something is in the chair. Then he asks them to make a statement to whomever is in it. In an English class, say, he may suggest that Macbeth is in the chair. He asks the students what they think Macbeth feels like when Lady Macbeth urges him to murder. They may stand behind the chair and double for Macbeth, or they may speak to him from their seats, giving him advice. This use of the empty chair helps participants to warm up to issues they can explore in an enactment.

The empty chair can also be used during an enactment. If in a sociodrama Albert is angry enough to punch James, bring in an empty chair and a pillow and let him pound the chair as if it were James. This allows the enactor to vent his feelings, yet not hurt anyone.

In either the enactment or sharing portion, you may use an empty chair to give group members an opportunity to show what they would say in the situation. After a sociodrama dealing with what to say to someone to convince him to sign a nuclear disarmament petition, the director may place an empty chair in the center of the group. She may ask members to imagine that a potential signer is seated there. Those who wish can demonstrate the approach they would use. One of the values of empty chair work is that one doesn't, of course, get the negative feedback or response that one gets from a human being. Therefore, people can often express themselves more fully than when confronted with a threatening person. Once they feel more comfortable expressing their feelings in this way, it is easier to do so with people. The empty chair, then, can be used in the warm-up, enactment, and/or sharing segment of a sociodrama.

Soliloquy

The dictionary defines soliloquy as a literary or dramatic form of discourse in which a character talks to himself or reveals his thoughts in order to form a monologue without addressing a listener. Perhaps one of the best known soliloquies ever written or spoken is the one in act 3 of Shakespeare's *Hamlet:*

> To be, or not to be, that is the question:
> Whether 'tis nobler in the mind to suffer
> The slings and arrows of outrageous fortune,
> Or to take arms against a sea of troubles
> And by opposing, end them.

In this, Hamlet searches his soul for the meaning of his life and how he should proceed. Perhaps few of us could ever come up with such immortal words as these, but we all have occasions when we need to reflect on our feelings and to express them openly.

In theatre, the actor emerges from the action of the play to reflect on his thoughts, feelings, and/or behavior. Either the actor is alone on stage or the action freezes, and he and his words are spotlighted. The soliloquy stands as a kind of time out when the character regroups his thoughts in order to return to the action with new resolve. Moreno adapted soliloquy for sociodrama. Realizing that soliloquy serves as a bracket in theatre, namely that the actor separates from the action to speak his thoughts, Moreno felt that this kind of bracketing of the player's feelings and taking a time out from the action would work well in sociodrama too.

Sometimes during an enactment, a participant seems stuck or not in touch with his feelings. In an intimacy workshop, Jack is playing the role of someone who had gone through a painful divorce two years before. Now, in a new relationship, he finds it difficult to touch and share his feelings, and Janet, his new partner, is pressing him to do so. Simply giving Jack a time out, removing him from the action, can be helpful. In these instances, stop the action, take the enactor out, and ask him to soliloquize about what he thinks and feels about the situation. You can also ask him to review his options and choose one to implement when he returns to the action.

At other times, so many people are talking at once in a scene that an enactor, and maybe even the director, seems to be suffering from sensory overload. Mindy, playing a high school teacher, looks overwhelmed as several students vie for her attention simultaneously. One student pleads for a change of grade; another is complaining that the boy behind him insulted him. Another wants to borrow lunch money, and two others are yelling to each other across the room. Here the time out is especially important.

Another type of soliloquy combines the physical movement of walking as well as talking. If you feel that the enactor is stuck, you can use physical movement to release his spontaneity. Moreno wisely realized that our physiology is connected with our feelings. He felt that it was less possible to remain emotionally stuck if the body is in action. With this kind of soliloquy, instruct the enactor to walk up and down and talk to himself aloud. This will help him recognize and clarify his feelings. After the soliloquy, make sure your enactors return to the same position as when the action was stopped. Your audience can help you here. It is important to give the group the sense that time has stopped during the soliloquy. Now, instruct the enactors to pick up the action when you call, "Action!"

The point of using the soliloquy is to help the participant overcome whatever is holding him back from total immersion in the enactment. When your enactor is totally absorbed in the action, is in touch with his feelings and is not overwhelmed, there will be no need to stop the action for a soliloquy.

Aside

The aside is like a soliloquy, but it is shorter, more like a parenthetical remark. The most common use of the aside is spoken by an actor in a play. He turns aside momentarily, steps out of the dramatic action, and briefly ex-

presses his thoughts aloud. Usually, he comments on the action that is occurring on stage. However, according to dramatic convention, the other actors
on stage do not hear him. For example, the villain, Silas Sinister, steps out of
the melodrama to tell us, "Little does she know that I have her hero, Gomer
Goodguy, tied up. He can't help her now. Ha!" He steps back into the action
as if his words were never spoken.

As a technique in sociodrama, the aside allows enactors to say what they
are really thinking and feeling without fear of negative reaction or reprisal by
their fellow enactors. For instance, in an enactment, Jerry answered Charlene
inappropriately. When she asked him to join her at a party, his answer was a
curt, "No!" Charlene could only conclude from this that Jerry had no interest
in her. But when Jerry was asked to express his thoughts in an aside, what he
said was, "I get real nervous at a party with people I don't know, and I don't
want Charlene to see me that way." When Jerry examined his aside, he was
able to rephrase his response to Charlene. He thanked her for asking him, told
her he couldn't go, and invited her out for the following weekend.

Another use of the aside often happens spontaneously when an enactor deliberately expresses the opposite of what he means, as in the following: Harold
says, "Wow, Celie, that's some gorgeous outfit," and then turns aside and says,
"If you like sneakers with a cocktail dress."

Walk and Talk

Walk and talk is similar to the walking soliloquy in that it too provides a
time out of the scene. The difference is that in the walk and talk, the director
and the enactor engage in a dialogue regarding the action. The physical movement out of the scene will often free the person from the tension felt within
its structure. The walk and talk provides an opportunity for a participant to
"take a breather" or "recharge his batteries" in order to return to the scene
with renewed energy or a refocused point of view. We all know that feeling in
life when we need to say, "Give me a minute." The walk and talk provides
for that. It also lets an enactor talk quietly with the leader about his feelings
and to "test the waters," if you will, before he attempts to verbalize his feelings
within the scene.

When you feel the enactor's need for a walk and talk, stop the action and
literally walk her out of the scene and around the playing area. Encourage her
to converse with you about how she is feeling at the moment. Help the player
discover what she wants and/or needs to say or do in the scene. Ask specific
questions about what went on in the scene so far, such as: "How are you
feeling now?" "What do you make of this situation?" "How did you feel when
Bob told you he loves you?" "What would you like to do at this point?" Once
the enactor feels ready to return to the scene and has an idea of what she will
do, move her into the scene and resume the action.

Occasionally, an enactor will stop the action because she is at a loss for words and will explain, "I don't know what to say." Walk her out of the enactment as you encourage her to use that feeling of inadequacy. Underscore the fact that everyone feels that way sometimes (Who hasn't?). You may ask her when she became bewildered or what is confusing her. These questions prime the spontaneity pump. You might instead suggest that she use that very feeling of confusion and turn it around to her advantage by going back to the action and asking the other enactor, "What do you want me to say?"

Perhaps one player cannot respond to another for some reason that is not apparent. Here is another good time for the walk and talk technique. You will get more information as to what is happening. Jeremy may tell you that he has been silent because he is annoyed with Father Flynn, and his parents told him never to speak disrespectfully to a priest. In another situation, the enactor may need reassurance that what she feels in the scene is perfectly acceptable.

At the opposite end of the spectrum, you can use the walk and talk technique if the action becomes too heated and threatens to erupt in violence. Taking one player out of the scene to walk him around and discuss his feelings may be just what is needed to defuse the high tension in the situation. Helping him move from the affective to the cognitive will cool down the situation. Ask him to analyze his reaction to his fellow player: "What triggered your anger?" "What did she say that evoked your response?" "Was it what she said or how she said it that disturbed you?" If both enactors are overheated, take out one at a time, so that each has an opportunity to vent and cool down.

When you use the walk and talk technique, you give participants a feeling of closeness with you, the director, and reinforce the structure of sociodrama. You are there to help them to discover alternatives in coping with whatever situation they are having difficulty with at the moment.

Freeze Frame

The freeze frame comes from the cinematic technique of freezing a single frame of the film on the screen, thus holding in place whatever action is occurring. In sociodrama there are times when you want the group and the enactors to see the body language of the scene as if it were a still photograph. That's the time to call, "Freeze!" Instruct the participants to stop and hold their positions in tableau for a moment when they hear the directive. Then you can ask enactors and audience what the still picture tells them about the scene.

This technique can be used in a variety of situations. Mainly, the freeze frame is a facilitator. It enables you to point out certain elements of the scene, such as, "Look at your body positions. What are they telling you about your feelings?"

You may employ the freeze frame to enable enactors to step out of the action and use one of the other techniques, such as soliloquy or walk and talk. Freeze frame is especially useful if the enactor seems overwhelmed by all of the action in the scene. For example, you can freeze the scene, bring him out, and ask him to look at the frozen scene. Ask him to comment on what he sees and to discuss how it feels to be out of the scene.

Sometimes you'll freeze the action because the structure for the action is lost. For example, ten people have volunteered to participate in a party scene. After a few minutes, everyone is talking at once, and it is difficult for the audience to focus on any specific dialogue. They just hear noise, and lots of it. Rather than stop all the action, the director may freeze all but one segment and allow those in the unfrozen segment to continue. After a while, he may freeze that segment and unfreeze another, and so on.

In addition, the freeze frame can be used when the director wants to elicit a reaction from the audience. Perhaps something is occurring between two participants that is more obvious to those watching than to the enactors in the scene. The director calls, "Freeze," and asks the audience what they see.

Let's say the scene is between a man and a woman. The man is trying to impress the lady with his urbane wit and charm. However, the woman's eye movements and body language clearly signal that not only is she uninterested in him but she's anxious to get away from him. What the man sees in the scene, however, is a woman looking for some company. He may interpret her behavior as encouragement to come on stronger. Once the audience tells what they see, the players can discuss what is happening to each of them and how each interprets the behavior of the other. Armed with this new information and understanding, they resume their positions and pick up the scene from there. Perhaps the lady becomes more receptive when the gentleman backs off some.

Freeze frame should be used in this way with the greatest delicacy and caution. It is all too easy for the audience to start analyzing and judging the actions of the participants. If you permit this, you'll find group members much less willing to volunteer for roles in the future: they will not want to open themselves to criticism. On the other hand, if a group is practicing an interpersonal skill and the enactors ask to be stopped and made aware of their actions, this particular use of freeze frame can be a great success.

Concretization

People often use metaphors to reflect how they feel. For example, a person may say, "Boy, Lou makes me sick to my stomach," or, "Sheila is a leech. I can't get rid of her." In sociodrama, the director can act as if the statement made is literally true and concretize it in action. A concretization is a literal portrayal of figurative or symbolic language or feelings. For example, if in a family sociodrama one of the enactors says, "I feel like low man on the totem pole," the director can ask the other family members to arrange themselves, head over head above the person.

When the director notices an enactor's physical responses, she can help the enactor to concretize feelings he is experiencing. Say that in a decision-making sociodrama, the director notices the enactor holding his head. She may ask why he's doing that. He may say, "My head is full of all the possible choices: reorganize the department; fire an employee; hire a new one; take a vacation; stay later at work." At this point, the director may bring in other enactors to play the alternatives, asking them to place their hands on the person's head and speak the alternative aloud. In this way, the enactor can externalize the cacophony of internal chaos and begin to deal with it piece by piece.

Sculpting

Sculpting is a kind of concretization in which enactors create a living tableau of interrelationships. In a family sociodrama, ask for volunteers to play members of the family. Say that five people volunteer: Harriet says she is Grandpa; Les says he is a seven-year old; Joan says she is his fourteen-year-old sister; Brenda says she is Grandpa's daughter and mother to the kids; Edie says she is Brenda's unmarried sister. They decide that all but Edie live together; she is visiting them. As a way of further warming up the enactors to their roles and role relationships, the director asks each to sculpt the other family members in relation to themselves, placing the others in positions that symbolize how they feel about the relationships. For example, Les loves Grandpa, so he places himself on Grandpa's lap. He can't stand his big sister, so he moves her to the edge of the playing area and faces her away from him with her hands on her hips. Les loves having all his mom's attention, so he places her with her back to sister and her arm around him. He is also fond of his aunt, and brings her close to him with her hand extended toward him.

In the middle of another sociodrama, the main enactor seems to be disturbed and withdrawn. Although she appears upset, she says nothing. In an effort to restore her spontaneity and sense of personal power, you may stop the action and ask her to sculpt the scene as it "feels" to her, how she perceives the relationships and the emotional tone of the interactions. She may, for example, feel like Kurt, playing her softball coach, is hovering over her and glaring. Her teammates have turned their backs and seem to be ignoring her distress. When she places people in these positions, she realizes why she felt so intimidated during the scene and resolves to assert herself with her coach and to seek out a friend for some support and acknowledgement of her competence.

Mirror

The mirror is a technique in which a player comes into the action, takes the enactor's place, and mirrors the enactor's verbal and nonverbal communication. Meanwhile, the enactor steps out of the scene to observe how he looks and sounds to others.

The mirror can be very helpful when the enactor seems to be overwhelmed by what is happening in the scene and is stuck. Taking an enactor out of the situation and allowing him to see it continue from a safe distance gives him a chance to figure out what is going on and what he wants to do next. The mirror, in effect, is marking his place, standing in for him, when he is out of the action.

Another way to use the mirror is to freeze the action when you see an enactor in an especially revealing body position. Call for a volunteer to assume that position in the enactment. Bring the original enactor out and ask what she observes and how she interprets the body language. Once she sees what she had been communicating nonverbally to others, she may want to adjust her actions when returning to the enactment.

This technique must be used with the greatest delicacy, so that the enactor doesn't feel mocked or judged. Direct the mirror to take the role of the enactor accurately and without caricature or stereotyping, and stop the action if this directive is not carried out.

Future Projection

Future projection is a technique in which the scene is set in the future so that the enactors can try out actions they have wished for, worried about, or planned. The future projection gives them an opportunity to see if things are likely to turn out as they hope, expect, or fear and how they will respond in the situation. A group of nursing students wants to see what it will feel like to be working as full-fledged nurses. They enact a scene where they play a nursing supervisor and two nurses on duty. On another occasion they acknowledge that they are worried about how to talk to the parents of a seriously ill child. They enact a scene where one of them encounters the father of a child who has just been operated on for acute appendicitis. On still another occasion, the students discuss their plans to become nurse/midwives. They decide they want to see what it will feel like to participate in the birth of a child and set up an enactment of the scene.

SUMMARY

The myriad techniques described in this chapter help to broaden and deepen the scope of sociodramatic enactment. With *role reversal* two people change places with each other in an effort to better understand themselves, the other, and their situation. When a person *doubles* for another, he or she expresses that person's unexpressed thoughts and feelings. The *empty chair technique* is one in which a chair is used as a projection tool. Group members are to suspend disbelief and imagine someone is sitting in the chair. They are then to speak to or double for that person as if he or she were actually present. In a *soliloquy,* an enactor steps out of the action and speaks his or her thoughts aloud at length. The *aside*, similar to the soliloquy, is a technique in which the enactor turns aside from the action and makes a brief statement. This is often either contradictory to what the person just said in the scene or is in some way a comment on what is happening. In the *walk and talk* technique, the director stops the action and brings one of the enactors out to walk and have a discussion about what is occurring in the scene. With *freeze frame*, the director freezes the action so that either the enactors or the audience can examine the scene differently. A *concretization* is a literal portrayal of figurative symbolic language or feelings. *Sculpting* is a technique in which an enactor places other enactors in frozen positions, making a living tableau representing interrelationships. In the *mirror* technique one enactor reflects the body language and vocal tones of another while the second observes. *Future projection* allows enactors to try out imagined scenes from the future. These techniques not only enrich the meaning of sociodramatic enactment; they also promote spontaneity and add the spice and excitement of variety.

7

ASSESSING NEEDS AND
MEETING GOALS

REVIEWING THEMES

Now that you are familiar with the techniques to structure the action of sociodrama, your next step is to assess the needs of your group and think about
what interventions might be called for in helping the group to meet those
needs. Focus on the group's theme for the day (shared central issue) and how
it may be developed in the enactment. Also, in deciding what to do next,
keep in mind the act hungers and open tension systems that were revealed in
the warm-up. Ask yourself if the group seems to need to experience catharsis,
insight, and/or role training. Once you have done these things, you are ready
to proceed with the enactment. Throughout the drama, concentrate on keeping your mind and the group's focus on the theme selected and the focus of
the enactment on developing that issue.

FACILITATING THE GOAL OF CATHARSIS

As stated in Chapter 2, catharsis in sociodrama refers to the deep expressions of emotions that take place in audience and enactors alike during a session. These purgings or outpourings may flow from such feelings as joy and
love, as well as from the less pleasant feelings of sorrow or anger. As participants release pent-up emotions, they experience relief and are freed up to look
at the situation in a new way.

In sociodrama, the leader encourages the enactors to allow themselves emotional spontaneity. She assists this process in a variety of ways. She establishes

a nonjudgmental atmosphere, noting to participants that emotions have no right or wrong; they simply exist. For example, many of us have been cautioned since childhood that anger is a *bad* emotion, one we shouldn't have. We may wish we didn't feel irritated, but most of us don't choose to be annoyed; we just find ourselves feeling that way. Since we don't deliberately create anger, *shouldn't* is immaterial.

Our emotions aren't the bad things. What we do in response to them is sometimes questionable, however. If you are hurt and express it directly and assertively, respecting the person to whom you are venting, it is likely there will be a positive outcome. On the other hand, if you are hurt and you bop someone over the head with the nearest object so that they can feel as bad as you do, your actions will carry a negative effect.

In addition to maintaining an accepting atmosphere, the director has many techniques available to facilitate catharsis. One of these is doubling. Say that an enactor is clearly feeling some deep emotion but is not expressing it. If one of the group members doubles for him, the enactor may feel the support he needs to acknowledge and speak out his feelings. Take a scene in which a married couple are disagreeing: a group member doubles for the man, "I feel terrible." He responds, "Yes, I do feel awful. Whenever you criticize me, Betty, I feel like a child again, and I hate that! I'm so upset!"

Another way to utilize the double is to reverse the enactor with his double and ask the enactor to express his feelings from the double position. This often feels like a safer place to vent emotions. The enactor position is experienced as the face we show the world, our persona; whereas the double position represents our truest self. Furthermore, when we are in the double position, there is a physical barrier (the person playing the role we have just vacated) between us and our antagonist.

We can also use a technique that Meg Givnish, who developed Problem Solving Theatre, calls the Magic Screen. Sometimes a person is having trouble saying what she feels because she fears the other person's response. In this situation, you can say that you are putting up a magic screen between her and the other enactor. Note that both people can see each other through the screen, and instruct the other enactor to act as if he cannot hear what she is saying. In this way, she can be free to say what she wishes without fear of reprisal. After the catharsis, ask the enactor if there is anything that she is willing to express to the other person directly. Remember, the other enactor may respond only to what the person says to him after the screen is down. When the person has decided what she wants to say to the other enactor, remove the screen with a wave of your hand and resume the action.

The soliloquy and aside are other techniques that can be used to facilitate catharsis. Gary was a person who was considered to be a mild-mannered individual. He characterized himself as someone who avoids conflict at all costs. He was anxious to learn how to handle himself in a difficult situation and volunteered to participate in an enactment where he had to stand up for his rights. The scene took place in a restaurant. A nasty waiter snarled at him to move from the table where he had just sat down with his date. Gary's first reaction was to do what he was told. The director, noticing Gary's face reddening, asked him to step out of the action and say what he was feeling. Gary said he was furious at the waiter for trying to push him around. He was also embarrassed at his own anger and felt ashamed that he hadn't stood up for himself. When he returned to the action, having expressed his feelings, Gary was able to respond in a new way. He told the waiter nicely but firmly that he had been shown to that table by the *maitre d'*, that he would not move, and would like his order taken now. He also breathed a sigh of relief at having removed the burden of silence and intimidation from his shoulders.

Sometimes a person's self-image prevents him or her from expressing strong emotions. In these instances, it is helpful to direct the enactor to reverse roles with someone in the scene who is able to express those emotions. At one point in the above enactment, the director reversed Gary into the position of the nasty waiter. He vented more of his own suppressed anger in the role of the waiter. He later said, "That felt great! I would never do that to someone and hurt their feelings, but it sure was a relief to say what I felt instead of shutting up."

Many sociodrama directors feel that an action catharsis is not only a purging of emotions, but it is also a creative moment. Through the purging, one is released to view and respond to the situation in a fresh way.

FACILITATING ACTION INSIGHT

Insight is another primary goal of sociodrama. It is the sudden comprehension or understanding in a situation. We see the light. We've all experienced the feeling of, "Oh, now I see!" In sociodrama, the insight occurs through action. From experience we know that any real change must express itself in action—in doing something, not just knowing, intending, or dreaming, but in action.

Often an insight will emerge spontaneously during an enactment. An enactor looks as if he's thunderstruck and will turn aside and say, "I just realized . . ." At other times when you feel an enactor wants to experience insight but feels unable to do so, you may freeze the action and bring her out for a walk and talk or soliloquy. You may ask her what she sees happening in the scene. You may ask someone to stand in for her while she either looks at the frozen scene or at the scene in action. Melody chattered away in an enactment, but her body seemed tense. The director froze the scene, called for a mirror and asked Melody to observe the scene and describe what she saw. "My body seems rigid in the extreme. I look nervous. I bet that's why I was talking so much. I didn't even realize that I was nervous."

Sometimes the double also facilitates the goal of insight. In an enactment, some enactors ask Bryce for arithmetic help. As he explains how to do the problem, his double says, "Hey, I really understand this." Bryce says, "Wow, not only do I understand it, but I never realized that other people saw me as someone who could do math! I also never realized that I could teach anybody anything."

The director can also call for role reversal to help an enactor gain insight. When a person changes places with another, he is often able to see the situation in a whole new light. In a job interview enactment, Alan is scanning the room with his eyes, shaking his foot nervously, and frequently shifting in his seat. After he role reverses with the person playing the potential employer, he says, "No wonder I don't feel like Ms. Martin will hire me. I'm not even looking directly at her. I bet my fidgeting is making her nervous. I'm going to make eye contact, stop thinking about myself, and start asking her questions about the job." As a result of the insight he gained in action, Alan learned to acknowledge his anxiety to himself and direct his attention toward others rather than focusing on his feelings of insecurity and worries that the interviewer won't like him. Alan's experience is one of many that illustrates that achieving action insight is a powerful impetus for change.

FACILITATING ROLE TRAINING

People tell us that experience is the best teacher. However, this kind of learning can be painful, embarrassing, and sometimes even dangerous. For example, with a gun directed at our heads in a convenience store heist, we may learn not to anger a hostile individual, but surely it would be better to learn that skill from a safer distance. Role training provides us with an opportunity to try on new roles and participate in new situations in a safe environment, away from the line of fire. We can make attempts at new behavior until we feel comfortable enough to try our newly learned skills in the world at large. The beauty of role training is that one actually experiences a simulated problem with another person who reacts spontaneously to what one says and does. Just as in life, one cannot anticipate what the other person will say or do in a given sociodramatic situation.

Role training is a goal that can be addressed in a wide variety of settings. Sometimes the purpose and contract of the group is primarily role training. Assertiveness training groups, rape counselor training groups, customer service training groups are a few examples of this. Rape counselors, for instance, learn through role training how to offer empathy and understanding as well as to acquire the pertinent facts for immediate follow-up. Although the counselor may know all the right questions to ask intellectually, when she is actually in the highly charged emotional situation, she will be better able to handle this crisis after successful practice in role training sessions.

Role training may be an enactment goal even in groups where it is not the focus or contract of the group. During a drama, an enactor may turn to you and say, "I don't know how to . . ." At this point you have several options.

You may ask if any other group members do know how to do it, asking them to make suggestions to the enactor, one of which he may want to try. You may also freeze the action, walk and talk with the enactor and ask him to consider what alternative steps to take to master the skill. When he has brainstormed some ideas, ask him which he would like to try out and return him to the action. If the skill the person wants to acquire is complex, the enactor may want to try the scene several times, modifying it each time to accommodate what he has learned from the previous trial.

Occasionally, several members of the group may want simultaneous practice. They may set up a scene in which most of the enactors are practicing new behaviors—for example, a group of day care workers learning to manage an out-of-control situation. Or you may want to set up a variety of situations for the enactors so that they receive an opportunity to practice as many aspects of the role as possible. In some ways this training is a rite of passage, as it were, for these people.

An interesting variation of the sociodramatic usage is role training using a troupe of trained enactors. A group called P.A.C.T. (Performing Arts for Crisis Training), operating out of New York City, performs training sessions for police trainees, social workers, crisis intervention counselors, and so on. The P.A.C.T. members enact the crisis situation and bring in the trainee to handle it spontaneously. An example of this is the young rookie cop who is called upon to talk a potential suicide victim off a window ledge. The scene is played with all its emotional turmoil and tension. The officer learns how he would react in such a situation. If he is displeased with any elements of his behavior, he can try the scene again, adjusting his actions accordingly.

We should remember that improvising in a variety of roles and expanding one's primary roles inevitably increase's one's ability to function satisfactorily in myriad situations.

GOING WITH RESISTANCE

Every group leader runs into resistance at one time or another. Sometimes members don't feel like doing an enactment. On other occasions, an enactor gets the giggles or says, "I can't go on with this." At still other times the enactor seems out of touch with his or her feelings. Sometimes we ourselves would rather be home in bed than out there directing a session. Whatever the overt reason, reluctance to act is connected with not feeling ready to put ourselves on the line and risk exploring our feelings, learning about ourselves, or trying something new. Moreno (1973) saw this as a diminishment or loss of spontaneity. This reluctance is to be respected. It is present because the person feels unsafe for some reason. When we can feel more confident that we will not come apart at the seams if we look at the underlying issue, we look at it. The director doesn't hammer away at people, trying to break down their resistance. Rather he assists group members to experience the safety necessary for taking risks. In *Acting In*, Blatner (63) quotes Moreno as saying, "We don't tear down the protagonist's walls; rather, we simply try some of the handles on the many doors, and see which one opens."

For example, with a group of teenagers who say, "I don't want to be here," simply ask them where they would prefer to be. After they have told you, set up a scene to correspond with their wishes. They will be better able to participate in the session if it addresses their warm-up.

Occasionally resistance emerges in the form of laughter. For example, an enactor might get the giggles apropos of nothing. Or he may laugh at himself playing the role, thus moving away from genuinely experiencing it. Usually this occurs because the enactor is afraid to allow himself to become fully involved in the scene. Here is where you might want to step in yourself and double, saying something like, "I'm laughing because I'm really embarrassed, and I'm afraid I'm making a fool of myself." As the enactor repeats the statement, he becomes aware of the source of his resistance.

You may also choose to concretize resistance in an enactment. Here is an example of how internal mixed messages kept an enactor stuck. Cheryl was playing the role of someone on a diet who is tempted to eat a piece of homemade cake her mother offered her. At one point she turned to the director and said, "Part of me wants to stay on my diet, and part of me wants to cheat. It's like I'm stuck some place in the middle." The director concretized the resistance by calling for two volunteers, one to play the part of Cheryl that wants to eat and the other to play the part that wants to lose weight. Rosanne played the devil part of Cheryl, as she called it, and tempted her to eat: "Go ahead, you deserve it. Just think how long it took your mother to bake that cake for you. Eat it! Eat it! Remember how delicious it tastes." On the other side of Cheryl stood her angel double who answered, "No, you can't eat that. Look how far you've come with your weight loss. You want to be thin and feel more healthy. Don't give in!"

The director can also internally double for the group to discover the underlying meaning of their reluctance. Once she has a sense of what may be happening, the director may do several things. For example, she may openly say to the group, "I get the feeling people would rather discuss something pleasant, and don't want to leave here upset. Who feels that way?" Once one person has had the courage to admit to reluctance, ask who else feels the same way, noting that if one person feels that way, probably others do too. If several members speak up, applaud their honesty. It is important to let them know that they are not alone in their feelings and that it is common to feel reluctant at times. If this reluctance occurs during the warm-up, the enactment may end up being about how difficult it is to do some things.

Above all it is important for the director not to personalize group members' resistance. They are not just trying to give you a hard time. They are themselves having a tough time of it, no matter how it appears on the surface. If you work with the resistance rather than oppose it, both you and the group will be able to resolve it with a minimum of stress.

FINDING THE BALANCE BETWEEN LETTING GO AND SELF-CONTROL

Throughout life we work to find the balance between self-control and letting go of our controls. Some of us most often feel at the mercy of whatever emotion we happen to be experiencing at the moment. If we are mad, everyone knows it. If we are happy, it is irrepressible. Sometimes we speak before we think, and people's feelings get hurt. Others of us tend to control our emotions to such a degree that no one seems to know what we are feeling. Occasionally, we don't know either. We would never make a scene. Sometimes we think so long about what to say, that the relevant moment for saying it has passed.

Frequently, people will join a sociodrama group with the specific purpose of becoming more comfortable in groups. They say, "I'm shy. I want to learn to speak up more," or, "I always say the wrong thing. I want to learn to be more sensitive to others." These people are not looking for psychotherapy, wanting to delve into the why and wherefores of their behavior. They simply want to learn new skills for communicating in a more satisfying way.

In order to provide the climate for people to feel safe enough to experiment with new behaviors, it is important for the director to set some ground rules for the group: members are not to judge each other's performance; no one is to verbally or physically attack another. The group members may also want to agree to some measure of confidentiality for the work they do, so that they may feel more comfortable expressing their feelings freely. Further, members are not to enact their own personal problems, since this violates the sociodrama contract.

There is a situation involving self-control that rarely happens, but needs to be handled delicately when it does. If one enactor is portraying a character vastly differently than the group has suggested, he may be doing so because he was in a similar situation in life and he wants to recreate that life situation in the sociodrama. However, it is not the contract of a sociodrama group to do direct therapy with participants. It is the director's responsibility as leader to assist the person and the group in keeping the sociodrama in an "as if" frame. No one should be acting out his or her own personal drama in a sociodrama group. What ends up happening if this is allowed to continue is that group members become annoyed at the member who is moving the action away from the shared central issue and resentful of the director. Also, the trust level of the group spirals downward. It is the leader's function to help the group maintain its contract. There are several ways to handle this situation. The director can freeze the action and point out to the enactor that he seems not to be responding to what people are saying but rather responding to some internal dialogue. She may ask the person if he has noticed this and if he has an idea what is happening. If the enactor is aware that he is dealing with his own issues and having trouble tabling them to play the sociodramatic role, the director may ask him if he would like to sit this enactment out and have someone else come in to play the role. Or, without saying anything about the enactor's personalization of the action, she can remind him of the shared central issue and see if that is enough to help the person correct his portrayal. If the person is still unable to adjust his character, ask him to play the double for the person and ask for a new volunteer to play the person. The importance of helping the group keep its contract cannot be overstressed.

On a macrocosmic level, group members learn new skills through involvement in the process inherent in sociodrama groups—namely, that people share their feelings in the warm-up and in the sharing segment, and they participate in a collective experience during the enactment. The director models sharing and encourages all opinions. On a microcosmic level, members learn how to let go or gain control through taking roles. Jeff realized that being outgoing wasn't really impossible after he played the role of a gregarious ship's captain. Betsy, on the other hand, learned to hold her tongue by practicing how to be present at a meeting without monopolizing the conversation. Whatever end of the continuum we are closer to, overexpression or overcontrol, the sociodrama experience can help us to develop the less-developed pole.

CLOSING THE ACTION

When time is running out or the action of the sociodrama seems complete, it is necessary for the director to help the group bring the enactment to a close. The first thing she must do is to make sure that all enactors are back in their original roles so they don't end the enactment in the role-reversed position.

Closing When the Action Is Reaching a Natural End

Most frequently, it is clear when a sociodrama is nearing its end. The enactors will have solved a problem; decided what action they will take; resolved a conflict; expressed the emotions they have needed to express; or practiced new behaviors to their satisfaction. In these instances, simply ask each enactor to say the last thing he or she wants to say for now. When that process is complete, the sociodrama is over, and the enactors return to their seats for the sharing portion.

Closing the Action When Time Is Up and the Action Is Incomplete

By the same token, there are occasions when time simply runs out and the action isn't finished. Perhaps the group is exploring a difficult and complex issue for which there is no quick answer or exploring a moral dilemma. Since sharing is vital, it is better to cut the action short than to eliminate the sharing segment.

When you become aware that time is up and the action is unfinished, there are several things you can do to facilitate closure. No matter what else you do, it is a good idea to let people know that time is running out, so that the action doesn't stop abruptly and leave them disoriented. You may freeze the action and let the enactors know that there are only two minutes remaining. Ask them how they would like to use the time. Or, after freezing the scene and noting that time is almost up, you may ask the audience rather than the enactors how they would like the scene concluded. If the focus of the enactment is on one specific enactor, ask that person how he would like to end the scene.

Another way to handle the situation is to ask the participants what they want to do that they haven't already done in the scene. Often the time constraint helps people to get right to the point they have been skirting around.

Sometimes it helps the group to acknowledge what they think would be necessary to conclude the action in a satisfying way, even if there is not time left to carry out the action in the session. For example, in an enactment in which the enactors seem to be at loggerheads, someone might say, "I think Jody and Gail need to speak to each other privately, away from their friends. Everybody's getting into the discussion, and it's making things worse."

Whatever choices you make, be sure that the significant enactors have the opportunity to say the last thing they want to say before they return to their seats. Saying the last thing gives the audience the same sense of completion they get from hearing a curtain line at the end of a play. For the enactors, saying the last thing helps them conclude their performance and return to their life roles.

It is important for the director to keep track of time and to get to know how to direct an enactment in the time available. This is a matter of personal style. If you know you have only thirty minutes left in the session by the time everyone is warmed up, what action can the group undertake that can be completed in enough time to allow for sharing time, too? Perhaps it may be necessary to do only a brief vignette (five to ten minutes). This may be either a scene or a sculpture of the issues to explore. A lot can happen even in a short enactment. It is helpful to let the group know of the time constraints so that they can help decide what kind of enactment will best suit their needs in the time available.

SUMMARY

Throughout each sociodramatic enactment, the director remains cognizant of the issues with which the group is dealing. After assessing the needs of the group, he or she facilitates the goals of catharsis, insight, and role training during the course of the sociodrama enactment. The director may need to help

group members overcome *resistance*. This is done not by directly opposing reluctance, but rather by providing opportunities for members to feel safe enough
to express themselves openly.

Regarding open expression, most people struggle throughout life to balance
self-control and *letting go*. In sociodrama, members can pool their knowledge
and expertise in this area and give each other support to develop whichever
pole of expression is weakest in them.

Whether the action reaches a natural end or must be curtailed because of
time demands, the director allows enactors to make a last statement in their
roles. If the action is incomplete, the director lets the group know that time
is running out and he or she devotes the last minutes of the enactment to
closing down the action.

8

TAKING STOCK AND MOVING FORWARD

SETTING THE TONE FOR SHARING

A vital part of the sociodrama experience is sharing after the enactment. During that time, enactors return to the group, and those who have viewed the action have the chance to say how it affected them. It is essential that the director let the members know what sharing means. It is a time to explore one's own identification with what has occurred. It is not a time to analyze or criticize the behavior of the enactors. As with the rest of the sociodrama session, the director encourages an accepting, nonjudgmental atmosphere.

The sharing generally has two parts. The first is the time for expressing feelings. The second is the time for returning to the cognitive: asking and answering questions; generalizing what has been learned, and planning new behaviors.

Returning the Enactor to the Group

In order to participate in the action, members leave their seats and the anonymity of the group. They assume roles, still further separating them from the group. Paradoxically, they must leave the audience in order to represent its themes and tensions. The risks they take in the drama benefit the group as a whole. After the enactment is over, it is essential to help the enactors derole and return to the body as members. This process is accomplished as people share how they were touched by the enactment, thus reconnecting them with the enactors. Also enactors are given an opportunity to shake off the role they have played and get back to being themselves.

Refocusing

During the warm-up, the focus is on group issues and the members' personal feelings. In the enactment, the focus narrows to explore specific facets of those issues and feelings. The group explores them through a hypothetical situation, enacted most often by a few people, not by the body as a whole. The sharing again provides time for refocusing on the group's issues at large, acknowledging one's personal feelings.

SHARING EXPERIENCES

Members watching the enactment connect actively with the participants and identify with their feelings. After its conclusion, ask audience members what they felt during the drama. As several members share how their lives are similar to what they saw, they discover they are not alone and feel less isolated. Frequently after members share their experiences, several will remark about how good it felt to speak openly and to realize that others have much the same feelings.

Audience members are sometimes embarrassed and surprised at the depth of their emotional reactions to the sociodrama. Again, sharing these feelings helps people to realize that they are not the only ones who reacted so strongly. Sharing helps people recover from what one alcoholism counselor referred to as "terminal uniqueness."

If the enactors don't share spontaneously what the experience was like for them, ask them to share what they felt during the scene and/or how it connected with their personal lives. Sometimes players will share feelings that are not at all obvious to those who were watching. For example, Dan spoke angrily to Shirley, who portrayed his wife in the enactment, but when it came time to share feelings, he said, "I yelled at Shirley because I was afraid . . . afraid she would leave me." This statement was a revelation to Shirley as well as to the observers. All any of them saw was Dan's anger. This sparked a discussion of how others in the group mask their fear with anger. This illustrates how important it is for the enactors to share their feelings after the scene.

Remind your group if necessary that an enactment is not a theatrical endeavor. The quality of the acting is unimportant and should not be discussed or analyzed in the sharing. What counts here is the process and not the product. Be careful not to allow any judgment to sneak in during the sharing. Occasionally, a member will want to analyze an enactor's behavior. This happens when the member is trying to distance himself from his own feelings. Gently point out that in order to make an analysis, one has to have first-hand experience, either because he has played the role himself or someone close to him has played it. Encourage him to share his experience rather than his analysis.

Sometimes, an audience member will be eager to give advice to the enactors. Advice-giving is another form of distancing that, like analysis, sets up a one-up/one-down relationship. The implication is, "I will give you advice, because I know more about this than you do." When someone gives us advice that we haven't asked for, we tend to get annoyed and start a power struggle with the advice-giver about why we can't do what he or she wants us to do. The whole process usually gets us nowhere, and everyone ends up feeling frustrated and edgy. It can be avoided by pointing out the difficulties "advice-giving" engenders. Then ask that instead of giving advice, the member shares what she has done and found successful in a similar situation. The person can still give the same basic information, but she isn't imposing it as a dictum on someone else. Maureen told Gina, "You should have told her you wouldn't baby-sit for her kids. Who does she think she is?" After being told to reframe the advice as sharing, Maureen said, "My aunt is always dumping her kids on me. It gets me so aggravated. This week, for the first time, I told her I'm busy and that I want at least a few days notice when she wants me to watch them. I still feel a little guilty because she used to baby-sit for me when I was a kid, but at least I finally spoke up." At this point the teens began to discuss how difficult it is to feel obligated. Thus, while Maureen's advice would have stemmed communication and probably started a power struggle, her sharing opened the group to discussing the sociodrama in greater depth.

In general, it is also important to discourage people's questions while others are still sharing. Asking and answering questions bounces us back to the cognitive and away from the affective. Questions are wonderful after everyone has finished expressing feelings and a great way of helping people cool down from the session. The problem is we don't want them to cool down before they have had a chance to say what they have felt.

Questions are generally of a few types. One kind is when someone wants to ask a question about process: "Could I get up and double whenever I want?" Another is one in which a member wants concrete information from the members: "Hey, in the enactment, someone mentioned a place to get tennis shoes fixed. Does anybody know of any place like that around here?" With both these questions, ask members to hold them until the end of the sharing, promising to give them time to make the queries then. Explain that questions serve to distract us and distance us from our feelings. The first part of the sharing is the time for feelings; the second part is the time to return to the cognitive.

Another kind of question is really a statement masquerading as a question: "Why did you tell Fred you don't want to be his roommate?" Most "why" questions are statements, usually hostile ones, in disguise. When such questions come up, explain that oftentimes we ask something when we really want to make a statement. You may point out, "It is valuable for all of us to know what you feel. What is it you want to say?" For example, when asked to transform the above "why" question into a statement, Riva said, "I felt hurt and annoyed when you said that to Fred. I was friendly with someone who agreed to share an apartment with me. I rented the apartment, and at the last minute she backed out, leaving me either to pay a rent I couldn't afford or to find a new roommate immediately!"

Occasionally, a member will ask an enactor, "How did you feel when ———— happened?" Give the enactor a chance to respond to this question, but after he does, ask the questioner how she felt when it happened. In this way, both people will have an opportunity to communicate and to express their feelings.

DE-ROLING

When the sociodrama is ended and the enactors return to their seats, most often they are back to being themselves. However, sometimes an enactor plays a role that evokes strong feelings and reactions in herself. When this occurs, there are several things that you can do to help the enactor de-role. The first and simplest is to ask her to say what she felt when playing the role. You can also ask how her own life is similar to or different from the character she portrayed and the situation in which she was involved.

You may also ask how the enactor liked playing the role. Occasionally someone volunteers to play a role that is somewhat distasteful to him. He may feel like a villain in the enactment. When the action is over, he may hurriedly assure the group, "I'm not really mean like that."

Another thing that we like to do to help enactors de-role is to shake out when the drama is over. Enactors shake their hands and feet and squirm around a bit. Or you can ask them to wave their arms and say, "Frog," "Erase," "Airplane," or any other word that has nothing whatever to do with the action. This physiological shift is most often enough to get the enactors out of role. Besides, people usually get a good giggle from this effective technique.

REACHING CLOSURE

It is important to reach closure at the end of each session. Reaching closure implies that the act hungers have been addressed and that the shared central issue has been explored to the group's satisfaction. It also means that the group is ready to conclude the session. Reaching closure does not necessarily mean that the group has solved all the problems that it explored. For example, after a values clarification sociodrama, members may not have come up with one right answer. However, they do see more clearly their own position on the subject or realize what facet of the issue they need to consider more deeply in the future.

Through sharing what they feel and thus discharging pent-up energy, the group members begin to cool down from the issues that were enacted. This cooling down through sharing is one of the ways that people reach closure. Two other ways to close are (1) to help people return to the cognitive frame and (2) to give them an opportunity to plan new behaviors. A *reminder:* Guide the group to share feelings first and to make cognitive statements only *after* everyone has shared what he or she wants to share. In this way, you will not stem the flow of members' identification with the enactment. It is through the identification and the sharing of myriad experiences that the learning base is broadened and deepened.

Returning to the Cognitive Frame

Much of the sociodrama addresses affective needs as does the initial part of the sharing. In order to reach closure, the group needs to step back from their emotional involvement in the enactment to the cool detachment of the observer. Often members are able to reach closure solely through sharing feelings and insights. This process helps to cool them down. When they have not done so, when group members want to ask questions or when you want to review skills learned during the enactment, you can help them to reach closure by focusing on the intellectual aspects of the session. For example, if you had asked people to hold their questions until everyone shared, you can let them know that it is now time for questions. Even if no one has asked anything during others' sharing, it is a good idea to see if anyone has any questions about what occurred during the session.

Occasionally at this time, members will ask for feedback about their behavior in a sociodrama. This is especially true when a person has been trying out new behavior and is unsure of it. For example, in a parent effectiveness group, Marie asked the members if they felt she was firm enough in setting limits for her child in a sociodrama.

Planning New Behaviors

When the group's focus in on skill building or learning of some type, it is helpful to give participants an opportunity to review what skills they learned during the session. They may want to discuss where they feel they can use those skills outside the group. They may even want to plan or discuss how they will act in a specific future situation.

TRYING OUT ALTERNATIVE SOLUTIONS

In addition to expressing feelings, the sharing is also a time for members to say how they approached the problem in their own lives and what they have done to understand it better or solve it. During this process, the group not only discovers that there are many appropriate ways to solve problems, but it also explores a variety of methods of doing so. Moreover, this practice of exploring alternatives provides a means of promoting insight in the participants.

After the sharing of feelings, if time remains, ask your observers what alternatives they could recommend for the situation. Begin with simple questions like, "What else could Dan have said?" or "How could Shirley tell Dan what she meant in a different way?" Preface the questions with a statement like, "What Dan and Shirley did was appropriate and right for them, but there are additional ways to handle the situation. Who can think of one?" These and similar questions will stimulate the group's thinking. Perhaps Dan himself has another idea of how to treat the situation differently from what he did in the enactment. He may want to try it out and see which solution he prefers.

Members may also brainstorm different approaches that they have not tried but that they think might work in the situation. Where you have additional time, give the members an opportunity to try out some of the solutions they have generated. Don't restrict the practice to the people originally in the roles, but allow whomever says she has an alternative to try it out. This not only increases learning; it also involves more people in enacting.

On the other hand, as people are discussing various alternatives, one of the original players, Shirley, for instance, may want to try out one of the suggestions made by a group member. Gloria said, "When Dan raised his voice to Shirley, I was frightened. I wanted to tell him that," Shirley said, "I was frightened, too. I want to replay the scene and see if I can tell him I'm frightened."

When searching for alternative solutions, encourage your participants to try out as many new solutions as they feel necessary. Some will be more comfortable for your enactors than others. Having the opportunity to explore one's own interpersonal style and see others' styles in action has a profound effect. We become clearer about who we are and how we behave, and we come to recognize and accept each other's individual differences and similarities. We also begin to become more accepting of ourselves and our own personal differences.

SUMMARY

The *sharing* is when the group reaches closure for the session. It is the time when members tell each other what they felt while watching the enactment. They also discuss how what they saw was similar to or different from their own lives. During this time, the enactors return to the group and are reintegrated. The *de-role* by sharing how they felt playing the role and how the role is different from or similar to themselves.

In the first part of the sharing, the group reaches closure through expressing feelings. Later members reach closure through asking questions, generating alternate solutions, and planning what behaviors to bring into daily life. If time remains, the director may give group members an opportunity to try out several solutions in mini enactments. If no time remains for this, the group may plan to try out the alternatives in the next session. If the group's goal is some type of skills building, the director may so plan the session that the group will be assured of time remaining after the sharing for behavioral rehearsal of the newly generated alternatives.

9

MASTERING DIRECTING SKILLS

WARMING UP FOR DIRECTING

Directing a sociodrama group is an exciting process. We participate from beginning to end in the many twists and turns of group dynamics. We facilitate education and transformation holistically. That is the good news. It is also the bad news in that such a heady opportunity and responsibility can be scary. Once a session begins, the director's first task is to help members become fully present—in other words, undistracted and paying attention to what is happening. Since he needs to help others to be in the "here and now," it is essential for the director to be in the moment from the start of the session. Therefore, it is important for the director to take some time to ready himself before the session begins.

Tuning in to One's Own Issues

In the same way that group members bring their own warm-up into a group, so does the director. If he has been caught in traffic on the way to the group, if he is worried about how to meet his mortgage payment, these will be part of the warm-up he brings to the meeting. Moreover, he may be warmed up to some anxiety about leading the group. Will he know what intervention to perform when it is needed? Will he be able to help participants resolve any interpersonal conflicts?

It is very helpful for the director to tune into his own issues for a variety of reasons. If you are unaware of your own warm-up, it is easy to become stuck in a session. For example, say I haven't acknowledged that I am afraid I won't know what intervention to perform in an enactment. The sociodrama chosen by the group deals with trying to be perfect and feeling inadequate. In the middle of the sociodrama, as one of the enactors says he doesn't know what to do, my own worst fears may arise and paralyze me. I don't know what to do either. I pushed my fears away without exploring them before the session, and now here they are mocking me. I have no idea what to do to help the enactor. On the other hand, if I have acknowledged my fears before the session and realized that I will survive even if I am scared, I can plan what I might do to help myself feel more comfortable. Before the session, I may decide to call for a walk and talk if I get stuck during the drama, or to ask the members what they think is happening in the scene, or to ask the enactors how they want to proceed. In that way if the enactor does get stuck, I needn't panic or grind to a halt as well.

Here is another reason for tuning in to your own warm-up. As part of the group, your personal warm-up may be similar to that of others in the group. Moreno described this phenomenon as a state "which the partners experienced and produced jointly" (*Psychodrama—First Volume*, vii). Moreno noticed that people who encounter each other intimately, whether in groups or dyads, often seem to be experiencing similar issues concurrently and to be generating concerns through the dynamics of their relationships. He referred to these processes as the "co-conscious" and the "co-unconscious."

After checking your own warm-up, then you may have a hint as to what issue the group may want to explore. One of the authors was leading a sociodrama group at a chronic care hospital. She had been feeling unsettled and anxious about something in her own life on a day when the group was to meet. Walking through the hospital corridors on the way to the group, she noticed that there was much more activity than usual. One of the patients had had a stroke during the night and was moaning and babbling loudly. In a usually quiet hall, someone else was shouting from one of the rooms. Further, she learned that one of the long-term residents had died that morning. Trays were clanking, and the muffled voices sounded tense.

When the group started, the director said, "I noticed all the commotion outside today. Does it seem more noisy than usual to you?" After the members answered, she asked, "How does it feel to have so much going on at once?" In this way, the author, having acknowledged her own warm-up, was more sensitive to the clamor in the hospital. She realized that possibly her consciousness and that of the members were aligned, and that Moreno's concept of the co-conscious was operating.

While it is certainly valuable to check your own warm-up and see if it matches the group's, it is equally important not to impose your warm-up on others or to assume that they will want to explore the particular facet of the issue that you would like to examine. That brings us to the point of tabling your own concerns.

Tabling One's Problems

Life being what it is, occasionally we have difficult things to deal with personally. We may be feeling sad, worried, angry, or upset. We may not be in the mood to direct a sociodrama session. Nevertheless, if we have accepted the responsibility of leading a group, our focus needs to stay on the members' needs and not our own while we are in session.

When times are rough for us and we are about to enter a session, it is helpful to acknowledge what we are feeling rather than hide our feelings from ourselves. There is less chance of our emotions overwhelming us in a session if we have acknowledged them. Once we have looked at what we feel, it is also helpful to tune in to what work we still need to do to better understand or resolve our problem. After that, knowing that the issue will still be available after the session, table your concern. The idea here is not to deny the problem, nor to obsess about it, but rather to notice it, contract with yourself to deal with it after the session, and put it aside for the present so that you can fulfill your contract with the group.

WARMING UP WITH THE GROUP

Whether the director has prepared a structured warm-up or chosen to allow members to warm up spontaneously through their interactions, once the session begins, he is readying himself for sociodramatic action just as they are. During the warm-up he is aware of himself and his feelings. He is cognizant of, and responsive to, the group dynamics. At the same time, he is listening for the shared central issue to emerge and developing a hypothesis upon which to proceed. One of the necessary characteristics of a sociodrama director is the ability to alternate between the roles of group member and director. In other words, the director is able both to be emotionally present and to distance himself enough to help the group meet its goals. This latter ability is called the *directorial function*.

When one first begins directing, it is hard to keep all the balls in the air at once. Some of our trainees complain of being so involved in the process themselves that they can't figure out what the group needs. Some others feel they couldn't possibly allow themselves to be in touch with their own feelings and also move ahead knowing what interventions to make.

If you are new at directing, keep in mind that no one starts out directing perfectly. We are always learning and improving. No matter how skilled, we can always grow. When we start out, some of us have great intuition. Others have great powers of analysis and seem able to determine what the group needs and what interventions to perform. Still others have such highly developed empathy that they easily build rapport with groups. Whatever your strong points, practice will help you to enhance them and to improve your less-developed skills.

Sharing Oneself Honestly

As the group is warming up and members are sharing thoughts and emotions, it is fine to let people know what you are feeling, too. Often your honesty can help to facilitate the group's process. For example, when there seems to be tension in the group that no one is discussing, it is appropriate to say, "I feel tense. Anyone else feel that way?"

Here is another example of both sharing feelings and facilitating group process. One day it was snowing hard outside. One of the authors went into her group and said, "Wow, it's frightening being out there. My car was slipping and sliding all over. Did other people have trouble getting here?" As members eagerly talked about their hair-raising experiences, a theme emerged: fear of losing control. Although the storm catalyzed the fear that day, the members later said that they had been feeling out of control anyway. Thus the director's honesty helped the group focus on the deeper issues.

Being Spontaneous

It is not only essential for the director to be spontaneous; it is also fun. The unexpected happens frequently. Whatever occurs, use it; it is an opportunity. If your warm-up is interrupted by a fire drill, when you return to the room, address how it feels to be interrupted. If members are not in the mood to do the warm-up you have structured, ask what they would like to do instead. If someone says something apparently out of context, help the person and group search for how it is connected. Also feel free to use your sense of humor and playfulness and encourage that in group members. We can all benefit from a good laugh. As the saying goes, "He who laughs, lasts."

Listening to the Group's Needs

It's important to listen carefully to *all* that members say during the warm-up segment. At this time, both verbally and nonverbally, people will let you know how they feel and what concerns they have. Try to stay open to both. poles of opinion and to how warmed up to action the members are. As you tune in to the various nuances of feeling, it will be easier to know how to assist the group during the enactment and sharing phases.

The more room there is in the group for expressing all shades of thought and feeling, the more effectively and freely group members will explore the issues. Sometimes, several members are very vocally espousing a particular viewpoint. No one seems to be disagreeing. Just because no one is arguing with them, it doesn't necessarily mean that the others agree completely. In fact, there are probably a wide range of opinions that haven't yet been expressed. You may ask if anyone disagrees and prime the conversational pump that way. Or, if no one responds during the warm-up, when the action begins, you can double for the opposite pole when you detect those feelings in one of the enactors.

During the warm-up as well as throughout the session, silently double for the group, tuning in to the various things members might be feeling. Once you have doubled, you can check out your perceptions with the group to see if they are accurate: "I felt excited when you said that, Mary. How did other people feel?" "Almost everybody looks exhausted today. Is that how you're feeling, or is it my imagination?" "I sense that people are annoyed that our trip was canceled. Is that true?" As members respond, you can adjust your perceptions accordingly, further readying yourself to direct the enactment.

CREATING A SAFE, NONJUDGMENTAL ENVIRONMENT

It is the director's task to create an environment in which the participants feel safe and comfortable, a place where they can share their thoughts and feelings without any fear of reprisals or criticism. In order to create this climate, any hint of negative, personal judgment must be discouraged. There is often a fine line between expressing opinions and making negative, critical judgments of others. The distinction that we make is that opinion refers to a person's thoughts on a particular subject—such as, "Prostitution should be legalized." Negative personal judgments are critical statements about members of the group, which someone expresses either directly or indirectly to someone else.

The director sets the tone for the group. That means she accepts all offerings no matter how apparently outlandish. Her manner, as well as her words, announce that everyone's thoughts, opinions, ideas, are of value. It is, in fact, true that they *are* valuable. When someone mentions something that appears to be off the topic, that person is the voice for important undercurrents in the group. The voice may reflect reluctance, fear, or the opposite pole of opinion. What on the surface seems unconnected may be connected at a deeper level. For example, in a group where members were discussing how annoyed they were about people they were supervising at work, suddenly Bonnie began telling about when she took her dog to the vet. Troy remarked, "Quit changing the subject. We're talking about people, not dogs!" The director, asking for patience, noted that everything members say is somehow connected to the process, whether apparent or not. She encouraged Bonnie to continue. As Bonnie spoke, she talked about how foolish she felt to have forgotten the vet's appointment. She also said she had apologized and offered to pay for the missed appointment. Even after her apology and offer to pay, the vet raked her over the coals, calling her inconsiderate and irresponsible. He also told her she should show him more respect.

As the other group members spoke of their annoyance at, and disdain for, their supervisees, Bonnie began to warm up to the role of the subordinate and to get in touch with how it feels to be the recipient of someone's angry feelings. Her story about the vet was her way of sharing the pole of feelings opposite to most of the group. After she spoke, however, members began to talk about how their disdain for their employees in part masked some of their own feelings of embarrassment and confusion. In encouraging Bonnie's expression, the director facilitated the exploration of a broader spectrum of feelings.

One of us has a favorite little speech for each new group: "Here's a place where we can try on new behaviors and problem solving, practice for upcoming life situations, experience difficult emotional encounters, all without the fear of consequences we have in our daily lives. In this safe place, we can try out new ways of handling difficult situations and discovering alternative solutions to problems. We are not judging whether these alternatives are good or bad, merely discovering and exploring as many as possible, so that we may find the ones most comfortable for us."

Modeling Acceptance of Divergent Opinions

Although there have been dozens of variations of this famous line, Voltaire said it first: "I disapprove of what you say, but I will defend to the death your right to say it." Don't worry! No leader is expected to go that far, but this famous line is a good one to quote and keep as a motto.

Each of us approaches the task of group leadership with a background of life experiences, with our own stage of personal development and our own values and biases. It is virtually impossible to be opinionless and certainly meaningless to be without opinions and be human. Nevertheless, we need not impose our own ideas and values on a group.

Any leadership role carries with it power as well as responsibility. Members often give special weight to the leader's ideas and opinions. A director can foster that power for swaying opinion or can encourage and accept the members' expression of a full range of views. It is our belief that a sociodrama group works best when people feel no need to rubber-stamp the views held by the director. It is essential that the leader allow for the expression and exploration of opinions different from his or her own. Members are more likely to express themselves fully if they have no fear of reprisals or ridicule.

For example, in a session where everyone seems to be involved, one person may say, "This is stupid." Try not to take it personally. He is probably just masking insecure feelings with hostile judgments. The emotions behind the statement are most likely, "I feel embarrassed. I'm afraid I won't perform well." There is no need to convince the person that the work you are doing is valuable. What he needs is acceptance of his viewpoint. Thank him for expressing his feelings, noting that if *he* feels that way, probably others do too. Ask who else feels that what is going on is "stupid." In this way, the person will be included in the session and you model for the group that all viewpoints are accepted and respected.

Guiding, Rather Than Imposing

There is no greater joy than discovering your own inner resources and learning how to put them to work. Here is the job for the director: guide each participant to discover his or her own resources for problem solving. One is reminded of the old adage, "You can lead a horse to water, but you can't make him drink." It is the same with a good sociodrama leader. She or he helps group members who are willing to step into the stream and guides them through the currents to a safe place to drink the water.

Avoiding Teaching Lessons

In sociodrama, the leader is a facilitator of the group's process and goals. He refrains from imposing his will on the group as to what sociodramas will be enacted. It is also wise to avoid being invested in a specific agenda for a session. If you find yourself wanting to teach the group a lesson or wanting them to come to a particular conclusion, check your own motives and feelings toward the group. Are you angry or disappointed with them? Do you want to change them or their values? If you can answer yes to any of these questions, it is important to recognize that you have placed expectations on the group that have to do with *your* wants and needs, not theirs. When such a situation occurs, it is important to acknowledge that the problem is yours and that it is our responsibility to work it out ourselves, not take it out on the group. One sociodrama director felt insulted by several members of his group because they frequently arrived ten to fifteen minutes late and disrupted the group's process with their arrival. He decided to teach them a lesson by setting up an enactment dealing with habitual lateness. Several members displayed obvious resistance to the theme as stated and to the enactment. Fortunately, the director realized that, rather than confront the issue directly, he had been trying to manipulate the group into punishing the latecomers. Becoming aware of what he really needed to do, the director stopped trying to force the group into a sociodrama and told the tardy members how he felt when they arrived late. A discussion arose in which those members and the others discussed how it feels to be late, how it feels to be interrupted, and so on. A sociodrama rose naturally from that discussion. Had the director insisted that the group do the sociodrama *he* wanted them to do, members may have rebelled or sullenly complied with his wishes and felt used. Either way, both he and the group would have lost. As it was, when the problem surfaced and was aired fully, the group proceeded with full spontaneity.

Discouraging Judgmental and/or Prejudicial Statements, Criticism, Personal Analysis, and Advice

Frequently participants sneak in criticisms and/or prejudicial statements almost unnoticed. For example, George criticizes women every chance he gets with comments such as, "You women are all alike. All you care about is money!" Here is where you can use your sense of diplomacy as well as your sense of humor. You have several choices. For example, "Come on, George. You know *all* women don't think alike on *anything.*" Or you may try a simple rephrasing of the comment, "Do you really mean 'all,' every single woman ever born? Don't they ever care about anything other than money?" You might also ask the group how they felt when they heard George's statement. He may be unaware that others feel differently or that others felt strong emotional responses to his statement. One such approach or another should guide the critic to a more objective statement.

Most of us are used to hearing criticisms, advice, and analyses of our behavior. We all know how unpleasant it is to receive unasked-for negative comments. Unfortunately, most of us are also good at dishing them out. Sometimes we are not even aware that we are being critical. We feel that we are just trying to help the person. In order to build trust, it is valuable for people to know that criticism, judgments, and analysis of another's behavior are not useful and, on the contrary, erode trust. If we sense that people will repay candor about our feelings with criticism, we probably won't risk expressing what we feel. In order to maintain a safe setting for sharing, it is helpful to set some ground rules for the group at its first meeting: explain why judgments are out of place, and reinforce those courtesies as needed during later sessions.

At some point during the first session, you will describe what sharing is, so that participants will know how to do it. We see this as an opportunity to explain how sharing is different from analysis and why we avoid it in sociodrama. Remember, when we say how the drama affected us personally, we maximize our involvement and ability to learn from the process. When we analyze another's behavior, we distance from the person, place him or her in a one-down position, and minimize our ability to learn from the experience.

Helping the Group Keep Its Contract

One of the ways to create a safe environment is to help the group keep its contract to do sociodrama. Remember, the sociodrama contract is one in which people agree to assume hypothetical social roles spontaneously, not the roles of the significant others in members' lives. Nor is the contract to do therapy. If the director doesn't take responsibility for keeping the contract, trust will erode or evaporate.

On rare occasions, a member will get very warmed up to his own personal issues and will be tempted to respond to the characters in the sociodrama as if they were people in his own life. When this occurs, the person is usually so overheated that he isn't fully aware that he is responding to the other enactors inappropriately. It is important that the director intervene and assist when the group is floundering in this way. Hank volunteered to be in a scene in which a young man and his mother were discussing his moving back home. Winnie, as his mother, was calmly attempting to negotiate with him what the division of household labor would be if he were to move in. Hank began telling her to stop yelling at him, stop criticizing him, and stop telling him to clean his room. Winnie hadn't done any of these things. It was clear that Hank was off on a tangent of his own. The director froze the action and asked Hank if he was aware that Winnie hadn't said anything about cleaning a room. He said he realized she hadn't said it, but that was what his own mother had said to him in an argument earlier that week, and he wished he had spoken up to her at the time. Hank was trying to shoehorn Winnie into the role of his own mother. At this point the director reminded Hank that Winnie was not playing the role of his real mother, but rather of a hypothetical mother. She asked him if he wanted to continue with the sociodrama, responding to what Winnie was saying and doing, and not responding to his own internal script. She told him that sometimes people are so concerned about something happening in their lives that it is difficult to think about anything else, so if it felt too difficult to separate Winnie from his mom, he could sit this enactment out and someone else could volunteer for the role. She also gave him the option of allowing someone else to step into the role of the son with Hank taking the role of the son's double. In this way, he could still be a part of the enactment, but wouldn't be able to respond directly to the mother. He chose to continue as the double. At the end of the enactment, the director mentioned to Hank that she noticed he had said very little as the double. She wondered why that happened. Hank said that while he was doubling and listening to the interaction from that position, he realized that Winnie really wasn't yelling and criticizing. He became aware of how his feelings had clouded his listening and responding to her earlier.

A word here to people who are knowledgeable in psychodrama: sometimes when a sociodrama group gets warmed up to its own issues, there is a temptation to do a psychodrama instead of a sociodrama. Knowing the beauty and power of the modality, a leader may think, "I'd really like these people to experience something as moving as psychodrama." However, remembering the contract and sticking to it are matters of both common sense and ethics. If a director abandons the contract as it suits him or her or even if several members say, "Yes, let's do a psychodrama," group trust is in jeopardy. Although it may seem a good idea at first, after the psychodrama is over, some members may feel their privacy was invaded. Others may be justly annoyed that the rules were changed and they had little or no input in that decision. Still others may be upset that they went along with the leader's recommendation even though they didn't really know what psychodrama was. Now after the enactment is over, they are feeling exposed and vulnerable. Of course, sociodrama itself can be moving and helps people to experience their vulnerability, but it is the process itself that gets them to that place. When one breaks the contract with the group, some of the vulnerability and affect result from the response to betrayal of trust rather than to the enactment itself.

FACILITATING GROUP PROCESS

A group session can be an exciting or dull experience, depending upon many factors, some of which are people's moods, their willingness to participate, whether they are warmed up to social roles or intrapsychic roles, or their ability to reach beyond themselves to interact with others. A new director occasionally blames herself when the group is not animated or when people seem distracted. It is helpful to recognize that however enthusiastic the director is, the group members may be totally engrossed in their own thoughts and feelings rather than interacting with each other. Although it isn't the director's fault that people are uncommunicative, when group process grinds to a halt, there are a variety of things a director can do to get things going again.

Reframing Statements

One of the functions of a group leader is to reframe statements to facilitate individual and group understanding. For example, in a group of teenagers, one says, "Charles is a pain in the neck. He's always bumming cigarettes from me." Another says, "The coach asked me to stay after practice to talk to him, and then he got busy and made me wait a half hour. I missed the last bus, and my mom had to pick me up. Boy, was she mad!" Someone else says, "My little sister always borrows my sweaters without asking, and I have to go searching for them whenever I want to wear them. Half the time, I find them, and they're dirty." The director hears these apparently diverse statements and looks for the thread of similarity. She fosters group cohesion by reframing the individual statements: "It seems that several people are feeling taken advantage of, today. Is anyone else feeling that way?"

Reframing can also be used to help participants shift their perspectives in positive ways. We sometimes feel stuck because we have conceptualized something as a problem. We feel swamped by the problem and overwhelmed since it feels bigger and more powerful than we are. On the other hand, if we can look at the situation in a different way and see it as an opportunity, we have gone a long way to resolving the difficulty. Therefore, when a group member seems stuck and overwhelmed about a problem in an enactment, the director may freeze the action and ask her what opportunity this situation presents. After the enactor has responded, the director may ask the enactor how she would like to shift the scene to maximize the opportunity. The enactor adjusts the scene accordingly and explores the situation anew.

Questioning for Cohesion

Throughout the sociodrama session, the director continually facilitates communication among members. Sometimes people speak freely and are eager to have a say. At these moments, the director can simply sit back and observe the process as it unfolds. At other times people are silent, and the director takes a more active role in fostering members' interactions.

People may be quiet for a variety of reasons. For example, they may be deep in thought. They may be afraid to disagree with someone who has been very forceful in representing an opinion. They may be confused or just shy. Whatever the reason for the silence, the director encourages discussion in a variety of ways. If someone makes a statement and no one else responds, he asks who agrees or disagrees. He may also ask who feels similarly or differently. After the second person speaks, the director keeps the process rolling by asking something like, "Who else feels this way?" If he senses responses grinding to a halt, he can ask, "Who feels differently?" or "Everyone seems quiet. What are people feeling or thinking now?" These simple questions are the keys to keeping group discussions going.

Allowing for Elegance

Although it is not a major aim of sociodrama to be aesthetically pleasing, individual enactments often are very satisfying in that way. There is a certain beauty that skilled directors foster. They listen carefully to what people have said, and they structure the action to allow that beauty to emerge.

Modeling Sharing

At the end of the sociodrama when members are sharing how their own life experiences were similar to or different from what occurred in the enactment, the director may also choose to share her own feelings and experiences. There are several benefits to the group when the director shares. First, if the director shares in a newly formed group, she can model for members how one does so without analyzing others' behavior. Further, when the director shares, members experience her as more human, more like them, less distant and unapproachable.

The director can also share in ways that facilitate group process. If, during the sociodrama, the director, through silent doubling, picked up some underlying feelings that members didn't seem to be addressing, she can share regarding those feelings. For example, the focus of the sociodrama was on a son telling his mother he needed to put her into a nursing home because he could no longer care for her with the help available to him. The mother didn't want to go, and the son tried to convince her of the logic of the decision. Although many feelings were discussed in the sociodrama, one major one was avoided: both the mother and son feared the mother's eventual death. The director searched through her own experiences for one similar to this situation. When the enactment was over and some members shared their feelings, there was a lull. The director noted how she worries about her own mother dying. Several members said they felt the same but had been afraid to say so since they thought they were the only ones who felt that way.

There are also times after an enactment when people seem to be deep in thought or not know where to begin discussing their feelings or experiences. When this occurs, the director may choose to share first to get things moving. If the time for sharing is limited, it is more important for the group members to share than the director. Also, if the group is animated and members are readily expressing feelings, there may be no need for the director to do so.

SUMMARY

As the director becomes comfortable with the rudiments of sociodrama direction, he turns his attention to preparing himself and the group to participate in a sociodrama session. He readies himself by tuning in to his own warmup prior to the session. He also acknowledges any pressing problems and concerns he might have in his own personal life. After recognizing them, he tables them until after the session so that he can focus directly on the group and not on his own issues.

It is essential that the director create a safe, nonthreatening environment. The director can do this through modeling acceptance and through discouraging verbal attacks and negative personal remarks.

Once the group is in process, the director helps keep the interactions moving. She asks open-ended questions. She also asks questions designed to connect members. For example, "Does anybody else feel the way Joan does?" or "Who else has something to say?" The director also reframes statements in such a way as to join members: "Both Ellie and John seem to have the same viewpoint" or "So, it seems that many of us feel suspicious when we're around people who have lied to us in the past."

Finally, the director joins with the group through the sharing of her own feelings and experiences. She successfully balances interacting with members and directing the group.

10

EXAMINING SOCIODRAMA UNDERPINNINGS

SURVEYING MORENO'S THEORIES

Moreno was a prolific writer and theorist. He wrote about philosophy as well as psychology and sociology. He developed a role theory, a theory of personality development, a spontaneity/creativity theory, and a theory of interpersonal relations (sociometry). Many of Moreno's theories are tied to the practice of sociodrama and act as its substructure. Here is a distillation of some theories relevant to sociodrama.

EXAMINING MORENO'S ROLE THEORY

While a variety of theorists have wrestled with the concept of role as a construct, Moreno's role theory forms the basis for using sociodrama. Moreno began looking at roles and role relationships as early as 1913 in his work with prostitutes. Although his theorizing is somewhat incomplete and his remarks on role are to be found in a variety of manuscripts, we have attempted to cull what we feel to be germane to the practice of sociodrama and present it here.

Defining Roles

Moreno defined role in the following way:

Role can be defined as the actual and tangible forms which the self takes. We thus define the role as the functioning form the individual assumes in the specific moment he reacts to a specific situation in which other persons or objects are involved. The symbolic representation of this functioning form, perceived by the individual and others, is called the role. The form is created by past experiences and the cultural patterns of the society in which the individual lives, and may be satisfied by the specific type of his productivity. Every role is a fusion of private and collective elements. Every role has two sides, a private and collective side (as quoted in Fox, *The Essential Moreno*, 62).

Role, then, is a unit of behaviors about whose parameters a society agrees. Making up each role is a cluster of behaviors. For example, the role *nurse* has several behaviors associated with it. Some of these are: taker of vital signs, pill dispenser, physician's assistant, solace giver. Some of these behaviors may be common to another role, but it is the specific clustering that we label culturally and, thus, recognize when we see the role enacted in life.

If a person in our culture says to us, "I am a nurse," we are not confused as to what that means. We may ask for clarification as to what type of nursing the person does—for example, pediatric, geriatric, or cardiac care—but we do know what a nurse is. On the other hand, if someone comes up to us and says, "I am a bryztnyp," we are certain to be confused, since we don't recognize "bryztnyp" as a role in our society.

Roles are important to us, since often we identify ourselves and others through the roles we play. "This is my friend, Tim. He's a computer programmer and sky dives for a hobby." In fact, Moreno hypothesized that we are composites of the roles we play. He felt that the way to study a person, get an idea of their personality structure, is to study the roles a person plays.

Perhaps this sounds simplistic, but when we think about someone, it is next to impossible to put together any meaningful thoughts or feelings about him or her without considering behavior. If I say, "Sue is really nice," what do I mean? Has this idea simply popped into my head out of the air? No, as I think about it, I realize that I feel Sue is nice because she showed her friendship to me through her role behavior. She stopped by one day when she knew I was feeling sad. She also volunteers at a local soup kitchen. Besides, she helps her nephew with his homework. The old maxim, "Actions speak louder than words," is operative whenever we take a look at personality. The "roles we play" is certainly not the whole answer to the question, "Who am I?" However, studying those roles and exploring how we coact with others when we play them goes a long way toward helping us understand ourselves.

Collective and Private Role Aspects

Moreno noted that each role a person plays has a collective component and a private component. The *collective component* of the role is comprised of the aspects of the role that are similar to the ways others play it. For example, Nell, Steve, and Jessica are all nurses. All of them work in a dialysis unit. All of them take patients' vital signs daily. All of them interact with physicians and patients. They have these duties in common with other dialysis nurses in other hospitals.

When they meet another dialysis nurse, they can readily begin conversing about the work they all do. After a while, though, based on what they have in common, they will probably each begin discussing their own particular experiences in the role, which brings us to private role components.

The *private component* of the role is comprised of the aspects of the role which the person plays in ways that are different from how others play the role. It is the private component that defines the purely personal way in which we put our mark on any role we play. Nell doesn't like physicians and avoids interacting with them as much as possible. Steve likes to read joke books to patients while they are on dialysis and does so whenever he has a free moment. Jessica has studied Therapeutic Touch and administers it to patients.

Moreno's idea of group work of any sort is based on the idea that we have more in common with each other than we have different from each other. Through tapping in to the collective role components, group members can find some common ground on which to interact. Specifically, sociodrama emerges from focusing on the collective components rather than on the personal role aspects of group members.

Psychosomatic, Social, and Psychodramatic Roles

Moreno further separated roles into three types: the psychosomatic, the social, and the psychodramatic, or intrapsychic, roles. Developmentally, the psychosomatic roles emerge first, so let's discuss them first.

The *psychosomatic* roles are physical roles such as eater, eliminator, crier. They are the first roles to develop after birth. The psychodramatic and social roles develop out of them. One might wonder why Moreno called them psychosomatic, the term indicating a psychological connection with bodily functions. Moreno realized that body and mind are inextricably connected. If the infant hears a loud sound and is frightened, for instance, she may cry (a physical manifestation) as a response to her fear (an emotional manifestation).

Moreno notes that when we are newborn, we are unable to make differentiations between ourselves and others. We are unaware that Mother is not I. We have the sense that we are all and everything is us. We don't know where we end and others begin. Moreno terms this the matrix of identity and calls the world surrounding the infant the first universe. At this time all is real to us. As we interact with our environment and gain greater autonomy, two parallel tracks develop. We begin to develop social roles as we interact with those who in reality surround us. Concurrently, we develop an imaginary life that is independent of objective reality. Finally, when we reach about 2.5 years of age, a breach occurs in which we become aware of ourselves as a separate being. At this point the child enters what Moreno terms the second universe, the world in which I and Thou are separate and where illusion and reality are two different things. Out of this breach, the psychodramatic and social roles develop.

Our *social* roles are those in which we interact with others: mother, friend, tailor. Our first social roles emerge slowly out of our interactions with our care givers. The hungry infant cries, and the mother feeds him. As this coactive process is repeated day after day, the infant begins to develop some sense of consistency and to expect in a limited way that his actions will evoke a recip-rocal response.

The *psychodramatic* roles, variously termed psychological and intrapsychic, are interior roles, such as the thinker, the problem solver, the inventor. Among the psychodramatic roles are also the roles we play in our fantasy life: the hero or heroine, the prima ballerina. One of the most famous and amusing explo-rations of intrapsychic roles is James Thurber's *The Secret Life of Walter Mitty*, where we see a Milquetoast with a mundane job whose fantasy life is rich and exciting. He imagines himself as a surgeon and an adventuresome pilot, among other things.

Our psychodramatic roles are of great importance in our lives. Through them we deliberate, reflect, and invent. Through our fantasy roles we receive role relief and recreation. We imagine ourselves doing things we have always wanted to do and sometimes cannot do except in fantasy. We also imagine ourselves performing roles we plan to include in our repertoire in the future. For in-stance, we imagined ourselves as authors of this book long before we actually sat down to write it. Having the intrapsychic role of writer/collaborator helped us to move toward actualizing that role in our external lives. It is to be remem-bered that, while some intrapsychic roles shift to become social roles, we also have intrapsychic roles that rightly remain internal, such as the thinker.

Moreno noted that we are warmed up to different types of roles at different moments. Think about times you have been an engrossed TV viewer, and someone tried to get your attention for a chat. You probably never even heard him talking to you. The realization that people can be warmed up to three different kinds of roles is important for a group leader. If you have ever tried to lead a group in a room that is excessively hot and people are dozing off (engaged in a psychosomatic role), you know how difficult it is to get a discus-sion going and social roles activated. In such a situation, you might want to open a window or use a physical warm-up to wake people up. On other occa-sions, you may walk in to a usually talkative group and find that no one seems to have anything to say. Perhaps people are warmed up to psychodramatic roles rather than social roles. After checking it out and finding people in fact are involved with their own thoughts, you can gear the group to addressing the intrapsychic role state. For example, in the dead of winter if people are silent, you might hypothesize that they are having escape fantasies. If they are, the sociodrama may end up taking place in the Bahamas. It is equally possible to find group members talking to each other so much that it is difficult to get their attention at the start of the group. When this occurs, ask them to share the topics being discussed. In this way you can use the interactions that are already occurring to allow the shared central issue to emerge. Whatever roles people are warmed up to, it is helpful to recognize them and adjust the work accordingly.

Role Taking, Role Playing, and Role Creating

Moreno defined three ways of assuming roles, ranging from most rigidly to most spontaneously, with the most rigid portrayal being role taking and the most spontaneous being role creating. *Role taking* is the term he used to describe assuming a role in its most routinized form. When a person role takes, he rigidly follows the parameters of the role as the culture established it, with little or no deviation. For example, let's take a certain telephone solicitor. He has a set script of what to say to the potential customer, and he follows it verbatim. If someone interrupts him, he starts over or checks the script so he can pick up where he left off.

Role playing, on the other hand, is the rendering of the role with a greater degree of freedom and spontaneity. Although still giving customers the essential information regarding the product, another telephone solicitor chats amiably with customers, weaving the information into the conversation and promoting their interest in the product.

Role creating is the rendering of a role with a high degree of spontaneity and creativity. When one role creates, she adds something new to the role or transforms it into a totally new role. Still another telephone solicitor begins to notice over a period of time that people she speaks to in the daytime are different from the people she talks to when she is on the evening shift. She gets the idea to create a new spiel, taking into account the varying populations she contacts. Another way that she transforms the role is to accompany her conversations with appropriate background music. In creating a new role, she figures out a way to participate in a personal computer network and begins to sell her product via computer conversations.

We can look at the idea of role taking, playing, and creating in a variety of ways:

1. Developmentally, when we learn a new role, we begin with role taking behavior. As we become more comfortable with the routines of the role, we move to role playing and finally role creating.

2. Each role as society defines it has its own demands for form and freedom. One role may demand a lot of structure, while another expects a person to be spontaneous and creative.

3. Every role has within it aspects of role taking, role playing, and role creating.

4. Whatever the role or its demands, we may choose to engage in it with role taking, role playing, or role creating behavior.

Let's examine each of the above items in greater detail:

1. In addition to how we engage in roles when we know them, there is a developmental procedure involved when we learn new roles, beginning with role taking, moving forward to role playing, and ideally ending with role creating. Let us take the role of pianist. When we first learn to play, we practice scales, learn when and how to move the pedals, and endlessly repeat simple pieces. We role take as we play pieces exactly as they are written. As we become more comfortable with the rudiments of piano, we begin to experiment with the dynamics of the piece, to play it faster or slower, louder or softer. We begin to develop a repertoire and vary when and how we play the piece. At this point we are role playing. As we become still more proficient at music theory and practice and more comfortable with our own style of playing, we become ready to role create. We may play a piece and riff off it into improvisation, or we may create a totally new piece.

2. When we examine certain roles in society, some demand and require more spontaneity than others. For example, it is our expectation that the mail carrier will deliver mail to our home according to our region's schedule. It might be very spontaneous for her to throw out whatever she deems to be junk mail instead of delivering it to us. However, we would be very upset if she did so. Maybe we would miss winning a million dollars from that publisher's house ad. On the other hand, a medical research chemist who spends all day making sure his beakers are clean instead of searching out a cure for disease will soon be out of a job. Thus there are some roles that require more role taking behavior; while others require more role playing or role creating behavior.

3. Each role has inherently within it all three: role taking, role playing, and role creating. For example, let us take the role of gardener. A gardener must know and follow certain routines in planting particular flowers and shrubs. He must water the plants according to schedule. If he is going to pot a plant, he follows the appropriate procedure. These are role taking activities. By the same token, there are many activities he performs that are open to more spontaneity. He may try a variety of plant foods and fertilizers. He may vary the arrangement of the plants from year to year and may add new plants to his garden. These are role playing activities. He may also be highly inventive as well and discover a new and different way of gardening, as happened when hydroponic gardening was developed. He may instead develop a new hybrid rose. He is taking the known and leaping into the unknown—role creating.

4. The manner in which we play a role may exhibit primarily a particular type of behavior—that is, role taking, role playing, or role creating. Whatever the role and its requirements, we may render it with rigidity or with spontaneity.

When we want to return some damaged merchandise, how many of us have run into a salesperson who says, "The seven days during which you can return the merchandise have passed. I'm not taking it back. After all, those are the rules. I don't care if the damage didn't appear until after seven days. Rules are

rules." The salesperson used role taking behavior here where role playing behavior would have been in order. She stuck rigidly to the store's policy without
taking into consideration that the product was defective. She played the role
as she always had, unable to engage her spontaneity enough to respond to the
problem with more flexibility.

Of what value is it for the director to know about role taking, role playing,
and role creating? The understanding of how we currently engage in roles can
help us to find satisfaction in what we do well. It can also help us to point out
for ourselves ways we would like to behave differently. Through sociodrama
we can explore roles and how we currently play them. We can also experiment
with our roles, practicing playing them differently. Further, we can help others
play their life roles with greater spontaneity.

EXPLORING SPONTANEITY THEORY

Spontaneity and creativity are the cornerstones of Moreno's theories and his
work. Moreno views spontaneity and creativity as a twofold process, with creativity as the germ of the idea and spontaneity as the goal or impetus to bring
the creative idea to its fruition in action.

Responding to the unexpected and trying something new are what spontaneity is all about. Moreno saw spontaneity and creativity as present and
essential in all of life, not just reserved for artists and inventors. He felt that
people couldn't make it through the day without using their spontaneity, since
the unexpected happens all the time. A person is on his way to work when he
encounters a nasty traffic snarl. What should he do: sit there and wait; fume;
try to turn around and find an alternate route; pass his time composing a
shopping list?

Moreno further believed that one of the greatest dangers facing modern humanity, particularly in technocratic societies, is the habit of approaching life
in a robotized way, not exercising one's spontaneity. He was concerned that if
people persistently acted rigidly and routinely in relation to their world, they
would diminish their ability to be spontaneous, creative, joyful, and deeply
satisfied in their lives and human interactions. He devised spontaneity training
techniques as a way of helping people enhance and restore spontaneity.

Defining Spontaneity

In *Who Shall Survive?* (336) Moreno said, "*Spontaneity* can be defined as the
adequate response to a new situation, or the novel [and adequate] response to
an old situation." Novelty and adequacy are the two criteria for true spontaneity. Totally new things happen in our lives from time to time, and we are
called upon to respond. Occasionally, something very unusual occurs, being
lost at sea, for example, but most often the new situations, though common

to others, are new to *us*, like giving birth to your first child. Whether the situation is earth shaking or mundane, how we respond is important.

Moreno distinguished between three types of spontaneity—true, pathological, and stereotyped. *True spontaneity* was defined above. As noted, novelty and adequacy are the criteria for true spontaneity. For instance, if you were lost at sea for the first time (and hopefully the only time), just about any response you could make to the situation would be novel for you. However, some responses to the situation would certainly not be adequate—jumping into shark-infested waters and trying to swim for it; yelling, "Help!" in an open sea with no one else in sight; or tearing your clothes into shreds and dumping them in the water. When a person responds to a situation with a lot of novelty and little adequacy, he is said to be using *pathological spontaneity*. Here is another example. One of the authors was at a New Year's Eve party where one of the party goers, an entertainer, was the center of attention. She was witty, funny, and spontaneous. The host called us in to dinner. As we all rose, the entertainer's boyfriend burst out of the bathroom nude and just stood there. The astonished guests gasped in disbelief. The young man later said he had been feeling jealous of all the attention paid his girlfriend. The only way he could think of to get some attention for himself was to do what he did—novel, but hardly adequate.

On the other hand, there are many times when we are performing a routine chore and we vary it in the slightest degree. This is *stereotyped spontaneity*—lots of adequacy, but not much novelty. Recently an article appeared in a national magazine about a Las Vegas performer. The journalist had followed him around for several days, watching his shows, trying to decipher his charismatic appeal. In the course of the article, the writer described one of the shows. The performer went out to cheering crowds, told the audience repeatedly throughout the performance how wonderful they were. He said that because they were so great he would change his show to please them. He told them that he didn't care what the management said, he was going to perform for them all night, singing their favorite songs. Together they would beat the management (a smart thing to say in Las Vegas). His show ended at 11:14 p.m. to thunderous applause. The next night the journalist was surprised to see a nearly identical performance, ending at 11:14 sharp. The only differences in the show were brief exchanges in which audience members spontaneously interacted with the entertainer. Here is an example of stereotyped spontaneity. There is a lot of adequacy—the show certainly succeeds with the audience—however, there is very little novelty.

The Canon of Creativity

In *Who Shall Survive?* (40), Moreno refers to creativity as the "arch substance" and to spontaneity as the "arch catalyzer." Each is necessary for the satisfactory completion of the other. They fit hand in glove. Imagine someone who impulsively throws himself into any situation that presents itself, without any thought as to what the situation requires or to his needs at the time. Disaster! Moreno terms someone possessing high spontaneity and no creativity as a "spontaneous idiot" (39).

On the other hand, there are also many people who have great ideas but don't bring them to fruition. A person has a unique idea for a new kind of chair that will be comfortable, attractive, lightweight, and inexpensive. The only problem is she never tries to build the chair nor hires someone else to build it. It remains in idea form. She is highly creative, but has been unable to summon the spontaneity necessary to actualize her creative idea. Moreno said, "There were many more Michelangelos born than the one who painted the great paintings, many more Beethovens born than the one who wrote the great symphonies . . ." (39).

Moreno pointed out the importance of warming up to one's spontaneity. As a person thinks about a new idea, he turns it over in his mind, trying to determine how to apply it. He may talk over his idea with someone else. Through this process, he readies himself for action. He warms up. When he has enough information and resources to actualize his idea, spontaneity provides the catalyst for creativity.

When spontaneity and creativity join, the result is called a conserve. There are various types of conserves: *social conserves*—social institutions and social stereotypes (e.g., the "typical" librarian); *technological conserves*—inventions; and *cultural conserves*—works of art. So, any interaction between spontaneity and creativity results in a conserve, whether the conserve is a new kind of hot dog, a speech, a government program, or a piece of sculpture.

Moreno believed conserves to be important in that they are not only the children of spontaneity/creativity; they are also the potential parents of future conserves. They are the basis for all creative activity. Let's take Mendelssohn's *A Midsummer Night's Dream*. The composer created a totally new work of art based on the materials of Shakespeare's play of the same name. Or consider a workbook for business success. Someone reads it and devises workshops based loosely on the concept outlined in the book. Even the book itself is based on conserves—other books, lectures, or materials the author used as a springboard to his own idea.

In an effort to depict graphically the spontaneity/creativity process, Moreno devised the Canon of Creativity. We have modified it slightly for greater ease of understanding (see Figure 1). S refers to spontaneity, CR to creativity, CO to the conserve, and W to the warming up process.

Spontaneity moves toward creativity. In their nexus, spontaneity catalyzes creativity. Spontaneity provides the goad for creativity to spring into action. The result of their interaction is the conserve. The conserve in turn warms people up to new ideas (CR) and to the impetus (S) to make those ideas a

Figure 1. Canon of Creativity

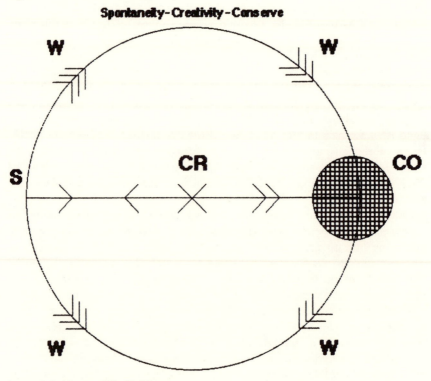

Source: J. L. Moreno, *Who Shall Survive?*

reality. Sometimes a person has an idea and repeatedly warms up to that idea, thinking about it and thinking about it. However, his spontaneity needs to kick in so that he can actualize that idea.

Understanding the spontaneity/creativity process is helpful for sociodramatists. Each session follows the model of the Canon. Group members warm up to an idea (the shared central issue) and to their spontaneity. As their spontaneity and creativity interact, a sociodrama enactment (conserve) is born. The enactment in turn warms the group up to sharing. In addition, the director uses sociodrama's many techniques (role reversal, freeze frame, doubling, etc.) to help restore spontaneity when it is momentarily blocked. She also encourages and fosters the spontaneity and creativity that group members bring by maintaining a safe, nonjudgmental environment.

While Moreno noted that conserves ideally warmed us up to creating new things, he also was aware that cultures sometimes deify conserves. They view a particular conserve as so perfect that they stifle their own creativity, not daring to change or adapt the conserve to the present needs of society. They take a rigid view, sometimes ignoring evidence that could help them restore spontaneous response. Examples of this would be those who believed our planet was the center of the universe and that Earth was flat. When Copernicus and Galileo challenged those ideas, they met with great hostility from fellow scientists, the church, and the government. Thus Moreno saw the conserve as the springboard to new ideas rather than the last word on any subject.

Training Spontaneity

Moreno noticed that people seem to be spontaneous in varying degrees. One person is paralyzed at a party while another is chatting away comfortably. One person is able to get up and dance freely, while another, who is no less talented, moves around the floor making sure he executes the steps correctly. Some people are aware that they have many choices available to them, while others feel stuck, with no options open. Not only does the degree of spontaneity vary between people. It varies within each person from situation to situation. Bruce is highly spontaneous when playing with his friends. However, when his teacher asks him a question in class, he is suddenly dumbstruck and can't think of a thing to say.

Moreno was further concerned that the stresses of living in a technological society were so great that people, in an attempt to cope, would find themselves going along every day, following rules, falling into a dull routine in most areas of their lives, warming up more to their anxiety than to their spontaneity. Moreno said that anxiety is blocked spontaneity. Bruce feels free and spontaneous around his friends in the school yard, but when his teacher asks him a question, he anticipates her disapproval if he answers incorrectly. His anxiety about her possible response stops him from venturing an answer.

In order to help people to restore and/or increase their spontaneous responses to situations, Moreno developed spontaneity training. He felt that if he gave people a safe environment in which to practice making spur-of-the-moment responses, they would be able to generalize the experience to the rest of life. Sometimes when people hear the term *spontaneity training*, they say it sounds like planned spontaneity, which is, of course, a contradiction in terms. Instead, spontaneity training is putting people in hypothetical situations and allowing them to respond on the spot (in the moment). Many police training programs employ spontaneity training as a core element of their work in crisis intervention. Trainers set up "as if" situations similar to those the trainees are likely to encounter on the job—for example, hostage situations, suicide attempts, crime investigation interviews, motor vehicle violation encounters, and family crisis situations. The trainees in pairs move into the situations and must respond spontaneously to whatever they meet.

One of the authors taught police trainees in this manner for many years.

The repeated feedback at the end of training was that the role training/spontaneity training element was the most immediately useful facet of their education. Over the years several follow-ups were done in which officers again cited the value of action training.

Clearly, spontaneity is a cornerstone of all sociodrama, so that in a way all sociodramas promote spontaneity. However, the director can also take specific steps to help people train themselves to be more spontaneous. Spontaneity training can be used with all kinds of groups and is often a lot of fun. For instance, in a group of fourth graders, the teacher may use spontaneity training as a warm-up to a sociodrama. She may ask each child to take the role of his favorite kind of bird or car or cartoon character.

Another of our favorite spontaneity training warm-ups is a game called Freeze that derives from theatre. Freeze is a variation of the childhood game of Statue. Divide participants into groups of three and ask them to count off. Tell them that in a minute you'll ask them to move around the space using large gestures and that after a while, you'll call, "Freeze!" At that point each person is to stop in her tracks, keeping her posture "frozen." Tell them that you will then call out a number. The person whose number is called is to check out her own posture and the posture of the others in her group and figure out a situation that these positions suggest. As soon as an idea comes to her, she is to start moving, talking, and interacting with her partners. They are to join her in the activity spontaneously, taking reciprocal roles to hers. Tell them to continue to interact until you call, "Freeze," again and call out a new number. For example, when the group is frozen, you call out, "Take it, Number 2." Jean, who is Number 2 in her group, looks at her own posture and that of the others in her group: all are looking at the ground. She drops to her knees and says to the other two, "Do you see it yet? I've got to find my contact lens. Be careful not to step on it." The others join in, helping her look until the director calls, "Freeze" again.

EXPLORING SOCIOMETRIC THEORY

Put simply, sociometry is the measurement of social choices. Moreno developed sociometry to study interpersonal and intergroup choice. The sociogram was one of the major measuring instruments he created.

Defining Sociometry

People constantly make choices. The choices people make that join them or separate them are often more complex than meet the eye.

- Gene chooses Joanne as his girlfriend. Joanne is still in love with Bob, but since Bob is dating someone else, Joanne starts dating Gene, whom she likes second best.
- Lynne is feeling stressed out and wants to go for a relaxed day at the beach. She

knows Betty is a pretty calm person who loves the beach, so she asks Betty to join her. She doesn't want to invite their friend Martha because Martha complains a lot.

It is time to pick teams for dodge ball. Tony, who is big and athletic, is chosen captain. Walt is also athletic, but he bosses the other kids around, so the other kids don't want him on their team.

Moreno was interested in the fact that people are constantly engaged in choice making. He observed that all of society was composed of both visible and invisible networks of choice. A group of people attending the same church would be an example of visible choice. Within that group of churchgoers, though, there would be an invisible network, joining and separating the congregants according to their attractions, repulsions, and feelings of neutrality. Mr. Benson and Mr. Chadwick don't like each other though they have never discussed it. Each avoids the other by sitting several pews apart. On the other hand, Mr. Benson and Mr. Goff are good friends and seek each other out every Sunday. Meanwhile, Mr. Janek feels neutral toward the other congregants and sits wherever there's an empty seat.

Moreno also noticed that a person positively chooses, rejects, or is neutral to another person based on particular criteria—such as Gene choosing Joanne as his girlfriend. Joanne is the one who is chosen and "girlfriend" is the criterion on which the choice is based. There may be other criteria imbedded in his choice of her specifically as his girlfriend. Joanne may be smart, friendly, warm, attractive, or spunky, for example.

Moreno developed the science of sociometry to study the phenomena of social choice. In *Who Shall Survive?* (51) he says, "Sociometry deals with the mathematical study of psychological properties of populations, the experimental technique of and the results obtained by application of quantitative methods. This is undertaken through methods which inquire into the evolution and organization of groups and the position of individuals within them." While sociometry describes social networks as they currently exist, Moreno also saw sociometry as prescriptive, providing direction for making future changes. Prescriptively, he used the results of sociometric studies to reorganize social networks according to the stated choices of the people in the network. In a landmark longitudinal study with Helen Hall Jennings, Moreno reorganized a whole community (The New York Training School for Girls) according to the sociometric choices of the inhabitants. While sociometry can certainly be used on a grand scale, it can also be used in everyday situations by ordinary people. For example, if an office manager asked each worker whom he would like to share space with, the manager could reorganize the office sociometrically, promoting a more harmonious work environment. Or in a sociodrama group, the director can ask members where they would like to sit and with whom they would like to participate in a warm-up, thus maximizing the chances that members will be able to work comfortably. Also the director asks the members to choose the issue and situation on which they would like to focus in the enactment.

The sociodrama director is very interested in the group's sociometry. She observes the attractions, rejections, and neutralities in the group. She notices the issues to which the group is drawn. She notices who the natural leaders are and whom people either ignore or reject. Through the process of sociodrama, she helps group members share the sociometric wealth and better understand and accept each other. She does this by encouraging participation of all, by valuing sharing as opposed to analysis and attack, and by use of the various sociodramatic techniques (doubling, role reversal, soliloquy, etc.) that help members make positive connections.

When the director uses sociometry in the above ways, she is doing so informally, choosing interventions based on her observations of group process. When Moreno devised sociometry as a science, however, he also developed a number of sociometric devices to map people's choices based on specific criteria. We will briefly mention a few of these here that can be of use to the sociodramatist.

Mapping Social Networks

Moreno created the *sociogram* as a way to chart social choices and interrelationships among people. A sociogram can be drafted on paper or can be completed in action. Since sociodramatists most frequently use the action sociogram, we will concentrate on that here.[1]

The action sociogram can be used as a warm-up to promote group cohesion and facilitate the emergence of group themes. The director instructs group members that he will ask them hypothetical questions, involving the choice of other group members. After he asks the question, members are to decide whom they would choose, based on the given criterion. Each is to indicate whom she has chosen by going to that person and putting her hand on the person's shoulder. Here are some examples of questions to ask. They vary from the playful to the more probing:

Whom would you choose to accompany you to a horror film? A comedy? A serious drama?

If someone stole your wallet and you needed to borrow $2.00 to get home, whom would you ask?

With whom do you have the most in common?

If you found your tire was flat, whom would you ask to help you change it?

Whom would you choose to help you with a research project?

If you were lost in a big city, whom would you want to accompany you?

If you were going to travel on a long trip in a compact car, whom would you choose to go with you?

If you had to cook a fancy meal, whom would you choose to cook with you?

If you wanted to change your hairstyle but were unsure of what style to try, whom would you ask for advice?

After people have made their choices for each question, give them a moment to tell the person they chose why they chose him or her. Not only does this get group members interacting; it also helps them to clarify misperceptions. For example, in a group where people didn't know each other too well, no one chose Ted to help cook a fancy meal. In the course of discussion, he told them that he is a gourmet cook.

Depending on the questions that are asked, biases and prejudices can also emerge through the use of the action sociogram. These feelings can then be explored through sociodramatic action. For example, Ted had received several choices from people to help change a tire. He pointed out that he knows nothing about cars. Linda, on the other hand, noted with some annoyance that she is a great mechanic but that no one chose her. She wondered aloud if people didn't choose her because she is a woman. This touched off a discussion on sex role stereotyping, which in turn led to a sociodrama on the issue.

Another thing that often happens spontaneously when doing action sociograms is that group members will say, "I have a question to ask the group, too. May I ask it?" This involvement of members sparks a lot of energy and facilitates the emergence of the shared central issue.

The *action spectogram* is another sociometric device. It promotes group cohesion, is a great icebreaker, and is often a lot of fun. The spectrogram is a continuum ranging from "like least" to "like most." The director tells the group that she is going to ask them how they feel about certain things, like pizza or skiing. She tells them that they have an opportunity to say how much they like these things and to see how others in the group feel about the same things. She instructs the group to imagine that there is a line on the floor that goes from one end of the room to the other. One end of the line represents "like most," while the other end represents "like least." The area in between represents the gradations of feelings between the poles. She asks them to position themselves somewhere on the continuum from most to least as she asks them whatever questions she chooses. Here are some suggestions.

"How do you feel about: bowling, Chinese food, chocolate ice cream, walks in the woods, classical music, hard rock music, gardening, exercise, talking about your feelings, computer games, reading, the beach, baby-sitting, pets, vegetables, gossip, holidays with your family, going to school, working?"

LIKE MOST ←———————————————————→ LIKE LEAST

As group members arrange themselves along the continuum, suggest that they notice who is near them and feels similarly about the question. You can also ask them to state why they placed themselves where they did. As the group continues to answer questions, you will begin to notice some patterns emerging that you and the group can transform into sociodramatic exploration.

If the director has prepared the group ahead of time for the spectrogram, group members can suggest questions on which they'd like to survey group feeling. Even if they have not offered suggestions earlier, members will often be eager to test some questions out on the group spontaneously.

The *social barometer* is a variation of the spectrogram. It focuses on the group's feelings regarding social issues. It is a wonderful tool for helping groups to begin exploring those issues. The social barometer employs a modified continuum. Again, group members are asked to imagine a line going from one end of the room to another. One end represents Pro, and the other represents Con. While the imaginary line represents gradations from Pro to Con, the midpoint of the continuum represents "I'm Undecided" as well as "Half and Half." For example, on the question of abortion, two people might place themselves at midpoint on the line. One person may be undecided as to whether or not women should be legally permitted to have abortions, while another feels abortions should be permitted under certain circumstances and not under others. The director performs the same function as with the spectrogram, but the issues called out to members are social issues—for example, euthanasia, safe sex, housing for the homeless. As group members literally see where each other stands on social issues, lively discussions ensue, and it becomes clear which issues feel most important to members to explore in action.

SUMMARY

Moreno was a prolific theorist and writer. Among other things he developed a *theory of roles* and a *theory of spontaneity,* and he created *sociometry.* He was intensely interested in the roles we play in life and our connections with others as we play them. One of Moreno's greatest concerns was that modern humanity could become robotized, enmired in routine and rules if we do not make efforts to exercise our spontaneity in daily life. Sociodrama is one of the methods he devised to help people restore their spontaneity, so that they could lead more varied and fulfilling lives, so that people could find ways to play their life roles with greater flexibility and could touch their native creativity in dealing with life's difficulties.

NOTE

1. For a more detailed explanation of sociometry and sociometric measurement, see Hale.

Part Two

Part Two illustrates how sociodrama can be used in specific settings, such as a language class, a town hall, or a management training session. Although Part Two focuses on particular settings, it is our hope that the sheer variety of suggestions will spark the reader's creativity to find ways to modify and adapt the suggestions to fit his own group's needs. Since sociodrama has its roots in theatre, education, and the community, we have devoted chapters showing how it can be used in these areas. Sociodrama is also used extensively in business and psychotherapy, so we have included chapters indicating how to use it in these settings as well. The final chapter is devoted to the experiences and insights of other sociodrama directors from around the world.

11

SOCIODRAMA IN THEATRE

DEFINING THEATRICAL AREAS

Sociodrama emerged out of theatre. It can, through its unique methods, give back to theatre, helping it to renew itself spontaneously and creatively. Although sociodrama does not have theatrical expertise as its aim, it may be used successfully in preparing for a variety of theatrical endeavors. There are three types of theatre experiences that are especially conducive to sociodrama: Theatre Arts, Theatre Arts Education, and Theatre in Education (TIE).

We define theatre arts as the use of dramatic literature and performance for aesthetic aims. The elements of theatre are script, actors, and audience. Theatre arts education includes all aspects of theatre aesthetics, focusing on training for actors, directors, and writers. It also involves training students to execute all other facets of theatrical production—for example, scenic design, costume design, stage management. Some programs stress professional training, preparing students for jobs in the theatre. This type of training is practical and specific. Other programs focus on the development of the artistic qualities in the student as a whole human being. This type of training is more humanistic in approach.

Gordon Vallins originated Theatre in Education in Coventry, England, in the mid-1960s. His vision was to dramatize nontheatre curriculum programs to enliven learning for both teachers and students. He organized teams of professional actor/teachers to assist him. These teams would go into a school and collaborate with local education authorities to decide on a project that suited their needs. The project might include the group's writing and performing a play in the school or conducting an improvisational performance based on a theme chosen by the authorities, such as welfare reform. After the performance, each actor/teacher would go into a classroom and hold a discussion on the topic of the drama with the students. This discussion could be followed by the students and actor/teacher interacting in several creative drama activities, including improvisation.

Although the TIE concept originated in England, the United States has a number of such companies. Perhaps the best known is the Creative Arts Team, known as CAT, a professional company of actor/teachers connected with New York University. Whether in the United States or Great Britain, the universally expressed goal of TIE is "to harness the techniques and imaginative potency of theatre in the service of education" (Tony Jackson, viii). A TIE team can move comfortably between improvisation and performance, meeting the educational goals with both.

USING SOCIODRAMA IN THEATRE

From the beginning of recorded theatrical history, playwrights have written social drama. For example, Aeschylus (525–456 B.C.) wrote about such problems as societal guilt, hereditary evil, and divine justice. His *Oresteia* is the only surviving Greek trilogy. It deals with the evolution of justice. Throughout the ages, such playwrights as Shakespeare, Molière, and the anonymous authors of the medieval morality plays wrote about universal themes. Any theatre historian could move through each era of human history and point out examples of many plays that tapped into the major political and moral concerns of their day. Good theatre is always a barometer of the social issues of its time.

Traditionally, sociodrama is not used in theatre, since theatre is scripted and sociodrama is not. However, both authors of this book have used it frequently in a variety of ways in theatrical production and playwriting. We see sociodrama as an additional opportunity for tapping spontaneity and creativity in generating theatrical materials. Playwrights can use sociodrama in script development, and directors and actors can use it in the rehearsal process in the development of characterization. Let's take a look at how they can do this.

CREATING PLAYS THROUGH SOCIODRAMA

Sociodrama is a natural tool for playwrights. Since social problems have provided themes for theatrical production from the beginning of recorded theatrical history, sociodrama can be successfully used to help playwrights explore themes in greater depth. This procedure offers comprehensive insights for the playwright. Through role reversal and doubling characters in a play, an author will gain a deeper understanding of what motivates each individual character as well as a clearer perception of the central issues of the play and other themes inherent in his or her work. While playwrights sometimes develop their characters first and then figure out the action structure for the piece, at other times they begin with a plot idea and flesh out the characters as they interact in a situation. Whichever they do, sociodrama can be helpful in scene building.

Several playwrights are working in a playwright's workshop; as part of the warm-up phase, the leader asks them to fill each other in on their projects. One says he is interested in what happens in a marriage if one of the partners is engaged in an extramarital affair, and he carelessly leaves clues around, encouraging his wife to discover his indiscretion. Another says he is interested in what toxic waste has done to endanger the water supply in a small town, and how the town reacts when it discovers the clandestine dumping. Still another says she is exploring what happens in a family after the parents have died, and the adult children are squabbling over the estate. What if one of the children, the executor, has syphoned off some of the father's funds in the final stages of his illness? As in any sociodrama session, the director listens for the shared central issue. Here, one main theme seems to be betrayal. If the playwrights agree that each is exploring betrayal, they can set up a sociodrama that examines the issue. They may decide to use one of the situations already suggested by one of them or can create a new situation. Whichever they do, they will be able to explore the theme in greater depth, thus sparking new ideas for when they return to their own writing projects.

Sociodrama may also be used to develop characters. One way to do this in a playwright's workshop involves the playwrights contracting with each other to spend a certain amount of time focusing on each work in progress. Say each of six playwrights has an hour of a two-hour session meeting weekly over a period of three weeks. When it is Playwright A's turn, the leader instructs her to focus on an area in the writing process where she needs the group's help. For example, she may be unsure about how the executor of the estate feels about his siblings and how he was treated by his parents. She may want to try out different approaches to see which best fits her vision of the play as a whole. The sociodrama experience clarifies and brings about a greater specificity to the theme and how each character feels about the problems. Using a double, the subtext becomes more obvious to the playwright, and she can explore several options in the dialogue. How does her character verbalize what he is actually feeling? Does he tell the truth or hide it?

When the playwright examines her theme sociodramatically, the spontaneity of the action often helps her realize what she wants to say. She explores her theme as a central issue. At times the playwright will see for herself that she needs to move in a different direction to bring about the desired results. Other times, just the opposite occurs. Through the enactment, the playwright may discover that the characters' motivations as she has developed them are correct. Even though here the group agrees to focus its attention on one person's work, the very process of sociodrama will reveal character and plot ideas for the other playwrights as well. Thus the experience of sharing the enactment can be inspirational to the entire group.

One of the most valuable assets in creating plays from sociodrama is the exploration of alternative lines of dialogue and/or solutions to the problems presented. When these alternatives are viewed as an action experience that comes from the affective rather than the cognitive frame, the playwright often sees his work more clearly. Although all playwrights by the very nature of their work have vivid imaginations, the spontaneity of the sociodrama enactment serves as an additional impetus for a creative spark to ignite a variety of new visions for the writers.

Using Sociodrama in the Rehearsal Process

When directing a play, sociodrama is wonderful for helping actors understand in greater depth the characters they are to portray. Sociodrama also can help actors identify with the characters emotionally and explore the interpersonal dynamics embedded in the play. Here is how.

During the beginning rehearsals, after the actors have read the script aloud, encourage them to discuss what they think the play is about and to do some preliminary script analysis. They may discuss theme, plot, and character relationships. You will discover that there are many unanswered questions. They may not be sure why a certain character acts in a particular way or what a character is feeling at a certain moment in the play or the meaning of an event or interaction. Rather than continue to discuss possible meanings and feelings, as the director notices the actors are warmed up to a particular scene or issue, he may ask them to explore the issue in action. After deciding where the scene is to take place, a sociodramatic exploration occurs. For example, in discussing Shakespeare's *The Tempest,* the actors wonder about why Prospero is so imperious and manipulative with Miranda and Ferdinand. They are aware of the reason Prospero has given—to get the young people to fall in love—but they feel there is more to it than what he says. The actors decide to improvise a scene in which Prospero orders Ferdinand about and is snappish to Miranda (the plot basis for this is to be found in the play). As they interact, the director asks Prospero to double for himself. The actor playing Prospero becomes aware that the old man has felt his whole life overturned by others' control of him. Now he has the opportunity to reassert his control and authority, and he wants to seize that chance, not hang back as he did years before, leading to his usurpation. He feels that the end he desires (his daughter's marriage to Ferdinand) will justify the means (his manipulation of the potential lovers). Further, he wants to test Ferdinand to see if he is noble enough for Miranda.

Another question the actors have is why Prospero doesn't kill his brother outright in revenge of the brother's betrayal. They decide to set up a scene between the two. It takes place years before the play occurs, when Prospero still rules and his brother covets his position. They also set up several scenes on the island with Prospero studying his esoteric books. Through doubling and role reversal, the actors might realize that Prospero feels somewhat guilty that he had chosen to spend so much time studying and so little time governing his lands. They may also see that, through his study since being on the island, he has tempered his rage with understanding and compassion. When he has the opportunity, he wants to startle his brother, but he doesn't want to kill him. The actor playing Prospero also experiences firsthand the conflicted emotions of love and anger that grip Prospero, when, as the play opens, he shipwrecks his brother but, through magical arts, keeps him safe from destruction. Through the sociodrama, the actor playing his brother, Antonio, realizes the depth of the character's jealousy and that his actions toward Prospero have hardened his heart. His subsequent actions, in supporting his treachery, have further removed him from grace.

Another way to work with sociodrama in rehearsals is to see what issues from the play interest the actors in their present lives. When the actors choose the issue, say breaking free from parental control, they can set it in the present day even if the play is a period piece, as with *The Tempest*. In this way, the actors playing Ferdinand and Miranda can explore the emotions and role relationships in a context that is more familiar to them. Later, when they move to developing the historical and stylistic elements of the characterization, they will be grounded in familiar and identifiable character emotions.

Another technique that is extremely helpful is asking the actors to create an action sculpture of their character's relationships to the other characters in the play. This sculpture is referred to as an action social atom, because it defines a person's social world and those who are significant in it. Through positioning the other characters in relation to himself, whether far away or near to him, whether positive or negative, he concretizes the attractions and repulsions he feels toward other characters and how he perceives their responses to him. After Caliban (the half-man, half-beast servant of Prospero) has positioned the other characters, the director asks him to reverse roles with each of them and make a statement to Caliban. Miranda's statement might be, "I'm afraid of you," for example. After doing this with all the characters, Caliban returns to his own role and listens to the messages as the other actors speak them. He may interact with them as they speak or just listen to the messages. Actors who engage in this process don't simply know, intellectually, how the other characters relate to his, they also profoundly feel the attractions and repulsions their characters feel.

Sociodrama, then, provides a wonderful tool for director and actors to explore the themes and character relationships in the play. Further, actors have an opportunity to experience the range of emotions the characters feel early in the rehearsal process. They are not only learning through script analysis or improvisation but are also tapping into emotions experienced, not "acted," with the help of role reversal, doubling, and other sociodramatic techniques.

USING SOCIODRAMA IN THEATRE EDUCATION

Sociodrama can be extremely helpful in theatre education. With its action and affective components, sociodrama engages and satisfies the mimetic urge that draws many people to the study of theatre. Acting students can learn to develop emotional expression through a new avenue. They can also role train how to audition with greater spontaneity and less stress. Further, plays can be used as warm-ups to sociodrama in dramatic literature classes.

Using Sociodrama to Train Actors

According to most current theories of acting, an actor must be able to feel and express emotions when in role. Much of actor training is devoted to helping student actors become able to feel a character's feelings on stage and respond naturally to the actions and expressions of the other characters. Acting coaches use exercises, theatre games and improvisations to achieve these ends.

One frequently hears acting students complain of knowing what the character *should* feel, but not being able to experience it themselves. Sociodrama is particularly valuable in helping them experience what it is like to express emotions in a role. There are several reasons for this. As you know, sociodrama emerges from the shared central issue of the group. Thus the students are warmed up to the emotions and role relationships of the chosen issue. Therefore, when they volunteer for a role, they are already attuned to the issue and perhaps to the specific role they have chosen to portray. When the sociodrama begins, their emotions become easily engaged.

Furthermore, in life our emotional responses are role-related. If you step on my foot, I will respond somehow. If I shout at you, you will respond to me in some way. When a person takes a role in sociodrama, his emotions emerge spontaneously in response to the other characters' words and actions in role. The acting student doesn't have to *try* to feel emotions or fulfill an intention; he simply does so as a natural function of the coaction within a social situation. This experience is what Stanislavski was referring to in *Creating a Role* (201) when he said, "Note that I execute *physical* actions, not feel them; because if they are properly carried out the feelings will be generated spontaneously. If you work the other way and begin by thinking about your feelings and try to squeeze them out of yourself, the result will be distortion and force. . . ."

Once an acting student has tapped his emotions in sociodramas, it is easier for her to access emotions in scripted roles. For one thing, she realizes she can experience and express emotions in a surplus reality situation. For another, she begins to realize the sense of role relatedness that she must become aware of when playing a role in a play.

Sociodrama is also helpful in training acting students in audition and interview techniques. The difficulties of getting work as an actor are legendary. Unfortunately, many theatre programs teach students how to *do* the job of acting but not how to *get* a job acting. Sometimes the best acting an actor has to do in an audition or interview is interacting with casting directors or agents, not reading the script. Sociodrama is a wonderful way to prepare actors for the stress of the audition process. Through enactment, they can explore and learn to manage their feelings about the often-scary experience of auditioning. They can examine how they block their own spontaneity and can find alternative solutions for keeping their creativity flowing and their own enthusiasm shining out. The role training aspects of sociodrama are great for giving actors an opportunity to practice how to handle a variety of difficult situations success-fully—for example, what to do if the casting director is hostile, or bored, or continually interrupted by the phone. (For a detailed program of training ac-tors in audition and interview techniques, see Garcia.)

Acting students usually are very much warmed up to their feelings regarding auditioning. Given the opportunity, they can go on for hours talking about their experiences at various auditions. It doesn't take much to get them ready for a sociodrama on the subject. One gets a palpable feeling of the group's relief as previously hidden emotions are expressed in sociodramatic action.

As a structured warm-up, the director might ask the students to separate into dyads. Person A plays an actor going on an audition. Person B takes the role of a difficult casting agent. Or the director can ask the students to take the role of the kind of casting person they fear most and mill around and talk to the other "casting directors." Conversely, the director can ask them to take the role of the kind of casting director they would most like to audition for, then mill around and interact with the other "casting directors." The students can also take the role of their idea of a great auditioner, someone who is calm and comfortable in the situation. This latter warm-up helps people to realize that if they can pretend to be relaxed and at ease in a mock audition, they can do so in a real audition too. Students are often shocked to hear the feed-back of others in the group that they didn't look nervous, no matter how they really felt. Whatever the warm-up, whether structured or unstructured, fledg-ling actors are eager to practice ways to become more adept at auditioning.

Using Sociodrama in Dramatic Literature Classes

Sociodrama is a natural for dramatic literature classes, especially since the themes of scripted drama are universal and sociodrama taps into collective experience. Sociodrama can be very useful in helping students explore the thematic and psychological issues in plays. For example, if students are study-ing Sam Shephard's *Buried Child*, they may choose to explore the family dy-namics in the play sociodramatically rather than simply puzzling over them in discussion. Not only does this process make the social and psychological issues of the play more immediate, being in role also helps students to gain insights into the characters that they might not have gained through just reading the play and discussing it. Further, it allows students to explore the themes for themselves and not simply rely on the professor's lectures for "gems of wisdom" regarding the play's meaning.

USING SOCIODRAMA IN THEATRE IN EDUCATION

Many TIE productions begin in a similar way to sociodrama by defining the group's problems rather than an individual's. Since their foundation is much the same, the authors suggest sociodrama as an additional technique for TIE companies. This would serve as another tool for these groups and allow the students and any other audience members, including teachers, to participate as enactors. This suggestion is not meant to be an "either/or" suggestion, but merely to be viewed as an alternative technique for TIE companies to incorporate.

For example, the well-known Creative Arts Team, affiliated with New York University, produced a play entitled *Tower of Babble*, scripted by James Mirrione. It was based on a group social problem, namely, the lack of effective communication among those who work in a school system (administrators, teachers, custodians, principals, and paraprofessionals). Ordinarily, after viewing a CAT production, the audience members discuss what they have just seen. How exciting it would be to move from that discussion to a sociodrama enactment, thus using the play as a warm-up to sociodrama! In this way, the audience members, as well as the actors, could actively participate in the enactive process, themselves exploring, and perhaps practicing, effective communication techniques.

The techniques mentioned in the preceding two sections are equally applicable for use in TIE. Sociodrama can help TIE companies create their plays and as a kind of epilogue, involving audience members.

SUMMARY

The authors believe that the techniques of sociodrama offer an invaluable connection for writing plays for the theatre and for use in Theatre in Education productions. Since TIE is most often used in curriculum drama and/or drama exploring social issues, this subject matter is especially relevant for sociodrama enactment. Several unique tools for character development, including the use of role reversal and doubling, offer invaluable insight and help the players build scenes through actions of the characters.

Furthermore, sociodrama is a fine method for directors and actors to use in exploring the themes and character relationships in a play. It also offers actors an opportunity to experience the range of emotions the characters feel earlier in the rehearsal process than they normally would. Finally, it assists actors in their own lives, helping them become more comfortable in the audition process.

12

SOCIODRAMA IN EDUCATION

GIVING BACKGROUND

Most people think of sociodrama in education as a new concept, but it has been around just as drama in education has since the 1930s. Sociodrama in the classroom was documented by Robert Bartlett Haas in *Psychodrama and Sociodrama in American Education* in 1949.

Our drama pioneer, Winifred Ward (mentioned in Chapter 1), offered creative dramatics in the classroom as a dynamic way of learning as far back as 1924. She said, "What children do is more significant than what they see." All creative drama in the classroom is based on the premise that students retain what they experience more easily than what they hear. An ancient Chinese proverb tells us:

I hear: I forget.
I see: I remember.
I do: I understand.

The pioneers in sociodrama, like the pioneers in drama in education, were not using theatre as an artistic endeavor, but rather as a means to holistic learning. Throughout our experience as educators we and our students have used sociodrama in a variety of classroom settings, with all ages from preschoolers to adult learners. We have discovered the power and joy of blending cognitive and experiential learning in this special way. In this chapter we will discuss a variety of ways to adapt sociodrama for use in classroom teaching.

USING SOCIODRAMA IN TEACHING HISTORY AND
SOCIAL STUDIES

How many times have you heard someone say, "I hate history"? Whenever you hear a statement like that, you can be sure that the person learned history as a series of names, dates, and places with no human element or dramatic conflicts made real for him. How different it would be to learn about the Civil War between the North and the South as a sociodrama enactment. What is the central issue here? Let's borrow Abraham Lincoln's famous words to say it: "A house divided against itself cannot stand."

Before a meaningful discussion can take place, everyone needs some role preparation. Students investigate the issues of the times—economic, cultural, social, and so forth. They research individual leaders on both sides, as well as what influential writers of the times had to say about the issues. Students explore various alternative possibilities to the war, some of which were tried, and perhaps others suggested by their research or prompted by their imagination. One or several students might research particular historical personalities in order to understand the person better.

A general warm-up regarding the issues of the historical period would allow the shared central issue to emerge, just as it would in any other group. For example, each student might be asked to take the role of the person whom he researched and to imagine that he is at a summit meeting with other Civil War figures. He is to walk around as that person, say General Lee, and interact with the other personalities present.

After the warm-up, when the students are talking about what they experienced in role, the teacher, who is functioning as the sociodrama director, listens for the main themes and act hungers of the group. Perhaps this group is especially dismayed at the idea that brothers turned against each other and fought on opposite sides. They want to explore what could lead to such a rift. Or they may want to know what it would be like to have the responsibility to declare war and exercise it.

When the teacher feels the group is ready and warmed up to the shared central issue, she will handle the sociodrama enactment exactly like any other, allowing for sculpting, role reversal, walk and talk, and any other technique she chooses to facilitate the enactment. For example, students might start an enactment by doing a living tableau of a Civil War photograph by Matthew Brady.

The sharing here is of particular importance. How did the enactor playing the role of Abraham Lincoln feel when he came to believe he had no other choice but to declare war? Even though we know what events actually happened historically, we can still be spontaneous and creative as at any other time in determining the feelings and emotions that brought a particular historical figure to the decision he made. Alternative endings here can be great fun.

Ask the students what alternatives they might like to enact. Through the discussion and sharing, meaningful and lasting insight is bound to come through.

Social studies can be handled in the same way. Again the research and role training involve the whole group. What are some of the main issues that are active in our world today? Which of these is a specific student group warmed up to dealing with on a particular day? Just a reminder here that the Living Newspaper format is just as vital today as it was in the 1920s and 1930s.

Learning to take a risk by playing a role as someone very different from oneself results in personal growth and insight. Oftentimes, insight occurs in a new or deeper realization of what is happening in our world today. Again, the sharing is vital and offers the students an opportunity to talk about what they felt and learned from the enactment.

USING SOCIODRAMA IN UNDERSTANDING CULTURAL ISSUES AND IN TEACHING LANGUAGES

The sociodrama structure offers a fine format to practice and experience the cultures of other nations and/or ethnic groups as well as to learn languages in addition to our own. Exploring the cultural issues of another country through sociodrama is not only an action-oriented kind of learning, but it is also a way of helping people think differently from their usual pattern. People are more mobile today, traveling to various countries for business and/or pleasure. Further, the United States has traditionally been a melting pot for cultures as people emigrate here from around the world. Moreno, himself a Jewish immigrant from Vienna, was vitally interested in exploring how cultures intermingle, how prejudices develop, and how to help people overcome their intolerance to cultural differences.

Understanding Cultures

In the same way that each culture has its own set of roles that characterize it, each culture also has its own customs and expectations regarding how those roles are to be played—for example, a loud public burp in an Arab country is a sign of pleasure and respect for your host, but here in the United States it is considered bad manners.

In working with intercultural communication, if there are students who come from various cultures, they can exchange information about how a particular role is played in their culture. For example, in a discussion about women's rights, a Moslem student from Saudi Arabia might talk about customs in dress and behavior in her country. She may point out that although there are many strictures placed on women, there are also ways in which women have more free time than in the United States.

In setting up a sociodrama in the United States, in order for students to understand a cultural issue involving a woman from the Middle East, for example, you will need to supply enough role information to give a context to certain behaviors. Here is a classic opportunity to supply additional cultural background that a student would want in order to be equipped as an enactor with enough knowledge to know how to deal with a given situation. This is a perfect example of a student putting himself in another person's shoes.

"But, I'd never behave that way," exclaimed a student when asked to participate in a sociodrama exploring an issue dealing with Moslem women. After examining the culture in which this woman lived, her limitations in the role were solidly set by this Moslem culture. There were no alternatives to submitting to her husband's wishes. Although this enactment was fraught with frustration for the female playing the role, she realized how the culture dictated her possible actions. Moreover, after the sociodrama was enacted, all the participants realized how limited the alternatives were in the context of the Moslem culture. They also began to explore the limitations imposed by their own culture.

When Jenny finally realized she had few options in the situation enacted, she said, "I guess it's like staying in character in a play, but I still don't like it. If I lived in that culture, it would be hard to stay in the traditional female role." Although Jenny did not like her situation, she did gain greater understanding of the Moslem culture.

If the students with whom you're working know little or nothing about the cultures you are discussing, it will be necessary to provide them with enough information about the customs that they will be able to enact and learn from a sociodrama. Their warm-up to a sociodrama may be a film, your lecture, their own research, or a videotape.

Learning Foreign Languages

When teaching foreign languages it is also helpful for students to begin to understand the culture in which the language is spoken. Linguists say the hardest part of learning a foreign language is developing the ability to think in that language. Once you can do that, you have mastered the new language. Others say that only when you dream in a foreign language can you tell you have mastered it.

Sociodrama can be an invaluable aid to bring about both of those conditions, because it helps us to place the language in its cultural context. Set up your sociodrama as you would any other. The only difference is the enactors play the enactment in the new language. Use any or all of the sociodrama techniques that you feel are applicable to the situation. Doubling can be especially effective here, with coaching from the teacher/director. After tuning in to the enactor's unexpressed feelings, particularly if the student seems stuck for words, the director can double, helping the student to express his feelings more accurately in the foreign language.

Conduct the entire sociodrama in the foreign language. Encourage all the participants to ask questions about where they were at a loss for a way to express something idiomatically. After discussing what expressions might be used in this situation, the students may want to replay the enactment utilizing the newly learned idioms. In this way, the need to learn a particular expression arises from the desire to communicate thoughts and feelings rather than simply to learn a few new vocabulary words. Thus by tying learning to need, students are more likely to retain what they have learned. Further, because of its holistic nature, through sociodrama students learn the new language both affectively and cognitively. Therefore the authors suggest the sociodrama structure offers a fine format to practice and experience the cultures of other nations and/or ethnic groups as well as to learn other languages.

Using Sociodrama in Teaching Health and Life Skills

Action methods other than sociodrama are used to teach a variety of health skills and lifesaving techniques. Anyone who takes a CPR (cardiopulmonary resuscitation) course practices on a mannequin in order to perform the technique. Other health crisis training, including lifesaving, the Heimlich maneuver, and first aid, also have behavioral rehearsal as a crucial component. However, there are many other less-dramatic health problems, which are usually described and discussed in classes, that would lend themselves ideally to sociodrama.

Historically, many of our health problems are permeated with moral and ethical issues. You will remember Moreno's work with prostitutes in Victorian Vienna, mentioned in Chapter 1. Although Viennese society claimed prostitutes didn't exist, there was no denying that the venereal disease they transmitted was a health problem. Although our understanding has advanced since those days, there are still many health problems people cannot separate from moral ones. Take the issue of abortion. How often is it a simple, clear-cut health problem? More often than not it becomes a moral one as well. Discussion on such an issue is fraught with emotion. Often there are more emotional factors involved here than a simple discussion can uncover.

Currently there are other health issues that produce a high emotional and social response as well—for example, alcoholism, drug addiction, AIDS, and even mental illness. Sociodrama is particularly well suited for exploring these health issues, especially those that are not easily talked about or openly discussed. The very structure of sociodrama offers a framework in which to examine any group problem. Think of how invaluable using doubling, concretization, and role reversal would be in any of the above situations.

While many schools combine health and life skills into one class, we separate them here. We see the life skills class as having to do with how people manage their day-to-day existence. It also is geared to helping students cope with the problems they face at their level of social and emotional development. Therefore, the issues discussed in a class of fifth graders would be different from those discussed with a group of high school seniors. Thus, for fifth graders, an issue of social pressure might cluster around what clothes are the "right" ones to wear, whereas for seniors, social pressure might involve whether or not to snort coke with your friends at a party.

How much more meaningful is an enactment exploring the problem of being teenage parents rather than a lecture on teen pregnancy? Or what about sharing the awkwardness of asking someone for a date? Or having the chance to practice what to say during a college admissions interview? These are life skills that can be explored holistically through sociodrama.

The ever-present school dilemma of whether to teach just basic skills or life skills as well is a growing problem. Some educators feel strongly that learning to read, write, and compute is not enough to give a young person the foundation for living his life with others in a fulfilling manner. Further, since more families have both parents in the work force and/or are headed by a single parent, youths have less contact with those authority figures who have traditionally helped them develop values. Therefore, many families look to the schools to help in this process. Educators around the country are beginning to ask for new ways to teach values clarification and/or ethical action strategies.

Why not give students of all ages practice in solving ethical dilemmas, give them the experience of clarifying their own values through a sociodrama enactment, complete with the spontaneity of the moment. One of the beauties of sociodrama is that rather than listen to a lecture on what is right and what is wrong, the participants can find answers that are right for them at their particular stage of development.

USING SOCIODRAMA IN TEACHING LITERATURE

Just as sociodrama is a natural for dramatic literature classes, so it is for teaching any kind of literature, be it prose or poetry. The themes of all great prose, as well as poetry, are universal and tap into the core of our collective experience. Reading and discussing literature is a valid method of teaching but how much more exciting and adventurous for students of any age to make their own discoveries through sociodrama. All it takes is a teacher willing to try.

Take a story such as *The Prince and the Pauper* by Mark Twain. Who has not dreamed of changing places with another and especially one who is royalty? This is the story of two look-alike infants who were born on the same day, one a pauper and one a prince. Many years later, they meet and, astounded by their resemblance, decide to change places for a while. In playing out elements of this story in a sociodrama enactment, the thoughts and feelings of the participants can be explored on both levels, through the many sociodrama techniques available to you. Interestingly enough, this plot would offer an unusual twist to role reversal since the characters reverse their identities in the story. Therefore, you would be reversing the reversal in a sociodrama. Complicated? Not really. Experiencing the layers of role reversal can be both profound and great fun. It will give students a lot to think about as they explore the theme of putting oneself in someone else's shoes, only to discover the value of one's own life.

Poetry is sometimes elusive for readers. We feel that some of the difficulties people have in understanding and enjoying poetry is that they don't experience the work affectively. They don't explore the feelings the poem evokes or follow its story if the poem is narrative. Through sociodrama, many of the complexities can be experienced and explored and the issues examined.

For example, take a poem like Edgar Allan Poe's "Annabel Lee," which tells us in essence that love is stronger than death. What kind of love did these two young people have, this love "that was more than love"? What made it so strong—"it was stronger by far than the love of those/who were older than we/Of many far wiser than we"? The poem, though speaking of a time archaic to students, nevertheless deals with emotions that are a part of modern-day experience. Students can warm up to many issues of interest to them that connect with the depth of loss and yearning the poem expresses. In exploring an issue sociodramatically, the students come to appreciate the poet's voice and deepen their response to the work.

Sociodrama can also be used to help students reconcile the conflicting feelings they experience when they have read a poem that affects them emotionally, yet they are not sure what the poem as a whole "means." As you know, much of modern poetry confuses students, with its lack of clear story, consistent rhyme, and narrative content. For instance, sometimes students read a poem and feel sad, but they are not sure why. They can explore the poet's imagery through sociodrama and discover for themselves what evoked their response.

Sociodrama is an additional way to explore the richness of literature. While not a substitute for experiencing the work of art, sociodrama as a learning tool enables students to return to the beauty of the work afterward with greater understanding and appreciation.

USING SOCIODRAMA IN TEACHING PSYCHOLOGY AND NURSING SKILLS

Many courses in both psychology and nursing are crammed with technical information that students must know. There is little time or reason to use sociodrama in a course where one is lecturing on the etiology of mumps. However, there are also courses in both these fields where communication skills and the affective realm are of paramount importance—for example, counseling techniques or psychiatric nursing.

Let us consider some courses where sociodrama would be of use. In a gerontology class, one teacher reported using the following warm-up. In order to help students experience the difficulties of aging, she asked each of them to stuff cotton in their ears. She asked those who had glasses to smear the lenses with petroleum jelly. She also gave some of them pieces of styrofoam packing material to place in their shoes to add to their discomfort. Next, she asked them to interact with each other and hold a conversation. During the sharing, students talked about their frustration at not being able to hear or be heard. Some complained about having back aches from walking unnaturally. Others were dismayed at being able to see only blurs. From the sharing a sociodrama arose regarding the difficulties of coping with the physical manifestations of aging.

Learning is a continuous process and extends beyond the classroom. For example, the head of nursing at a large teaching hospital felt her nursing students on the pediatric oncology unit needed some special training in how to handle the highly charged emotional situations they dealt with daily. Not only were these nurses faced with the death of their young patients every day, but also the further responsibility of consoling the families of these youngsters. Talking about their feelings helped but just wasn't enough. She ran a series of sociodrama sessions to help these care-givers understand and cope with their own feelings and experiment with different ways of consoling grieving parents. In addition, these nurses wanted to learn how to help family members without becoming overwhelmed by the pain of the situation. Through sociodrama, they learned how to offer solace to the grieving families, while at the same time maintaining their own inner strength.

USING SOCIODRAMA IN ADULT EDUCATION

Adult education courses are more popular than ever before. Schools are offering a plethora of courses, including academic subjects, hands-on skills courses (such as word processing and woodworking), leisure-time activities courses (like golf and sailing), and also courses in self-improvement (like conversation skills and being single again). While sociodrama is probably not appropriate for teaching surfing or calculus, courses that involve behavior change, human interaction, or role expansion can benefit from using sociodrama.

Let's take a look at a course in assertiveness training. Although role play is a popular modality used in this learning, the authors suggest that sociodrama, with its variety of techniques, would aid students to better understand their feelings and the feelings of others as well as to verbalize them. Assertiveness is not simply a matter of speaking up when you have a mind to do so. The distinctions one makes in training for assertiveness are those between aggression, passivity, and assertion. Explaining the differences is not enough, however, especially since participants may be accustomed to responding either aggressively or passively in interactions and may be unaware that they are doing so. The mirror technique may be useful here for helping participants to view their behavior from a distance and plan ways to correct it as desired.

USING SOCIODRAMA IN RELIGIOUS EDUCATION

Throughout the years, we have known many who have used sociodrama in religious education. Each told us that before using sociodrama, their students' eyes would frequently glaze over as their minds wandered from the topic. The teachers chose sociodrama as a way of making their religious teachings more immediate to pupils. Sociodrama is an ideal intervention for enlivening stories from Sacred Scripture, whatever the religion. One Sunday School teacher used the story of the Last Supper and the betrayal (Matthew, 26) as a warm-up to a sociodrama. She also asked the class to look at a print of Michelangelo's "Last Supper." Then the group came up with the central issue of betrayal and discussed its many forms. They examined the difference between the betrayal of Jesus by Judas and by Peter. The sociodrama that ensued produced some heated emotions and conflicting opinions as well as personal disclosure from students about their own experiences with betrayal.

Sociodrama is also wonderful for helping participants explore ethical issues and clarify values. Another good source for sociodrama warm-ups from the Bible is the Book of Proverbs—for example, Proverbs, 14, 20: "He that walketh with wise men shall be wise: but a companion of fools shall be destroyed."

SUMMARY

Using sociodrama in education is the core of what it is all about. When Moreno began his work in sociodrama, he hoped to change the world into a more responsive, humane, and compassionate society through the use of sociodrama techniques. Although we have a long way to go in fulfilling Moreno's dream, many of us believe that we are just beginning to discover the many areas in which sociodrama can succeed. It can bring history to life; investigate economic, cultural, and social problems; as well as examine emotional reactions in a variety of life situations. Sociodrama presents an ideal format to explore the culture of other nations, to learn other languages, and to help us understand intercultural differences and similarities. Sociodrama gives us practice for exploring issues in any number of subject areas for every age, without fear of the consequences of a wrong answer, a fear that often paralyzes students from participating in the traditional classroom.

13

SOCIODRAMA IN THE WORKPLACE

USING SOCIODRAMA IN BUSINESS AND THE PROFESSIONS

Sociodrama has been used in the workplace for decades. It is a wonderful modality for training all levels of personnel, especially those who must interact with others as part of their job. Sociodrama is helpful in training managers and executives, but it is equally useful as a tool for managers in training those whom they supervise. Sociodrama functions well in other ways besides training. Where a work team has been organized, sociodrama facilitates the trust and resource-building process so necessary for smooth completion of tasks. Further, it provides workers with opportunities to understand and respect each other's contributions. Sociodrama can also be used with great success to foster creativity and help people generate alternatives in the workplace. All too often one gets so immersed in one's job that all sense of perspective is lost. Sociodrama, in allowing people to play, provides enough relief from a difficult work situation that one can go back to it refreshed and with new ideas.

Because of the nature of the business situation, it is essential to respect people's right not to disclose personal information (i.e., information about their life outside the job). The purpose of sociodrama in the workplace is to explore work issues and train work-related skills. Its goal is not therapy or self-exposure. While it is fine for people to express themselves regarding work-related issues, it is not appropriate for the director to encourage personal disclosure.

In groups where employees and managers are both members, the group leader needs to be especially aware of the power the manager has over his or her supervisees to promote, recommend, dismiss, or apply sanctions. The relationship between a supervisor and supervisee can be anything from friendly cooperation, to master/slave, to hostile animosity. The director must provide an environment in which people are not pushed to put themselves in jeopardy by personal disclosure. For example, John the manager finds abortion distasteful and wrong. If Sue, his employee, discloses she had an abortion to end a teenage pregnancy, he may find reasons to complain about her work where he would otherwise have been satisfied.

Usually, people in workplace groups have a natural reserve about exploring personal issues anyway. So it is mostly a matter of the director's respecting and supporting that stance. In order to emphasize the collective issues without personal disclosure, the director can encourage the group to choose enactments that are work-related. For example, the issue of fear of criticism can generate an enactment about a child lying about his test grades or one about an employee going to great lengths to explain every project delay to her supervisor. Clearly, the latter is more likely to arouse sharing that is germane to work issues.

Confidentiality is as much an issue in the workplace as it is elsewhere. Even though people do not discuss their personal lives, they are still sharing thoughts and feelings and are taking the chance to practice new behaviors. If the director can facilitate the group's decision to keep the contents of the sessions confidential, members will feel more comfortable participating fully in the group. Confidentiality takes away some of the fear that "others" will find out if it takes "me" a while to learn a new communication skill.

The possibilities are endless for discovering business and professional groups where sociodrama would be beneficial: librarians, executives, day care workers, police, door-to-door canvassers, social workers, desk clerks, teachers, administrators, hospice workers, salespeople, attorneys, and so on. We hope that the examples given here will spark your interest to find still more settings and applications for sociodrama in the workplace.

USING SOCIODRAMA TO TRAIN PERSONNEL

Sociodrama provides a training method to explore a variety of new situations, try on different roles, and expand existing skills to handle current and future tasks. Through the spontaneity of an enactment, group members can explore management decisions in a manner they thought heretofore impossible or were resistant to try. As was said above, this action method can serve a wide variety of groups from nuns to dishwashers, fire fighters to chorus girls. One key to why sociodrama works so well in business and professional training is that it encourages individuals further by offering the security of the group and the support of others in the same boat—everyone is learning new behaviors. Mastering skills through sociodrama is a safe and secure method no matter what the occupation and/or profession.

Warm-ups in business training situations, as in other types of education (see Chapter 12), may be either cognitive or affective. The director may lecture about the skills to be learned, providing needed background information. For instance, in training employees to prioritize tasks, the director may provide some specific information on time management. On the other hand, the director in a staff training group of hairdressers may ask the participants to take the role of demanding customers and interact with each other regarding their complaints about their hair.

Training Executives and Administrators

Sociodrama is useful in training administrative and executive staff in leadership skills. Some specific concentration areas are: delegating authority, prioritizing tasks, communicating with employees and peers, conducting employee reviews, reorganizing and deploying staff, and motivating workers.

With action training, participants have an opportunity to assess their own present skills as they experience how they perform as leaders in enactments. They do this both through playing the role of a leader and by role reversing and seeing how they appear from the employee's position. For example, take an executive who routinely used sarcastic criticism as a way of motivating his employees. He was shocked at the discomfort he felt when playing an employee of a sarcastic administrator.

Meanwhile, since participants can role train in sociodrama, they have the opportunity to correct behaviors with which they are displeased and to practice new ones. The sarcastic executive, then, could try out alternative ways to motivate others. When a person cannot imagine another way to play a role, the director can freeze the action and ask the group if anyone can think of an alternative. The group can be helpful in offering suggestions, some of which the person may elect to examine in sociodramatic action. Even if the person doesn't try one of the suggested alternatives, just hearing the ideas of others often inspires one to come up with still another idea to try, which better suits his or her own personality. Someone may suggest to that executive mentioned above that not taking employees' mistakes personally might be helpful. That suggestion may lead the executive to remember his own fine sense of humor. He may decide to use his humor without its cutting edge to lighten tense situations and motivate employees.

Another way for administrators to learn new skills is to agree that they will deliberately try to perform the skill as incorrectly as possible, so that the rest can explore what went wrong and why. This use of sociodrama is fun, since many in our culture work so hard to do things "right" and experience shame and embarrassment for any errors. It provides wonderful role relief for people deliberately to do something "wrong" without any consequences. From this, members can also generate more adequate alternatives to explore in future enactments. Let's take a group of managers dealing with the issue of delegating authority. The enactor playing the manager shows the group how responsibility could be delegated to insure failure rather than success. He waits until the last minute to ask for help and then blames his staff for not meeting the deadline. After the enactment, as people share their responses, you may notice that some people sheepishly confess that they have occasionally done the same thing. If members do that, ask them if they have tried it differently and/or how they would like to try it differently. Then, if time permits, allow members to try out their suggestions.

Throughout the course of sociodrama enactment, executives and administrators also learn from the skills modeled by other members as they portray the role of leader. In a session where several executives agree to set up an enactment about communicating with secretaries, each may decide to try handling a given situation differently. For example, the executive will try out various ways to approach an assistant who has not succeeded in getting a new phone line hooked up in his boss's office. One may ask what has impeded the progress of the phone's installation. The boss may also ask if there is any way she can help the assistant to speed up the process. Another may say, "John, you're so efficient with these things that I'm sure something outside of you must be bollixing up the works. What is it, and is there anything we can do about it?" After the enactment, participants can discuss which options they preferred and generate others if they wish.

An exercise that helps participants warm up to dealing with difficult employees is to ask administrators to take the role of a typical troublesome worker. Having taken the role, they are to interact as if they were at work. A variation of this warm-up is to separate the group into pairs. Person A takes the role of a difficult employee, and B is the administrator who must deal with him or her spontaneously. Each pair may want to create a setting for the action. They are to interact for five minutes. At the end of that time, they are to stop, and B becomes a troublesome employee and A, the administrator. Sharing from this warm-up is sure to be animated and generate a spirited enactment.

Training Staff

Many employees have to deal with people as an integral part of their work. In any field where direct interpersonal relations are involved, sociodrama can provide that transition from awkward beginner to polished professional. While the uses of sociodrama with workers are virtually unlimited, for the purpose of simplicity, this segment is divided into *sales* staff and *service* staff.

Some people may be born salespersons, but, more often than not, it takes training and experience to do the job well. Role training through sociodrama can provide a rehearsal for beginners to learn how to handle a variety of different situations and customers with equanimity. Training a group of salespeople through sociodrama is much less threatening than trying to tell a new salesperson all the details and procedures he or she must follow. Such issues as maintaining a pleasant demeanor, finding ways to help the customer, staying patient when people keep repeating questions or can't make up their minds, and learning to hear, "I'm not interested" without feeling rejected are some of the many issues ripe for sociodramatic exploration.

For example, take the issue of rejection. Trainees may take turns creating rejecting customers for each other to deal with in action. Further, one may find that some people feel more comfortable selling to individuals, while others like selling to groups. A person who is accustomed to selling products in large groups may do well enough overall so that he isn't upset when individuals don't buy his product. However, when selling one to one, although selling proportionately as much, each "no" is magnified, and he feels personally rejected. Through sociodrama he can build on roles he already played successfully and modify those skills to fit the new situation.

The sociodrama group provides a forum for the members to explore various facets of a sales job. It offers feedback from the others in the group, including praise and possible alternatives in dealing with different types of people.

Another area that provides challenges for salespeople is how to warm themselves up to selling on days when they are in bad moods or otherwise don't feel like getting out there, making sales and being nice to customers. It takes very little for people to warm up to this issue, since it is a part of virtually everyone's experience. When doing an enactment on this subject, the group will often benefit from concretization of a "bad mood" or the kid's voice in all of us that says, "I don't want to work. I want to play!"

In concretizing a bad mood, either someone can volunteer to enact the role or the group can sculpt a bad mood together using several enactors. In this way, the enactor playing the salesperson can interact with the bad mood. Regarding the role of, "I don't want to go to work. I want to play," people love playing that role and often spontaneously rise to double as a way of participating in the role of the resistant child. The director may want to encourage audience members to double as a way of facilitating group catharsis and role relief.

Now let's talk about service personnel. Clearly, there are many jobs in which an employee provides services to others. We will consider how sociodrama can be used in two of these.

Maybe you have been in one of the new hotel chains where everyone on the staff from the desk clerk to the chambermaid treats you like royalty. This gracious hospitality seldom comes naturally. Rather, employees in most large hotels are trained in cordiality and patience as well as how to handle crisis situations calmly. In a sociodrama session, trainees may decide to explore how to act if the hotel catches fire or what to do if a guest's dog bites someone. They may also role train numerous problems that are more commonplace in hotels—for example, dealing with irate customers, handling unusual requests, dealing with guests who want to change their rooms or day of departure. Any of these situations is easier to handle in life after it has been explored in a sociodrama session.

Sociodrama can even be useful in such unexpected places as dental offices. Dental hygienists, dental assistants, and receptionists meet people in pain daily. They intervene in crises, and they are aware that many people associate them with pain. Through sociodrama enactment, staff can explore how the patients' discomfort affects them. They can learn to deal with fearful patients and people in pain more effectively. Through role reversal, they can experience what a patient feels like and get in touch with what might help the patient to feel more relaxed and less frightened. They gain an awareness of what may comfort a patient in pain. Through role training they can practice ways to interact with patients that they might not have thought of or believed they could do.

Using sociodrama to role train staff helps participants explore and expand their work role in a relaxed, nonthreatening environment. Because of the way the process works, with ready interaction among participants, members tend to spark each other's spontaneity and creativity. An idea, which may never have come to a person sitting alone in a room pondering an issue, may bubble up naturally simply through the synergy of sharing thoughts and feelings in the group. Further, in role training, participants learn through their own action trials and through observing and participating in each other's attempts as well.

USING SOCIODRAMA FOR TEAM BUILDING AND NETWORKING

Sociodrama provides an excellent opportunity for team building. The term *team building* refers to individuals' efforts to join together as a well-functioning work unit. One may either be building a team from the ground up or be intervening where a work group is assessed as needing improvement. According to William G. Dyer in his *Team Building: Issues and Alternatives*, adequate team building necessitates developing trust and respect among members. This process means that over time the group will share leadership roles, become able to resolve its conflicts, to accept each other's differences relative to the work at hand, to know that each other's ideas and opinions are valued, and to feel free to speak up honestly and assertively.

Sociodrama helps the team builder kill two birds with one stone. The sociodramas that the group chooses to do may be situation-specific to the work the team is actually doing, thus helping group members learn to deal with each other regarding the project. At the same time, the very act of role reversal goes a long way toward the more global goal of building empathy and understanding among members without overtly focusing on those issues or specifically focusing on a task. Here are a few examples of how sociodrama can be used to facilitate team building.

As a way of taking stock and promoting interaction, the director in a team-building group may ask members to imagine the group as a body ranging over an area of the room, with the head in one place and the rest of the body arranged in relation to it. He may then ask them to reflect upon what part of the body they feel like. After they choose the part that represents them, they are to go and stand in the corresponding area of the room. After the members have sculpted themselves into a group body, the director can ask them to share why they put themselves where they did. Interesting discussion and enactment can arise not only from how people see their place and function in the group but also from any vital body parts not occupied by any group member.

The team leader, in using sociodrama to train a group in conflict resolution, may preface an action warm-up with a lecture on the principles of conflict resolution. He may next move to the affective by asking people to do an action spectrogram. He may ask them how they feel about conflict, instructing them to place themselves along an imaginary continuum from "like most" to "like least." He may also ask them how they feel about how they deal with conflict. After asking these and other similar questions, the members can share why they placed themselves where they did. From their comments, a sociodrama will emerge in which the group can explore in greater depth the issue of conflict resolution.

As with any kind of sociodrama group, the director accommodates himself to the group's needs and wishes. If one member of the team expresses that she experiences discrimination toward herself and other women in the company, there are undoubtedly others who have also experienced discrimination. Because of weight, height, race, religion, ethnicity, or whatever else, each of us has experienced exclusion or excluded others. Through sociodrama, the group can explore how it feels to be excluded and why one is moved to exclude another. The open exploration of such issues is essential for the building of a strong working team.

For years people associated networking with the "good old boys network," which usually referred to businessmen's cliques, based on class and socioeconomic distinctions. However, in recent years, the term *network* carries more the connotation of an organization, whether formal or informal, comprised of people with similar and/or complementary knowledge and interests. Our world is full of networks: television, organized religion, corporations, clubs, schools, and so forth. Certainly, team building is a part of networking, but here we are also considering networking as encompassing people relating to each other in the larger professional community outside the individual's immediate workplace. For example, an arts administrator in Houston has received a call for information about graduate programs in arts administration. He may have to telephone several colleagues or his former professors to find out the information he will pass on to the caller. The person who called him tapped into the arts administration network, and the administrator has in turn further used the network to unearth the necessary data.

Among the factors necessary for adequate networking are admitting that one needs information that one doesn't already have; dealing with shame about not knowing "everything"; finding out who else might have the needed information or skill; deciding whom one can trust with one's uncertainty; overcoming shyness to approach someone else for help; feeling free to ask the necessary questions; and willingness to help others who might need help.

All of these abilities are ripe areas for sociodrama exploration. As with all other types of sociodrama groups, at the outset the director must assess the group's strengths and needs, so that she can help participants to build on those assets and guide the group to fulfilling the needs it wishes to explore. Depending on the group's needs, the sociodrama director may help participants warm-up to any networking issue. Let's take the arts administrator mentioned above. Say he shared in a group that he felt ashamed that he couldn't provide his caller with current information on the spot. Therefore, promising to call her back, he made excuses to the caller as to why he couldn't give her the answer. After the conversation, he procrastinated about calling his colleagues and professors, because he "should" know about all the graduate programs and didn't want to expose his ignorance. If others in the group have had similar difficulties, an enactment will emerge in which the group will have the opportunity to explore their thoughts and feelings and to practice handling the situation differently.

USING SOCIODRAMA TO UNLOCK CREATIVITY AND GENERATE NEW CHOICES

Most often executives seem to be the only ones lucky enough to be offered creativity sessions on the job, but clearly sociodrama is useful to all personnel. The human value of attending to creativity is that workers feel renewed vigor in approaching their work and perform their job functions with higher excellence. The monetary value of attending to creativity is that a worker who approaches problems creatively and with enthusiasm is more productive.

When helping people to enhance creativity, it is important to remember that many of us have routinely had our spontaneity squelched in our youth. We have been told to "grow up," "act mature," "be quiet," and "not make a fool of ourselves." These attempts, by adults and other children, to stifle our playfulness oftentimes work only too well, so that we come to adulthood feeling like the fun has gone out of our lives. Coupled with that is the sense that work is work and not to be enjoyed in the way that leisure time is enjoyed. The problem is that most of us spend about one-quarter of the week working. That is a lot of time to spend not enjoying what we do. Sociodrama is a wonderful antidote to feeling stuck at work. It provides an environment and structure for re-creating. Because so many of us have forced our playfulness underground and are ashamed of it, sometimes the director will have to begin slowly, to shake off the cobwebs, as it were. Guided fantasy and physical warm-ups where people all rise and move together are good for this. It might also be necessary to give members an opportunity to discuss how they feel about their creativity and how they feel about play. As with other kinds of groups, the warm-up in creativity groups may come from the director or from the spontaneous interaction of group members. Whatever the warm-up, the enactment will still explore the group's shared central issue.

The sociodrama director who wants to enhance creativity will often use spontaneity training warm-ups so that participants respond to situations on the spur of the moment. He may, for instance, use a warm-up called Pass the Face. The group stands in a circle. One person makes a silly face as if it were a mask. He passes the face to the next person, who must repeat the expression and then transform her own face into another silly face, which she, in turn, passes to the next person, and so on around the circle.

Another spontaneity training warm-up that never fails to evoke interesting and exciting sociodramas is a mask warm-up in which the director brings in a number of masks, each having a different expression (plain plastic character masks are wonderful for this warm-up if they are available in your town). She also brings in a hand mirror. The director asks for volunteers to come up and put on a mask. After they have done so, she asks them to look at themselves in the mirror and take on the persona the mask indicates—happy person, sad person, angry person, buffoon, or whatever. After each has taken on the persona, holding the mask to the face, they are to interact spontaneously. When the warm-up is over and people have shared, a sociodrama may arise regarding how the masks that we wear in our lives help or hinder us in the work setting. Members may even decide to explore congruity by enacting a scene alternately wearing different masks and then removing the mask and continuing with the enactment without the mask.

The director might also ask the group to imagine that they have become great wizards. They have the power to create or transform any aspect of the world they choose. After sharing what they would transform, the director may ask them what aspect of the work situation they would transform and how. After sharing, the group may elect to have a wizard try his hand at changing a hypothetical work situation.

Generating new choices and trying them out in action is a future projection technique that gives participants an opportunity to do trial runs in a safe environment. A work team that isn't sure which course to take may enact each of the known options, one at a time. They can imagine it is six months from now and the option is in place—for example, the new computer system is in place, or two new workers have been hired to work on a special project. As they enact each option in this way, they may become aware of benefits and/or drawbacks they had not considered. They may also generate new options that occur to them from enacting the possibilities they had been considering.

Whether in a creativity workshop or not, all sociodramas deal with creativity in that people agree to assume roles and enact hypothetical situations spontaneously. Participants have no script to rely upon, only their own spur-of-the-moment responses. They are called upon to figure out what to do in the situation as events occur and as others interact with them. Thus it is an easy and highly enjoyable step to combine sociodrama with creativity enhancement.

SUMMARY

Sociodrama can be used in the workplace in a variety of ways and with all levels of personnel. It can be used in management training to help administrators and executives perform their work roles with greater efficiency and aplomb. It can be used to train personnel in sales and services. It is equally valuable in facilitating interaction among workers as with team building and networking. Finally, sociodrama, with its roots in spontaneity and play, is a stellar modality for stimulating and expanding people's creativity.

14

SOCIODRAMA IN THE COMMUNITY

FOCUSING ON ORIGINS

Sociodrama has its origins in Jacob Levy Moreno's social activism. In a sense, all sociodrama is about social action, since it mobilizes people around social issues and helps them to explore those problems and the human interaction surrounding those concerns. In this chapter, dealing with sociodrama in the community, the authors are directing their attention to sociopolitical issues and how they can be explored sociodramatically.

Moreno believed that the theatre had an incredible potential to stir the human heart, influence and activate people. However, he felt that theatre had become leaden and sterile because it relied upon the conserve of the play. He also felt that, while humanity was open to the use of technological tools (e.g., the computer, the food processor, the automobile) for external progress, it was less open to using social tools (e.g., sociodrama, sociometry, psychometry) for internal progress. He wanted to join theatre and the community, believing that the synergy between the two would be enormously powerful in helping humankind evolve to a more loving, more spiritual, less hating, less destructive, global community.

From its inception, the Theatre of Spontaneity (1921–1923) was open to the public and dealt with the issues of the day. By 1928 Moreno had emigrated to the United States and was working with New York City school children. Under his leadership they learned democracy in action as they enacted scenes from a Democratic political convention.

In "The Concept of Sociodrama," first published in 1943, but later appearing in *Psychodrama–First Volume,* Moreno said, "The true subject of socio-drama is the group. It is not limited by a special number of individuals, it can consist of as many persons as there are human beings living anywhere, or at least as many as belong to the same culture" (354). When his Impromptu Theatre was in operation in Manhattan, the *Patterson Press-Guardian* is quoted in 1930 as saying that the whole audience rose and became part of the enactment at one performance the reporter attended (Moreno, *The Theatre of Spontaneity,* 107).

Throughout the years sociodrama has been used as a modality for social action.[1] In the late 1940s, Bert Hansen of the School of Speech at the University of Denver carried on experimental work in community sociodrama. He taught two classes in his program: community sociodrama and communication and community problems. He also conducted a study that included four related sociodramatic approaches to community intervention. One project dealt with community problems in various service, social, political, and religious organizations in Denver. Another project concerned blacks living in segregated areas and the problems caused by being forced to live in this way. The fourth project was carried out with community problems in a small community close to Denver. Bert Hansen, in his essay, "Sociodrama—A Methodology for Democratic Action" (Haas, 161), tells us, "Community sociodrama is founded on the conception that the problems of a group find better solutions within the group than from without the group." He goes on to say further,

Ours is a world of people badly in need of a medium of communication which brings to folks sympathy and understanding from a mutual exchange of ideas that have the warmth of simple human relations. If in such a world, community sociodrama can help serve that purpose, then that is enough to justify it. It so completely ties up with our long tradition of democratic action, because the fundamental philosophy of both is based on the conception that community judgment, unhampered by individual authority shall prevail (162).

EXPLORING SOCIAL ISSUES, RESOLVING COMMUNITY PROBLEMS

Sociodrama can go anywhere. It can be used at the site of problems as they arise, whether in the street, the schools, the community center, or the seat of government. Sociodrama provides a forum for exploring options, feelings, and interests. Today, our communities face many problems that deeply affect us. We often feel impotent to solve them, either because we're not sure how they should be solved, because we feel small in relation to the magnitude of the problem, or because we feel the government or someone else in power is unresponsive to our needs regarding the issues.

Among the important social issues before us currently in the United States are substance abuse, the disruption of divorce and its aftermath, spousal and child abuse, mistreatment of the elderly, violent crime, white-collar crime, nuclear disarmament, AIDS, racism, abortion, toxic waste, homelessness, child custody, teen pregnancy, U.S. military involvement in Central America and elsewhere. Each of these large issues has numerous components that are loaded with emotional and social ramifications that are ripe for enactment.

Community problems are often caused by inadequate communication and understanding or a combination of both. Frequently, groups can receive information regarding a problem and fail to process it in such a way that it brings about understanding. Oftentimes people are hesitant to voice their opinions in a public gathering, but when the format is a community sociodrama, most people talk more freely. Through sociodrama, members of the group can express their feelings on current problems that concern them as individuals and/or as members of the group.

It is important to note that frequently a community sociodrama is a one-time event in which people congregate relative to a particular sociopolitical issue. Since the group is usually heterogeneous and composed of people who may be together only once as a group, it is especially important that the director carefully construct the warm-up to take this into consideration. A good warm-up will help people connect quickly.

The sociodramatist may direct his or her own group and deal with social issues within that group as they arise. Or a group of people interested in exploring a particular topic can be brought together. For example, a group might be formed to explore the possibilities of setting up a neighborhood cooperative day care center. Oftentimes, though, directors are invited into other community groups with the express purpose of directing a sociodrama. With a brief introduction to the techniques of sociodrama—ten to fifteen minutes—virtually any group can participate in enactments. Generally, either before or after the warm-up, the director can explain briefly what sociodrama is, how to role reverse and how to double, and the group is set to go. Any other techniques the director chooses to use can be briefly described as needed during the enactment.

The sociodramatist may be invited to lead an already formed group. For instance, a sociodrama director comes to a government task force studying inner city violence for the express purpose of leading enactments. On the other hand, a sociodramatist may lead a group of interested people who join together for the specific purpose of exploring a stated issue sociodramatically. For example, a school system may bring in a sociodramatist to explore the issues of substance abuse or teenage suicide at its high school assembly. Or a community may contract with a sociodramatist to explore with its members the impact of spousal and child abuse at a town meeting open to the public.

The sociodrama of social action often emerges spontaneously in any kind of group. No matter what the purpose of the group, on the day the Challenger went down or the day that Kennedy was assassinated, people were able to think of little else. The director at such a time follows the spontaneity and needs of the group to explore the immediate social crisis.

Whether called in to direct a sociodrama or originating the social action group oneself, the sociodramatist uses the opportunity to help participants to explore the issues honestly and as fully as time allows. He or she is aware that the shifting of attitudes in one small group has ripples in the larger community. Those group members coact with others outside the group, bringing Moreno's dream of making the world a better place through sociodrama one step closer.

EXPLORING PREJUDICE THROUGH SOCIODRAMA

In *Psychodrama–First Volume* (363) Moreno told us: "The exploratory value of sociodrama procedure is only one-half of the contribution which it can make, the other and perhaps the greater half of the contribution is that it can cure as well as solve, that it can change attitudes as well as study them." It is in this area of changing attitudes that sociodrama is so fine a modality for diminishing prejudice. In 1948 Moreno used sociodrama in this way when he devoted several sessions to exploring the problem of racial riots that occurred in Harlem.

No one is totally free of prejudice. Somewhere along the line everyone picks it up from family, friends, bad experiences, or simply misconceptions about others who are different from oneself. Prejudice is based on fear, on the feeling that others will take something from us, and on feelings of insecurity. It is also based on taking isolated experiences or information and generalizing from that to an entire group. On the other hand, the prejudiced person doesn't allow new or conflicting information to change his or her viewpoint about the group as a whole. For instance, how many of us have heard something like this: "I know all Mexicans are lazy, but my friend Enrique is an O.K. guy." Or, "All gays are limpwristed jerks. A macho guy like you can't really be a fag."

Whenever we meet individuals or groups whom we perceive as radically different from ourselves and therefore threatening, feelings of prejudice are in danger of becoming aroused. These differences can be something obvious that we can see like race, sex, age, physical disability, weight or body shape, and even some types of developmental disability. Other forms of prejudice, equally strong, but not as obvious to the observer, are religion, sexual preference, ethnic background, social or economic level, and intellectual and artistic ability.

A sociodrama group may come together specifically to explore a crisis, as with the bombing of an Asian's home in a black neighborhood. Or the issue of prejudice may be a problem for which a community seeks sociodrama as a means of promoting dialogue and interaction and of resolving the problem— for example, parents in a school district trying to reach some consensus about busing. In setting up a sociodrama to explore prejudice, it is particularly important for the leader to present the participants with as much factual information as possible. Present the group with a common shared experience. Tell a story. Read a newspaper article. Bring in an expert to impart factual information. As a warm-up for the group, ask them to free associate their feelings and experiences with the subject of prejudice. "Have you ever been labeled in a discriminatory manner?" "Have you ever labeled or discriminated against someone else?" "Do you know someone who is prejudiced?" These kinds of questions prompt an open discussion that will generate several possibilities for group action. If you need to prime the pump, ask people to make a list of discriminatory words that have been applied to them. This will lead to feelings behind those labels and what it is like to be saddled with one of those prejudicial terms.

An interesting action warm-up is called Circle Exclusion. Ask for a volunteer to remain outside the circle and try to break in. He may do this physically or verbally. Ask the other members to link arms and not allow the person to get in. After the warm-up ask members to say how it felt to be outside the circle or to keep someone else out. The sociodrama can emerge from their responses.

An immediate problem today deals with AIDS. There are many questions and prejudices surrounding this whole area. Let's say you want to explore prejudice in training AIDS counselors. These trainees will be dealing with a variety of prejudicial responses to the patients, such as sexual preference, promiscuity, drug use, and the most significant of all: fear of the unknown. A trainee might want to explore his own prejudices in relation to the disease first, so that he will be better prepared to handle the prejudices of others. He may feel, "I'm not prejudiced," but through a sociodrama he may come to realize that he is and work to resolve those feelings through enactment. Again, the director would first gather the factual material and see that his trainees were familiar with it. The sociodrama could explore a variety of situations: telling parents about their child's illness; talking to the patient and calming his fears; warning a lover of the possibility of infection and offering specific information/suggestions for that person's testing and safety. Through this type of training, the counselors won't solve the primary problem of curing the disease, but they will be able to help others become more sensitive to the issues involved.

Very often people are unaware of their own prejudices. One way a sociodrama group can help is to reveal unacknowledged prejudice. Individuals may be hooked into a certain type of thinking about one group or another without even realizing it. For example, one of the authors directed sociodramas with a group of disabled and nondisabled college students. The group decided to explore prejudices they had met regarding disabilities and began by brainstorming on the subject, "Exploding the Myths of Disabilities." Some of those myths were:

Blind people can't hear.

Blind people need someone to lead them around.

Blind people are sloppy dressers.

People in wheelchairs are invisible.

People in wheelchairs can't travel on public transportation.

People in wheelchairs have to be carried up stairs.

All deaf people are beautiful.

All deaf people have super eyesight.

All deaf people only communicate with their own kind.

Learning disabled are other words for retarded.

All learning disabled persons have trouble with math.

Learning disabled people can't read unless they hold up a mirror to a page.

And the biggest myth of all: disabled people have no interest in sex! One student in the group put it this way: "Just because people have a disability they're not supposed to be interested in sex. Well, it's not true! We have the same sex drive, hormones, and even sexual fantasies that everyone else has."

When the group explored ways of dealing with prejudice about disabilities, they uncovered a most interesting truth. The disabled members were surprised and a little upset to discover that they too had prejudices against others. The blind students were able to share that when the group was first formed, they were resistant to participating in a group with others of such varying disabilities.

When directing a group dealing with prejudice, group members should be better able to communicate with each other as a result of their work. In most instances, they will even resolve their prejudice and disagreements as they appear in the group interactions. It is to be noted, however, that in rare cases, people whose values are diametrically opposed become more polarized after interactive work and role reversals. Moreno noticed that this was true in life generally as well as in sociodrama.

After they leave the group, some members will undoubtedly encounter prejudice directed toward them, in particular if they are members of a minority on which prejudice is traditionally heaped. Therefore, in addition to learning about their own prejudices and those of others, group members can explore how to best and most safely protect themselves from prejudice that is likely to be directed to them in the future. For example, take a group of black women community activists who want to set up an abortion clinic in their area. First they must garner the support of the community for the project. In order to do this, they must educate others, regardless of sex and race, to the need for such a clinic, and they must convince the community at large that this is a worthwhile project. Chances are these women are going to meet prejudice and probably downright hostility along the way. Some people will be prejudiced against this group because of their sex, their race, or because of the project itself. Still others will be prejudiced against them for all three reasons. How can these women learn to protect themselves from discrimination directed toward them as they move throughout the community in an effort to get their project accepted?

Here is an example of how the sociodrama process can arm a group with inner strengths and controls through *role training*. The director may begin the warm-up by asking members to brainstorm derogatory and/or inflammatory words or name-calling prejudicial labels, such as, "dumb broad," "black bitch," or "baby killer." Then each participant picks out the ones that bother her most or cause her to become angry. The leader is not trying to goad them here. What she wants is to help the participants identify what triggers their emotional response or ignites their anger.

Next, the leader asks members to come up with as many offensive questions about the clinic project as they expect to encounter. Armed with this information, the group can set up an enactment in which they field offensive questions and practice protecting themselves from prejudice. During the enactment, the director can use soliloquy and walk and talk to help the enactor gain some distance or perspective if necessary. She can also freeze the action and generate alternative coping behaviors from the audience. In addition, the director and group members may decide to keep a sharp eye out for the words and/or actions that escalate the emotional reactions of the enactors. These will be the words and actions the enactors build their defenses against in their role training. Through this behavioral rehearsal or role training, the women learn how to protect themselves from reacting in ways they don't want to react and find ways to deescalate a potentially explosive situation.

SUMMARY

Sociodrama is intrinsically connected with social issues and social action. Moreno used it as far back as 1921 to mobilize people. He proved its value in various projects as exemplified in the Theatre of Spontaneity and his Impromtu Theatre. The goals of community sociodrama are to examine social issues and precipitate direct action by the participants to resolve community problems. It can be practiced anywhere that people come together.

Sociodrama is also useful in helping people explore prejudice, their own and that of others. It helps them examine how their negative expectation of others contaminates communication. Through such techniques as doubling, mirroring, and role reversals, participants can initiate or restore satisfying interaction.

Moreno had a grand vision of sociodrama making the world a better place to live for all mankind. He felt that each sociodrama could influence participants to influence others. The ripple effect over time could create a new order in which people interact with each other honestly and with good will. May his grand vision become a reality.

NOTE

1. The reader can turn to Chapter 16 to see how some leaders currently use sociodrama for social action.

15

SOCIODRAMA IN PSYCHOTHERAPY

GIVING AN OVERVIEW

Although sociodrama is an educational rather than a therapeutic modality, it can be extremely useful in facilitating the therapeutic process. As psychotherapists are so keenly aware, many clients seek treatment because they have problems for which they see no solution: they feel immobilized. Others seek help because they are depressed and lack some degree of self-esteem. Still others have difficulty setting limits or controlling or expressing uncomfortable emotions, such as anger and pain. Since sociodrama mobilizes spontaneity and provides people with an opportunity to generate alternatives and try them out in action, it is a wonderful adjunctive tool for the counselor or psychotherapist.

Sociodrama is great at getting things going in an otherwise quiet or resistant group. It can be a lot of fun, and it energizes participants through their involvement. The authors cannot remember directing or viewing a single sociodrama where people didn't become involved in the process.

Further, because sociodrama focuses on hypothetical roles and group issues, people can work on therapeutic issues, anonymously as it were, without having all of the group's focus on them and their personal problems. Sociodrama is especially helpful, then, with a timid group of people or with people who are downright terrified of the issues with which the group is dealing. An example of this is a group for rape victims. A sociodrama dealing with some aspect of the issue would help the members explore what might otherwise be too painful or shameful to examine.

Sociodrama is useful for all kinds of clients. This chapter will include material for work with low functioning as well as medium and high functioning clients.

DEVELOPING SOCIAL SKILLS

The social skills that many of us take for granted may seem like foreign and confusing territory for a low functioning client. Many people who have had repeated psychiatric hospitalizations have either lost some of their socialization skills or may never have acquired them in the first place. For example, the client may not know how to begin or maintain a conversation. He may not use eye contact, but rather slump over and look at the floor. He may not know how to give or receive a compliment. He may not know how to conduct himself on a job interview or how to send back a burnt steak at a restaurant. He may not know how to make a request or complaint appropriately.

This lack of social competence further insures that the individual will continue to have difficulties in the world. It is not enough for the therapist to help the client find and work through the roots of his or her problems. The client also needs tools to be able to interact with people in the present while that longer, more arduous process goes forward. Through sociodrama, clients can learn and practice social skills in a safe setting.

One way to do this is for the director to contract with a group to work on social skills for a certain number of sessions. The group would give input as to what social skills they want to acquire. In this way, the director could structure warm-ups that would attend to the group's needs and interests. The warm-up could be a lecture/discussion about how to perform the skill, or it could be an affective warm-up designed to fit the topic. For example, if the skills were giving and receiving compliments, the director could divide the group into pairs and ask them to say three positive things about their partner. After the warm-up, the director can ask the members to say how they felt giving the compliments and receiving them. She might also ask what makes it hard to say positive things to others and to receive positive statements about oneself. Out of the members' responses, a sociodrama can arise in which members practice how to give and receive words of praise.

One of the authors directed a socialization group for members of a day treatment program for young people who had been hospitalized once. Most had held down jobs before their hospitalization, and now only a couple had returned to work. The group had concerns about how people would receive them when they went back to their old jobs. Did their co-workers know where they had been? What should they tell them? Would anything in their affect give them away? One member complained, "I act weird sometimes, and I don't want to do that." Group members decided to enact scenes dealing with different aspects of encountering people at work. As they enacted, group members worked together, helping each other build the needed skills. They were no longer strictly reliant on the therapist for wise advise. In addition to gaining social skills, they experienced the esteem-building power of being able to help others, of having good suggestions to offer and support to give.

Something to keep in mind when helping a group to build social skills is to chunk down the larger skill—for example, holding a conversation—into several smaller skills—for example, showing interest in another person—which can be handled more easily than the larger, more complex skill cluster of holding a conversation.

While low functioning groups may have a crucial need to develop social skills, higher functioning clients can often benefit from learning to communicate more adequately as well. For example, the person who flies off the handle every time she feels criticized, or the one who seldom speaks up and says what he needs, can both benefit from assertiveness training.

Although assertiveness training was discussed in the "Using Sociodrama in Adult Education" section of Chapter 12, the focus of the group can be somewhat different in a psychotherapy setting in that the therapist and client may be on the alert for issues to be worked through later. For example, in an enactment, as a woman is trying to tell the gas station attendant that she asked for $5.00 worth of gas and will only pay that amount rather than the $6.50 he put in while chatting with his friend, she may become aware that she is experiencing a familiar anxiety. She may gain an action insight that her fear of speaking up comes from her relationship with an angry, overbearing parent. This realization can be the seed for some new and fruitful therapeutic work or may reinforce and advance the process that is already germinating.

REDUCING ISOLATION

One of the most common complaints of clients is depression. They feel not only isolated and alone, but also helpless to do anything about their situation. Furthermore, they are sure that no one else has ever felt like this before. Usually these clients have little or no adequate support systems for themselves, no one to talk to, and no place to turn for help. If they do have a support system, they may be unable to tap into it. They think of themselves as totally alone in the world and isolated from every other human being in it. They sometimes feel that they are so awful that they should stay away from others, for fear they will contaminate those whom they love and need most. The therapist's job in this situation is to help the isolated persons discover there are others who feel just as isolated as they do, and for many of the same reasons. The first step is verbalizing these feelings within the group. Once these individuals realize there are others in the same boat who feel just as alone as they do, a connection begins. The director must reinforce commonality or connection among all members. The very process of sociodrama reduces isolation. One warm-up for people feeling isolated would be to write the word *isolation* on a flip-chart in front of the group. Ask members to think of any other words they associate with isolation and to come up and write them on the chart. After they have written down all the words they can think of, ask them which word most closely represents their feelings and why. A sociodrama can arise from their responses.

The liberal use of doubling is especially helpful in reducing isolation. The director can encourage members to rise from their seats and double during the enactment by stopping the action for a moment and saying, "Who thinks they know what Marcie might be feeling? If you do, come stand near her and make a doubling statement." As group members cluster around the enactor, isolation is literally as well as symbolically reduced.

RESTORING SPONTANEITY

We all suffer from blocked spontaneity at times. When our spontaneity is down, it can be very frustrating or very boring. Either we don't want to stir ourselves, or we can't seem to get ourselves in gear. Or worse yet, even if we could convince ourselves to get moving, we don't know in what direction to start. Some clients seem to spend large portions of their lives in that state of locked spontaneity.

It is not only the low functioning client who suffers from this difficulty and brings the complaint to therapy, but many higher functioning people do so as well. Sometimes a person is suffering from overwork and overcommitment. He simply can't do another thing. Spontaneity grinds to a halt, and the person zones out in front of the TV night after night. Most often, though, spontaneity is blocked because either the person or those important to him squelched or devalued his spontaneity. That situation may be occurring in the present as well. Roy's parents always told him to grow up and act like a man. Now, he has trouble playing with his own kids. He feels foolish and can't seem to stop himself from shrieking at them to "shut up!" when they get giggly. Betsy's mother repeatedly criticized her behavior. Now, Betsy can't seem to make a career choice and stays stuck in a dead end job.

Sometimes therapy itself grinds to a halt because the client's spontaneity is at such a low level, and the client can't see that any options are available. Unfortunately, sometimes the therapist gets discouraged and begins to feel the same way. Whatever the reason spontaneity is lagging, sociodrama is a marvelous antidote. The director can use spontaneity training exercises, fantasy exercises, or physical exercises as warm-ups. One fun spontaneity training warm-up is a variation on the child's game Spin the Bottle. The director writes down silly actions on pieces of paper, such as "Sing Dixie," "Hop up and down three times and say something serious," "Make a funny face," "Whistle a tune." She folds the pieces of paper and puts them in a bag. Someone spins the bottle. The person to whom it points chooses a slip of paper and does what it says. Then he spins the bottle. And so on. If the group runs out of slips of paper before everyone has had a chance, the person spinning the bottle can give a silly action for someone else to do.

An example of a fantasy exercise is to ask people to take the role of their favorite cartoon or fairy tale character and to interact with the others in the group as that character. A physical exercise that enhances spontaneity involves balloons. The director releases balloons in the room and asks people to bounce them around a while interacting as they wish. Then he asks them to get a balloon from one side of the room to the other without using their hands. If people are not fearful of touching each other, he can ask them to pick a partner and move across the room with the balloon between them, again without using their hands or talking. They can make sounds but not talk.

The director can foster spontaneity in participants during the enactment also. She can do so by freezing the action, moving one of the enactors out for a walk and talk and asking the person to generate other ways to deal with the situation at hand. Or she may ask for doubles from the audience to double for an enactor. In this way, she is mobilizing audience spontaneity.

If an enactor, in dealing with an authority figure, seems timid, the director can bring in a chair and ask the enactor to continue the dialogue standing on the chair. This intervention allows the person to be in a physically more powerful position. Further, the surprise of shifting place often helps a person to get unstuck. The director might also use a concretization of the underlying action of the enactment. For example, in an enactment dealing with two people engaged in a power struggle, the director may ask them to join hands and try to pull the other person over to his or her own side while continuing the conversation. As an alternative, if a rope is available, the enactors may use that.

Restoring spontaneity is energizing. The therapist using sociodrama sees affect change as if by magic. Clients can tap into the wellsprings of their creativity and enhance their strengths, so that they can turn their attention to the problematic aspects of their therapy with renewed energy and confidence.

EXPANDING ROLE REPERTOIRE

In the Moreno folklore, there is the story of a young woman being brought to him by her wealthy parents. She had been given up for lost by other mental health professionals and sent to Moreno since he worked so well with impossible cases. When she arrived at his Institute in Beacon, New York, with her parents, she was carried in and deposited on the floor, dirty, disheveled, disoriented, and growling instead of speaking. Rather than ask the young woman what was wrong with her, Moreno called in a nurse and told her he had a new nurse's aide for her. He turned to the young woman, informed her that he was hiring her as a nurse's aide. She'd have to get up, go out with the nurse, get washed, and put on a uniform. He instructed the nurse to train the woman as an aide and start her immediately. With that, the young woman rose and

walked docilely off to learn her new role. This is a wonderful example of
expanding role repertoire.

In a less dramatic way, sociodramas provide many opportunities for people
to take roles different from those they normally play in life. One finds participants eager to set up enactments in which they can try on roles they want to
play in their future lives. In taking these roles in enactments, the person becomes desensitized to taking on the new roles in life. For example, a home-
maker who has never been employed outside the home, but who now wants
to get a job, can benefit from playing the role of a businesswoman. Or the
young man fearful of marriage can take the role of a husband in an enactment.
In a therapeutic setting, the director may suggest to a client that he play a
specific role in a sociodrama, since she feels that his playing the role will help
him. This practice is referred to as a *therapeutic role assignment*.

The technique of role reversal can also be used in expanding role repertoire.
For example, the worker can play the boss and vice versa. Clients find it more
difficult to say, "I can't" after they *have* done something new.

ENHANCING SELF-ESTEEM

In Francois Rabelais' *Words to the Reader* (Book II, Chapter 29) we learn,
"So much is a man worth as he esteems himself." Yet many clients in therapy
suffer from a lack of self-esteem. Although every human being starts out in life
as the center of his own universe, somewhere along the line he begins to
believe and accept what other people say about him. This loss of self-worth
often begins in childhood and comes from a variety of sources: parents, siblings, teachers, and peers. The unfortunate result of this feeling is that it is
self-perpetuating. A parent tells a child, "You're no good," and since these
words come from the central authority figure in that child's life, she begins to
believe it. A sibling cries out in frustration, "Daddy loves me more than he
loves you." A stressed-out teacher losses her patience and blurts out, "Don't
be so stupid." When this type of feedback is persistently given, the person
begins to process the negative information he received from others and con-
cludes that he is "a no good, unloved, stupid person." If he accepts this of
himself, he will begin to act as if this were true, and these labels become an
unexamined part of his self-concept despite any further evidence to the contrary. In effect, the person interjects negative authority roles and uses them
against himself, telling himself from those roles, "You're stupid," and so on.
Meanwhile, there is also a part of the person, although perhaps very well
hidden, that knows, "I am a worthwhile human being." In order to protect
himself from being hurt further, the person pushes these feelings as far down
inside himself as possible. The sociodrama director can help the client to work
through the negative injunctions and feel free to experience the integrity of
who he really is.

The trick here is to discover some strengths, any strengths, as a focal point with which to begin working. A good warm-up is to ask each group member, one at a time, to say the line, "One thing I do well is . . ." and fill in with his or her own words. You might want to add for variety, "One thing I wish I did better is. . . ." Another good line to complete that also focuses on the client's strength is, "One thing I like about myself is. . . ." If the client draws a blank, ask others in the group to help out: "What do you like about John?" or even, "Let's go around the group and everyone say something you particularly like about John." This can provide the jumping off place for an enactment about self-esteem or self-love.

Moreno (*Theatre of Spontaneity*, 8) said, "When spontaneity is at a zero, the self is at a zero. As spontaneity declines, the self shrinks. When spontaneity grows, the self expands. If the spontaneity potential is unlimited, the self potential is unlimited."

If you need fuel to fire the imagination and ignite spontaneity, there are numerous quotations that promote discussion, such as the one by Rabelais that begins this section or the well-known line from Shakespeare's *Hamlet*, "This above all, to thine own self be true" (act 1, scene 3, line 75). Another familiar saying, from the Bible, is "Love thy neighbor as thy self" (Leviticus XIX, 18).

One of the ways that we enhance self-esteem is to take a more competent role and acknowledge that we have done so. It is also helpful when others give us positive feedback on our new behavior. For example, in a sociodrama, if Maureen plays the role of a warm, understanding friend, she can recognize that the role she played is available to her in life as well. Others in the group might further reinforce her behavior by spontaneously saying, "Maureen, I always thought you were so quiet and didn't like us, but you'd really make a great friend. I'd like to have a friend like you."

The group modality of sociodrama is an ideal way for individuals to gain support and respect for and from each other. By discussion and enactment, clients discover their ideas and opinions have worth, that they are not alone in their feelings, and that those feelings have value. Therefore, they too have value as human beings. Through the group process, clients realize that they have something to give others as well as to learn from others. As one client put it after her first sociodrama experience, "I never thought my opinion was worth anything. Now, I realize I have something to contribute, and it feels good." She paused for a moment, and then said, "I'm not so bad after all."

LEARNING NEW BEHAVIOR

Learning new behavior is different from learning new roles. One way to learn new behavior is to modify one's manner of acknowledging and expressing certain emotions—for example, dispelling fear and managing disappointment. Another aspect of learning new behavior occurs when a person modifies how he plays a role that is already in his repertoire. For instance, a teacher who practices being more firm with his students regarding deadlines for reports is not learning a new role but learning new behaviors to play an old role with greater satisfaction.

A common complaint of many people is anger and how to control it. For some, the only way they know how to vent that feeling is by violence. Most of us, through the process of becoming civilized, learn to control the expression of our anger to some degree. However, what we don't always realize is that the same situation that infuriates one person may have little or no effect on someone else. We all have different boiling points, so to speak. Most of us have heard some of the traditional advice on how to handle anger, such as: count to ten, take a cold shower, go for a walk, or eat something sweet.

A good warm-up to vent anger by physicalizing it is called the "silent scream." Direct the participants to stand in a circle and imagine screaming with their right hands and arms. Send the silent scream up and out through the fingers. Repeat with the left hand and arm. Then give the same direction for the right leg and foot. Repeat on the left. Next, send the silent scream up and out through the whole body. Lastly, repeat the silent scream with the whole body and exhale a voiceless air stream. Clients report that this warm-up offers all the same physical/emotional benefits that a good loud scream does with none of the adverse effects of a sore throat. This warm-up affords relief for those who need to learn control as well as those who have the opposite problem with their anger—keeping it bottled up inside. The exercise gives participants an acceptable way to release their anger and ready themselves for an enactment. After the activity, encourage group members to talk about their anger and what makes them angry. The group can discuss various ways to deal with anger and to vent it. From here group members can set up an enactment to deal with the issues that arise.

With regard to playing an old role in a new way, we will take the example of the teacher mentioned above. He has difficulty setting limits in most of his relationships. If he were in a group with others having the same problem, the director could create a warm-up in which participants practiced saying, "No." Here is an example of such a warm-up. Participants are in a circle. The first player turns to the one on his right and says, "Please." That person says, "No." He then turns to the person on his right and says, "Please." That one also responds with "No." The process continues around the circle with each person responding with "No" and asking the next person, "Please." After the warm-up, group members can share how they felt in each position. From their discussion and the emergent shared central issue, an enactment will arise. In the enactment the director can provide opportunities for group members to explore and experiment with new behaviors. He can also allow them to practice these behaviors until they become comfortable enough to use them outside the group setting.

Sociodrama offers many ways of learning new behaviors in a safe, nonjudgmental environment. Through the many warm-ups and enactments, clients have the opportunity to experience new ways of behaving in a variety of situations without fear of consequences.

SUMMARY

Sociodrama has many applications as adjunctive to psychotherapy. Because it focuses on the collective aspects of roles, it is a fine intervention to help even the most resistant clients gently slide into expressing their thoughts and emotions. Through the sharing of feelings, connections are made that link individuals together as part of a whole. In this way sociodrama reduces isolation among its members and assists in the enhancement of self-esteem. Further, sociodrama offers practice in developing and/or honing social skills, an area essential for better communication. Also, clients can practice new behaviors and try out new roles in a safe setting. The director can facilitate this process through the use of *therapeutic role assignment* in which the client is asked to play a role the therapist feels will be beneficial. Because the entire premise of sociodrama is based on spontaneity, clients participating in enactments often restore their own spontaneity without ever needing to focus on that as an issue.

16

PULLING IT ALL TOGETHER

HEARING WHAT EXPERIENCED LEADERS SAY

There are many practitioners of sociodrama, each with his or her own unique style and approach. Some sociodramatists work with troupes of trained enactors interacting with an audience, while others work, as the authors do, utilizing members of the group solely as enactors. There is enormous richness available in the field. Since inspiration comes from many quarters, the authors have asked some prominent sociodramatists to contribute their thoughts and experiences here. While this list of contributors represents only a small segment of those directing sociodrama, the reader will see a variety of exciting and inspiring uses of the modality. These sociodramatists come from the United States, Canada, England, and Australia.

Sociodrama in Australia and New Zealand
G. Max Clayton (Australia)

The purpose of sociodrama is to create in each individual an experiential knowledge of themselves in relationship to the essential nature of groups, whether these groups are families, subcultures, cultures, or the social structure of the entire world.

From 1971 until the present, I have been responsible for the introduction of the sociodramatic method in many of the major cities of Australia and New Zealand. I have utilized the sociodramatic method with a wide range of groups, including educational institutions at the secondary and tertiary levels, businesses, government departments, cultural organizations, church and spiritual groups, recreational groups, and family groups. I have also taught the sociodramatic method to a wide range of professional people, including educators, organizational consultants, staff trainers, business executives, counselors, psychotherapists, and clergy.

The learning is always very great because group members enter into the view of life and feelings of people who are quite different from themselves. This comes about through group members being warmed up to act the roles of others and to portray those roles with increasing accuracy and depth of warm-up. I place great emphasis on the interviewing for roles. In my interviewing, I bring out the basic map of the universe that is implicit in the role or set of roles being enacted.

In one sociodrama, a person was acting the role of a man who has been extremely significant in the creation of cultural norms in this part of the world. This influential man thought that the world operated best if males were removed from their sensitive, feeling levels. As soon as the group realized the approach to life was inherent in the "great man's" behavior, members probed the meaning of many aspects of their own functioning. As a result of their conscious thinking, they realized the importance of developing in themselves a much wider range of roles and integrating the masculine and feminine levels in themselves. Based on these convictions, they acted out a new commitment to expressing their sensitive, feeling levels.

Group members explore and experience cultures that are quite different from their own. On many occasions, group members have warmed up to and enacted the roles of early pioneers who migrated to Australia or New Zealand and established a new culture there. They have developed new perceptions of the vast differences between the forefathers and their children and grandchildren. In other cases, group members have played the roles of government ministers, heads of departments, chairmen of boards. This has resulted in a deepening of appreciation of the work that such people perform and a personal sense of our own contribution in the evolution of our culture.

There is no doubt that in many sociodrama groups there has been a broadening and deepening of experience, a greater flexibility in functioning, a greater appreciation of the values and attitudes of others, and an enlargement of one's role repertoire. There has been a greater understanding of the structure of groups and subcultures and a greater ability to plan and execute interventions to improve the everyday working of those groups.

Management styles have altered as a result of participation in sociodrama sessions, and this has led to higher productivity in businesses. Classroom management in schools and tertiary institutions has also changed, leading to increased learning and satisfaction in those settings.

There are a number of professional people in every region of Australia and New Zealand who have been training in the practice of sociodrama. Standards for such practice are laid down by the Board of Examiners of the Australian and New Zealand Psychodrama Association. Standards not only call for a high degree of expertise in dramatic production, social investigation, and in the bringing about of new perceptions and new solutions to old social problems, but also emphasize the development of sociometric awareness and the ability to make adequate assessments of social systems. There is little doubt that the sociodrama method will continue to gain in prestige and power in this part of the world.

The Human Drama of Sociodrama
Linda Gregoric Cook (United States)

For the past twenty years I, a traditionally trained theatre artist and educator, have been engaged in the sometimes pioneering, often unorthodox, and ever-evolving process of sociodrama. My first "stage" in the late 1960s was the maximum security prison libraries of Connecticut and Rhode Island where groups of fifty inmates would gather to express their feelings through original poetry, enact their sociodramas, and critique their roles on video. The enactments were improvised from the issues facing the inmates. The video camera functioned as both recorder and player. The challenge was to develop communication skills and trust while maintaining administrative support and cooperation. A process had been born.

For the prison years, video was essential. Giving definition and ventilation to faceless, despairing men, the sociodramatic process generated enactments so real and rich in implications that burned-out parole officers incorporated the content of the inmate videos into their own training tapes, also developed through sociodrama. The process again had provided an opportunity for ventilation, clarification, and enhanced communication between parolees and their counselor-cops.

From the sociodramas, original material emerged entitled *The Uncaged Mind*. The inmates dramatically presented this dialogue in a series of community tours. The result? Such interest was generated in the public that university students flocked to the prisons to learn. An MA program in sociodrama was established at the University of Connecticut at Storrs through the Department of Dramatic Arts to provide supervision, structure, and basic training in the field. Sociodrama, in practice, had by now evolved into an instrument of therapy, training, and education.

During the Title XX years (when block grants were given to states for social services) rehabilitation gave way to staff training, and the process found application in the training of such staff as Planned Parenthood, drug and alcohol abuse programs, Puerto Rican agencies, battered women's shelters, and children's and youth's services. In each instance, the formula remained essentially the same: identification of group problems, sociodrama and videotaping, structured role plays (solutions), and evaluations through instant replay. In each group it worked because individuals could stand at a distance and objectively watch roles in action, recognize the struggle, and, right or wrong, see choices being made. Through sociodramatic action they could better understand the players and the enactment.

Perhaps the most rewarding partnership was in a pioneering program at Connecticut Correctional Institution at Somers with clinical psychologist A. Nicholas Groth, an expert in the field of sexual assault. Over a period of two years, sociodrama was used to break down identified barriers in the treatment of sexual offenders. Through sociodrama, missing or damaged emotional links could be explored, repaired, and experienced. Traditional treatment could then resume.

Currently, my work takes me to more traditional settings—overpopulated public school classrooms, where at-risk children learn coping skills through the problem-solving situations and techniques of sociodrama; and at a psychiatric hospital, where adults seek identity and direction. The major change in this chameleon-like process is that for now, the camera, once central to the process, has been removed. The schools have no equipment, and the patients suffering from seriously low self-esteem are frightened by the video image. No matter; the process still works. The sociodrama is based in the ever-changing boundaries of the human condition and the drama in human life.

Private Truths in a Public Context
Ken Sprague and Marcia Karp (England)

Sociodrama shows the multifaceted nature of truth. When a group issue is examined in depth through dramatic action, people are able to look at a problem from several roles and thus are able to see the problem through the eyes of many. The process of the drama helps people experience and become aware of the whole system involved.

In the Holwell Centre training program for psychodrama and sociodrama (in Devon), storytelling in action is used extensively. Personal stories related to their social context have been particularly meaningful in recent years. The following examples are themes that have been used in sociodrama: the social dilemma of AIDS, the role of the psychotherapist in Britain's class-divided society, dealing with the pain and bewilderment of the war between Britain and Argentina, and in teaching young people with severe learning difficulties.

The Social Dilemma of AIDS

The first time we used sociodrama to explore AIDS, it arose spontaneously through fear and prejudice within a training group. A group member who had been caring for people dying with AIDS was suspected by others of being infected and therefore would infect them. It was the early days in the AIDS phenomenon and, as always, a little knowledge was dangerous. We brought the issue into the open in order to hear the individual fears and suspicions and to look at the subgrouping developing. We then separated fact and opinion. Through scenes of social experience, the group pooled its knowledge in action. We were able to see ourselves in the ostracized group member and in that way brought him back into the group. It made the issue a social concern of many, not just the experience of one. AIDS is a recurring theme in our training program.

The Role of the Psychotherapist in Britain's Class-Divided Society

Class position—working class, middle class, or upper class—is an integral part of British society and often comes between patient and therapist as well as therapist trainee and teacher. Role reversal is a crucial tool of insight. We have found that many therapists are ascribed a professional role that is perceived to be middle class. The individual behind the role may, in fact, be from working-class or other origins that are hidden or fail to connect with the patient or training colleague. Through sociodrama, we utilize the democratic ideals of Moreno that each person has a right to speak from his or her own perception.

Dealing with the Pain and Bewilderment of the War Between England and Argentina

Holwell is situated in an area that had one of the highest casualty rates during the war fought in the Falkland Islands in 1982. Our neighbors' sons were fighting while other neighbors disagreed with the war and had divided loyalties. Sociodrama was a perfect tool to look at the roles of parents, press/media presentation, the military, government officials, and peace activists from both Argentina and Britain. We ran these sessions in both countries as an attempt to bring to light mutual awarenesses. Visual materials such as photographs and newspaper headlines were used to express the multiplicity of opinion on the war. Enactment and role-reversal gave opportunities for people to ventilate their own ideas and become enlightened to others. Negotiated settlements were made between members, and a small move was made toward Dr. Moreno's aim of nothing less than world peace.

Teaching Young People with Severe Learning Difficulties

We use sociodrama at our local college to teach young people how to survive in a world basically unsympathetic to their condition. Action methods are used to help find more adequate solutions to a lack of self-confidence and self-worth. Presentation of self and other preparation for life skills are part of this project.

Sociodrama, then, is an action method useful across class and ethnic boundaries and in a variety of settings. It helps people to experience each other and gain new insight about the systems of which they are a part.

Sociodrama: *The Social Systems Approach to Institutional Change*
Dale Richard Buchanan (United States)

Most typically, sociodrama has been used within St. Elizabeth's Hospital and the Commission on Mental Health Services for the District of Columbia to moderate attitudes and behaviors characteristic of total institutions and to promote spontaneity and creativity on the part of all members of the system.

Using a social systems approach, the Commission realizes that institutions are typically resistant to change and even dedicated personnel can be impersonal in the delivery of services. Often communication, exchange of information, and consultation between members of the system become minimal for a variety of reasons, including lack of adequate funding, overcrowding, staff turnover, unreasonable and conflicting expectations on the part of the community at large, stress, and lack of appropriate discharge placements for patients. Rational, realistic therapeutic intervention based on an understanding of the individual and group becomes almost impossible.

The sociodrama groups are conducted with the entire population of the treatment unit, including patients, mental health professionals, and support personnel (e.g., dietary, housekeeping, secretarial staff). Session content varies. The central concern model is used, and all participants are encouraged to suggest topics for the sociodrama. Roles are played by all representatives of the system, with a tendency to cast persons in new roles (e.g., generally it is preferable to have staff play patients and patients play staff).

One place where sociodrama is used is on an acute admissions unit. Generally, pervasive themes on such units are denial, anger, and hostility concerning unwanted hospitalization and acting out or withdrawn behavior on the part of the patients. The staff are usually extremely busy and forced to deal with numerous crises daily. At times there are institutional pressures for staff to focus on documentation of treatment rather than provision of quality services that may result in their barricading themselves in the nursing station and writing copious medical records.

One particularly poignant sociodrama on an admissions unit dealt with the staff and patients' frustration at the nature of the revolving door of treatment. The sociodrama was precipitated by a patient returning on a suicide precaution less than twenty-four hours after discharge. The staff, who had had a difficult time placing the patient, were frustrated and angry that the patient acted out by using PCP and having to be rehospitalized. The other patients felt helpless, depressed, and angry that the patient had not been "cured." Rather than conducting a psychodrama dealing with this particular patient, a sociodrama was enacted concerning a "typical" patient who had to be readmitted to the hospital for an unwanted hospitalization. Staff and patients played a variety of roles in the sociodrama including mental health professionals, police officers, community members, family members, and a revolving-door patient. We also managed to get individuals to play the president of the United States and the mayor of the District of Columbia. The goal of that particular session was to break through the rigid role expectations and boundaries in which patients were viewed as "crazy" and helpless and staff were viewed as omnipotent.

Other recurrent topics of sociodramas center around the value/use of medication; asking for and finding help; the stigma of being institutionalized; various topical sociodramas triggered by current events or theatre/film. The current event- and drama-inspired sociodramas are often concerned with issues of racism, justice, compassion, ageism, and sexism.

After viewing and being moved by the film *Mississippi Burning*, one of the patients warmed up the rest of the group to the issue of racism as manifested by segregation and lynching. The sociodrama explored these issues and provided a deep emotional catharsis for the participants, many of whom had themselves been victimized by segregation. It was an equally powerful enactment for those group members too young to have experienced that form of racism in their own lives.

After the social system sociodramas, participants are generally more able to identify realistically their strengths and limitations. Expectations are more equally shared between staff and patients, and roles are examined, clarified, and redefined as are relationships, status, sanctions, and value systems in terms of social dynamics and treatment goals.

Sponte and Sociodrama
Madeleine Byrnes and Barry Stevens (Canada)

Sponte (pronounced SPON-tay) is a troupe of nine performers and psychotherapists who came together in 1980 to create healing theatre. What excited us was applying psychodramatic forms to theatrical performance. After a couple of years of experimenting, we came up with our highly participatory and improvisational theatre form.

We enter singing, usually a song about change. We warm up the audience by staging quick images of mini-experiences that they volunteer. Then we do our version of sociodrama. Finally, we create pieces of improvised theatre, each based on a personal story told by an audience member. (This form is based on "Playback Theatre," developed by Jonathan Fox and the Playback Company.) We incorporate doubling and soliloquy.

For us, sociodrama is key to our goals in Sponte. From the beginning, we wanted to make social and political issues immediate and personal. We wanted to empower our audiences and ourselves. We were all taken with role reversal and its power to overcome polarization. Our version of sociodrama enables audience members to express strongly their point of view and then encourages them to "walk in someone else's shoes."

Perhaps the best thing is to give an example from a recent show. The context was a weekend psychodrama conference. The closing session was a Sponte performance. At the beginning of the conference, we had asked for examples of groups polarized because of role differences (e.g., teachers versus students); identity differences (e.g., native American versus white); or ideological differences (e.g., prochoice versus prolife). The troupe identified the three examples most frequently chosen by the audience. We then planned the key elements of a scene for each.

In performance, a member of the troupe, the Conductor, asked the audience to vote for one of the three. The audience chose Alternative Expressions of Spirituality versus Traditional Forms. The scene we staged featured a couple's planning of their wedding over dinner. They had invited the woman's Catholic parents and the Unitarian minister that they had chosen to help them design their nontraditional service. The husband-to-be was a nonobserving Jew; the woman wanted to incorporate spiritual forms like crystals and meditation; and the mother was very traditional. When the inevitable conflict had reached a climax, the Conductor called "Freeze!" He then encouraged the audience members to get up and stand with the character with whom they most identified. About fifty joined in, speaking their piece to the other characters in the scene. Then, when all who wanted to had spoken, the Conductor invited the audience to stand with the character with whom they least identified and continue the dialogue from that experience.

The subsequent Playback stories mostly revolve on the themes of the sociodrama. In one story at the conference, a woman told her conservative Catholic mother that she planned to divorce. A fight ensued. Another story was about a Jewish woman's anger at her granddaughter for dating a Gentile. The theme of conflicting spirituality had emerged as a challenging issue during the conference. In choosing it, the audience found some group catharsis and closure for the conference.

Sponte has performed for feminist conferences, gifted schoolchildren, peace groups, health professionals, a brewery, as well as for the general public. (In public shows, the suggestions for polarized situations are made on the spot, and the actors develop the sociodrama scene cold.) Sociodrama issues have included disarmament, capital punishment, sexual monogamy, pornography, parenting, splits in the women's movement, and more. We have had as many as 200 people noisily joining in. Both the troupe and our audiences find sociodrama enormously exciting theatre.

Experiences in Sociodrama with Elementary School Children
David F. Swink (United States)

I was using sociodrama in a classroom of fifth graders in what we called a Social Living class, a concept created at Saint Elizabeths Hospital in Washington, D.C. Sociometries had been analyzed throughout the year, and it was clear that one little girl from a different part of the country was a rejection star on many criteria. No one seemed to want to play with her or talk to her, and kids often made fun of the different way that she dressed. The little girl had retreated into a protective shell, not choosing anyone else to do things with. A metaphorical sociodrama was created. I told them a story about a fishing village in Africa whose welfare depended on catching fish. Their whole culture revolved around making nets and going out each day to fish. A hunter from a different tribe moved to the fishing village but didn't know any of the village's customs and the village did not easily accept him.

I had the class act out the story. I assigned the role of the chief of the fishing village to the girl who had moved from the other city (the isolate) and I assigned the role of the hunter to a girl in the class who was a positive star. Upon acting the story out it was discovered by the children how lonely and rejected the hunter felt. All the children felt that the people in the fishing village should accept the hunter and teach him their ways. They enacted this and the hunter, in return, taught the fishing people how to hunt and play animal games.

The sharing phase went beyond the metaphor with the girl who had felt isolated explaining that she felt like the hunter sometimes. The class, with the knowledge they had taught themselves in the sociodrama, discussed how they should teach the new girl their games and learn more about where she came from. The girl's sociometric position as isolate changed tremendously over the rest of the school year. She was chosen on a number of criteria, and she appeared to be much happier.

In this case, sociodrama played a useful role in preventing isolation from causing potential psychological damage. If any preventive mental health paradigms are to work, they need to be implemented early, and the schools are the place to use them. The above story is more than just anecdotal. That class served as the experimental group in a study I conducted that showed that the class, as compared with a control class, significantly increased its internal locus of control over an eight-week treatment period. $F(1,48) = 11.46$, $p < .01$ (Swink and Buchanan). The control group showed no significant change. Internal locus of control is associated with the belief in one's ability to solve one's own problems and it is also associated with many other correlates of personal adjustment.

The Sociometry of Social Chaos
Ann E. Hale (United States)

I am mostly known as a sociometrist. Sometimes people new to the field get sociometry mixed up with the word sociodrama. What is really fascinating to me is that sociometry and sociodrama are so powerfully connected. The potential sociometry and sociodrama have to effect change in everyday lives, and eventually globally, is very serious indeed.

When a sociometrically trained person consults with a group she learns about which roles have high value and which are more peripheral. She helps a group investigate who has access to roles, and to what degree personal preference is being satisfied. She studies the feelings and motivations underlying choices for interactors—all kinds of interactors: whom to go to with a question, in whom to confide, whom to invite out. A sociometrist devises opportunities for group members to train their perception and to be conscious of the less-obvious criteria on which people are making choices. She teaches skills of encounter. It is not enough to know what needs fixing through investigations. When unresolved issues and projections surface, she must devote time and energy to helping participants learn to know others as they perceive themselves to be. She must also help the group to communicate authentically.

What I have learned as a sociometrist is that when a person does not have access to roles that he or she most values, and has neither the skills nor the connections to be chosen for them, a tremendous act hunger is present. There is a striving for a particular place in one's own world and when that place is denied, or deemed unobtainable, the energy that might have been released in role is contained. The tension that results can build up to explosive proportions, or seep away into apathy or depression. When this dynamic comes into focus collectively, a sociodramatist can become the healer for the individual, the group, and the society.

The sociodramatist provides dramatizations (structures) that maximize access to roles. When there is suddenly a place where there was none before, the act hunger explodes, and what is observed, rather fearfully by the novice, is a kind of chaos. The sociodramatist anticipates this phenomenon, works knowledgeably with it, and facilitates the return to safety and awareness of others. In the sociodrama the hero and the heroine are the group members who realize from the enactment that they have a strong desire to bring about change. Each person seeks support and accepts assistance from the people present. It may mean learning new skills; it may mean giving up blaming and resenting; it may mean confronting and taking risks. The hero and the heroine find their temporary solutions within the sociodrama and seek ways to implement that resolution in their day-to-day existence.

James Gleick, the author of *Chaos: Making a New Science* (27) wrote of Edward Lorenz, that "he saw a fine geometrical structure, order masquerading as randomness." And further (23):

In science as in life, it is well known that a chain of events can have a point of crisis that could magnify small changes. But chaos meant that such points were everywhere. They were pervasive. In systems like the weather, sensitive dependence on initial conditions was an inescapable consequence of the way small scales intertwined with large.

The sociodramatist addresses these "points of crisis" and is often the balancing point in the resulting chaos. Sociodrama directors are necessary and vital contributors to social healing when they bring forth the heros and heroines of the sociodramatic action, for it is here that "small scales are intertwined with large," that order is "masquerading as randomness," and that what we do has impact.

Where the Owl and the Pussy Cat Wanted to Go, but . . .
Warren Parry (Australia)

The owl in the tree looks down, "There is blood on the ground this morning; there was yelling and shouting in the night." The tree, waking up, feels the weight of the bodies lying among its old, entangled roots. "There was terrible fighting," the tree says. "Some of them wanted to kill her. My grandmother told me they used to burn witches in the old days."

The local farmer, looking over his shoulder at the forest, is filled with fear. "It's the quickest way to go through the forest," he said to the traveler. "But most people don't go that way anymore. You are a priest, are you? It's dangerous for fellers like you to be wandering around at these times."

The story continues, "Where are we?" You as the reader might also ask this: "the Russian plains? Vietnam? Southern Europe? Which age are we in? Is it now, back in time, the Middle Ages, perhaps?" The director continues talking to the group. He is asking questions, building on the answers, weaving them into the story, appointing people in the group to take up roles as the story unfolds.

The session takes place in a white room with red carpeting on the floor. A circle of chairs forms an enclosure for the action in the middle of the room. The group members go on setting up house, buying produce from each other, going about their daily business in this medieval village. There is a complete world contained in this room. You can go to any time or any place. It is real being there, at the same time you are yourself, here in this room. This is a sociodrama session.

Dr. Moreno clearly defined sociodrama as "a deep action method dealing with intergroup relations and collective ideologies" (*Psychodrama–First Volume*, 352). Sociodrama allows the unconscious layers of the group to become visible. Members spontaneously take roles. There is a permission to act out the "shadow sides" to discover the collective depth of feeling and role—the owl, the priest, and the farmer. There is a depth captured beyond stereotyped social roles.

The two forms of sociodrama have difference of focus. The protagonist in a group-centered sociodrama is "the group." In the sociodrama mentioned above, layer after layer of medieval life, the violence, the passion, and the power in the unconscious levels of the groups is expressed. In the roles, there is an individual experience and simultaneously experiential awareness of the "whole." There is a collusion among all in the cocreation of the murder that took place moments before in the enactment. This form of sociodrama brings out the multisided nature of truth.

In a protagonist-centered sociodrama, the reality of the world is explored via the life experience of one individual—for example, the world from the owl's point of view. What does he tell his wife, his friends at the owl club? What did mother owl say about the way the humans are? Who in the forest is the president right now, and what is his policy on human relations? What does owl think as he goes to sleep that night?

And the person playing the pussy cat? Having sat back and worked it all out using systems theory and role theory, she can't wait to get in on the action. The ending? You never would have believed it!

The Living Newspaper: One Expression of Sociodrama
Abel K. Fink (United States)

One excellent way to overcome the couch-potato syndrome—settling before the TV until one's joints ache and one is overwhelmed by the mayhem and nonsense—is to explore current events by becoming a part of them. Although much of my personal involvement with the living newspaper has taken place in my own college classes, I have shared such experiences with community and professional groups also, and these sessions have left lasting impressions. Having been part of the scene leaves powerful memory traces in all who participate because, psychologically, "I was there; I moved through it, felt it in my gut, and had to think on my feet to get through it."

—I well remember the night when our airline was highjacked and we had to confront the terrorist who was waving a pistol in our faces.

—And the day I lay dead in a field in Vietnam surrounded by family and friends, lying there but thinking out loud about how unbelievable it was to have our friends, the American soldiers, firing at us at point-blank range, feeling the bullets hit, and not understand why.

—And that early morning as a crew member of one of the first space flights, watching the earth recede in the distance and wondering if we'd ever return and be able to talk about our experience.

—And the night when my friends and I were interviewed on television and asked to describe how it felt to be arrested by the police as participants, even though we had come as observers to witness what was supposed to be a peaceful protest.

—And the sweet smell of the poisoned fumes on the gentle breeze that killed my entire family at Bhopal, India, while we slept in our small shack near the wall of the chemical factory. And how we felt as we lay there and listened as company and government officials came and protested that our deaths were not their fault.

—And the night when the pope visited our class and we had a chance to dialogue about why women can't become priests.

—And the night when Mahatma Gandhi sat with his feet crossed in the center of our circle and explained to us why means and ends are inseparable, particularly if you want to bring peace to the world.

—And the afternoon when we relived the struggle of a South African child caught between her parents' racism and her grandparents' humanity. All this strife, just because she wanted to have a black friend.

I remember the first time I heard about J. L. Moreno's early sessions in a New York City theatre using a group of actors to reenact newspaper headline stories and how intrigued I was with this idea. How gratifying it has been for me over the years to lead and participate in these sessions. Indeed, I can't think of a more interesting way to spend an evening with friends and colleagues.

Role Exploration and Cognitive Flexibility
Adam Blatner and Allee Blatner (United States)

We use the concept of "role" as the key to sociodrama. Every role has its own set of advantages, disadvantages, and typical events that lead to feeling happy, sad, angry, or frightened. The challenge is to discover "what is it like to be . . . ?" Our approach to sociodrama is to help participants explore the various emotional issues inherent in a given role.

We have developed a method we call "The Art of Play," in which basic role categories become stimuli for the enactment of imaginative characters (Blatner and Blatner). Our method is an integration of the make-believe play everyone first learned in childhood with the more mature skills of sociodrama. It may be used as a pleasurable art form and opportunity for recreation and social enjoyment, and it also has clinical applications. Learning to understand the deeper emotional dynamics of others requires a utilization of one's own imagination and feelings. The role-taking exercises in The Art of Play can facilitate learning basic empathic skills, and we therefore use it in the training of medical and mental health professionals. This educational process demands a degree of emotional involvement, and as a form of experiential learning entails some risk-taking. In the early phases, then, one of the core ideas in The Art of Play, that of working with imaginative characters, offers some psychological distance, while its intrinsic fun enhances the group's motivation for the task. At other times we use our approach to introduce students to psychodramatic methods and to develop their spontaneity and imagination.

Because our objective is to maximize spontaneity and create a "fail-safe" context in which risk-taking is supported, we use the following principles in our work: (1) enactments are done for the experience of discovering the dimensions inherent in the role, rather than performing for an audience; (2) competitiveness is discouraged; (3) we avoid psychologically "analyzing" the role explorations.

"Role distance" occurs when an actor is operating a meta-role level. The actor no longer identifies with the role being played, which fosters a capacity for greater creativity. The medium of drama encourages a shifting of perspective and includes not only the roles being played, but also the meta-roles of "director": thinking about other ways the situation could be played; "audience": sensing how the enactment is experienced by others; and "playwright": choosing which scenes and interactions are indicated at the time. By exercising these meta-roles, a more flexible and multileveled cognitive style can be developed.

An important aspect of the theory behind our work is the concept of "metacognition." We define this as an ability to reflect on and creatively work with various points of view. Engaging in sociodrama fosters habits of thinking in this metacognitive fashion, and this ability can help resolve conflicts more effectively and improve interpersonal and intergroup relationships. Finally, role flexibility fosters an increased capacity for celebrating the pleasure and vitality of life.

Sociodrama Comes Full Circle
Rosalie Minkin (United States)

Within the last decade, there has been a significant trend toward an age-segregated society in which residential, educational, and recreational patterns isolate the young from the old. Many children grow up with limited exposure to old people. They not only develop unhealthy myths and fears about the aged and the aging process, but they also find themselves unprepared for the adjustments they will have to make both to their own aging and to the aging of their parents. On the other hand, the elderly, when segregated from the mainstream of society, begin to question the meaning of their past experiences and feel they are denied a stake in the future. Isolation of one age group from others deprives all persons of perspective on their own lives and restricts them from the resources, skills, and experiences of those at other stages in the life cycle.

Since 1983 I have been working with an intergenerational sociodrama group, called The Full Circle. Intergenerational cooperation, bringing young and old together for their mutual benefit, has emerged as an effective way of maximizing resources and strengthening the collective community. The benefits accrue both to members of the troupe and to all those who view their work.

The sociodrama group has helped both age groups. Young people in the troupe (ages 13–21) have gained access to adult role models, obtained help with specific problems, developed a sense of responsibility, and attained a more holistic perspective on life. The seniors in the group (ages 65–80) have gained an increased sense of belonging, mental stimulation, an improved self-concept, and a sense of pride as they transmit their skills and experiences to a new generation. Through group interaction, role play, character development, and improvisational skills, age-related myths and stereotypes begin to disappear, and a sense of cooperation and interdependence emerges in the sociodrama community.

It is this needed concern to restore caring connections between the generations that has motivated me to continue working with The Full Circle Intergenerational Sociodrama Troupe in Philadelphia. The group performs improvised scenes to audiences in community centers, senior centers, religious institutions, and schools. The purpose of the performances is to confront, challenge, and educate the audience by increasing their awareness of age-related stereotypes and fostering their understanding of other people. Usually, there are mixed age groups in the audience.

The improvised scenes, developed out of the actor's experiences, are presented as conflict situations. The conflicts are viewed from several perspectives and reflect situations often faced by audience members. To add to the dynamic nature of the performances, the cast and director actively initiate a dialogue between the audience and the players. Audience members suggest alternatives and are encouraged to challenge or defend the actions of the characters. Sometimes a scene is replayed as an audience member searches for a satisfactory resolution to the scene. During performances, audience members may brainstorm, address, and confront such issues as respect, loneliness, loss, family relationships, sexuality, body image, and drug abuse.

As The Full Circle begins its sixth season, the group performs improvised scenes about socially relevant issues, concerns, and topics to audiences in order to challenge, confront, and educate in an environment of safety, creativity, and spontaneity. The sociodramas extend beyond The Full Circle to encompass the collective concerns of audience members themselves. Everyone truly is embraced into The Full Circle of life through sociodrama.

SUMMARY: DRAWING CONCLUSIONS, BEGINNING ANEW

Sociodrama has myriad applications as was seen through the ideas and experiences shared by sociodrama directors from around the world. It offers participants a renewal and affirmation of the life process itself. By returning to the natural state of spontaneity and by unlocking creativity, individuals gain new insight into themselves and others. Through enactment, group members put themselves in someone else's shoes and gain understanding and insight into what other people think and feel. They can expand who they are by trying on new behaviors and new roles.

If you are new to sociodrama, the authors urge you to get started. Learn to trust the process, and it will work for you. Learn to trust yourself and your own spontaneity. Through its many techniques, sociodrama illuminates the connectedness of all humanity. This modality can literally transform one's life by changing the way he looks at himself and others. Further, it can help a person realize and discover that alternative solutions are available for the problems that arise in life. Not only is the sociodrama experience beneficial for group members, participating in this process with groups is an exhilarating, energizing, and growth-producing experience for the director as well.

For those of you already working in the field, we have been delighted to share with you some of our experience, understanding, and love of sociodrama. May we all continue to work together to bring sociodrama to more areas of life and help others discover its unlimited power.

ACKNOWLEDGMENTS

The authors wish to thank all of the contributors to Chapter 16 for writing an essay to reflect their experiences as practitioners or teachers of sociodrama.

APPENDIX

A number of warm-ups are listed below. Some we have developed ourselves; others are warm-ups we have seen other directors lead; still others are warm-ups our students devised and shared in classes over the years. Aside from the warm-ups for new groups, which have their own section, the others are grouped together. At the end of each warm-up in the second section, the reader will find L, M, and/or H, to indicate whether they are appropriate for low, medium, and/or high functioning groups. For still more warm-ups, the reader can look at Hollander and Hollander's Warm-Up Box *and Viola Spolin's* Improvisation for the Theatre.

WARM-UPS FOR NEW GROUPS

Name Game

The first person is to say her own name. The second person is to say the first person's name and then his own. The third person is to say the first person's name, the second person's name, and then her own. The fourth person is to say the first person's name, the second person's name, the third person's name, and then his own. And so on. It is important when doing this exercise to follow the order. Otherwise, the folks with the most names to remember become hopelessly confused. After you have gone around the whole group, you might want to ask if anyone can go around backwards, saying all the names. Or ask people to change seats and ask for volunteers to say all the names. A variation of this exercise is to ask people to tune in to what color they feel most like today. When they say their name, they also say what color they feel like; I'm Sarah, and I feel mint green.

The Talk Show

Divide the group into dyads. Give people five to ten minutes to get acquainted. Instruct them to find out at least three interesting and/or unusual things about their partner. When time is up, bring everyone back to the circle. Ask each person to imagine that he is a talk show host and is introducing his partner to the public. A variation of this is to introduce the partner as if he were running for the office of president of the country or the town mayor.

The Line-Up

Ask members to line up alphabetically, then by height, then by house number, then by birth date (month and day), or size of hand or foot, or by length of time living in the area, or whatever else you can think of to ask them.

Tape Territory

Have masking tape available. Ask people to stake out territory in the room, defining their own space with masking tape and the furniture in the room. They may adorn the space with masking tape however they wish. Discuss.

Pass the Prop

Seat the group in a circle. Pass around a simple object such as a block, a blackboard eraser, or a scarf. Ask members to say what else the object could be, something that is the same general size and shape. For instance, the block or eraser could be a candy bar, a calculator, a bar of soap. With the scarf, the players may change its shape and see how many different things it could be used for: a flag, a sling, an apron.

Unusual Objects

Pass around strange and unusual objects that are relatively unrecognizable as they are (these may be unidentifiable pieces of larger objects). Ask each person to choose one, make up a story of what the object is for, and try to sell it to the group. Encourage them to come up with the most outlandish ideas they can. Obviously, there is no right or wrong with this warm-up; thus there is a built-in success factor. After everyone has had a turn, discuss.

Shake and Freeze

This is a variation on the childhood game of statues. However, here the leader calls out, "Shake—shake—shake—and freeze into . . . the funniest position you can think of." Or "the scariest position," or "the most complicated position." Then move into emotional words like, "angriest," "saddest," "happiest," and so on. This exercise is especially useful for children, although it need not be limited to them.

In or Out Continuum

Draw an imaginary line on the floor. One end stands for "in the group." The other stands for "out of the group," with the space in between representing degrees of feeling in or out of the group. Starting with all members standing at the "out" end, ask them what makes them feel ready to enter a group and what helps them to move from "out" to "halfway in," to "all the way in" the group. Ask them to move along the continuum as they tell the others how they tend to enter a group. After all members have done this, ask them to place themselves along the continuum in relation to where they feel they are at the moment. Discuss.

Hopes, Fears, and Expectations

Have slips of paper on hand. Pass them out to participants. Ask people to reflect on their hopes, fears, and expectations as a member of this group and to list these in order on the piece of paper they have been given. Ask them to write legibly. You may need to differentiate between a hope and an expectation. Sometimes people get wishes and "shoulds" confused with each other. After they have written their hopes, fears, and expectations, ask them to fold up the paper and give it to you. Once you have collected all of them, allow each person to choose one, putting it back if it was his own. Then instruct members to imagine that they are the person who has written what they see before them on the paper. One at a time, they are to take the role of the other person and in their own words discuss what is on the paper. After the process is complete, ask people how it felt to take someone else's role. Also ask whether they could figure out who had represented what they had written. Ask how it felt to have someone else represent what they wrote. Ask if they were surprised to discover how many people had similar fears. If several listed as a fear, "making a fool of myself," point out that everyone just experienced taking a role, and no one was "foolish."

WARM-UPS FOR ALL GROUPS

Changing Places

Participants are seated on chairs in a circle or stand shoulder to shoulder in a circle. Ask for a volunteer to be "It." The person who is It stands in the center. He will call for people to change places by saying something like, "Everyone wearing blue, change places." The person who is It must himself have on whatever he calls out. If he said, "Everyone wearing glasses, change places," he would also have to be wearing glasses. Every player who has on what was called out must change his place in the circle. The object of the game is for It to take one of the other player's places when he calls out, "Change places."

After several rounds of this game, of course, players catch on to things that everybody—or at least most people have on—for example, "Everyone wearing underwear, change places," or "Everyone wearing shoes, change places." This is a simple game that gets everyone moving and promotes spontaneity among all players, whatever the age. (L, M, H)

Trash Sculpture

Divide the groups into teams of four or five people. They will have five to ten minutes to collect throw-away objects. Make sure you underscore that they may not include anything that can still be used. When they return with these objects, they will create a trash sculpture with them. When each team agrees that the sculpture is completed, they agree on a title for it. After this process is completed, each team shows the others its sculpture and tells its title. (L, M, H)

Follow the Leader

This is a simple adaptation of well-known childhood game. However, here each player places his right hand on the shoulder of the person in front of him. The leader begins to move, with all players connected in this manner. Each player who wishes to, takes his turn at being the leader and creates a sound and a movement for the other players to follow. This exercise is a playful activity that promotes spontaneity within the context of a physical connection. (M, H)

Dreams and Gradiose Schemes Bag

Have a brown bag available. Ask members to jot down on pieces of paper their fantasies and/or grandiose schemes. They fold the pieces of paper and put them in the bag. Each picks one and acts as if she has achieved the dream or scheme written on the paper and tells the group how it feels to have achieved it. After the process is complete, you may want to ask some questions, such as, "How did it feel to hear about your dream?" "How did it feel portraying someone else's dream?" "Who got warmed up to someone else's dream or scheme after you heard it portrayed?" (M, H)

Objects

Pick an inanimate object. Introduce yourself to the group as if you were the object. (L, M, H)

Hero/Villain

Think of your favorite superhero or -heroine. Step into his or her role. Imagine that you are at a convention of superheroes. Interact with someone. After a few minutes, call, "Freeze." Ask people to say the last thing they want to say to their partner and move around silently. Once everyone is moving silently, ask them to keep moving and think of their favorite villain and to take the villain's role. They are now at a villain's convention and are to interact. After a few minutes, end the exercise. Discuss. (L, M, H)

Fortune Teller

Tell the group that in a minute they are going to have the chance to take on the role of a great fortune teller. They will also have the opportunity to have someone tell them about their future. Encourage them to have fun with it and trust their spontaneity. Instruct them to choose a partner and decide who will be the fortune teller first. Person A spends five minutes telling Person B her fortune. Encourage them to be fanciful and playful with the exercise and to allow any offbeat or silly ideas they have to emerge. After the five minutes are up, Person B tells A's fortune for five minutes. After the whole process is complete, you may want to prompt discussion with such questions as, "How did it feel to be the fortune teller?" or "How did it feel to have your fortune told?" "Did anyone feel like something accurate was said?" (M, H)

Visitors from Outer Space

Ask people to choose partners. Instruct the pairs to select a planet in the universe that they come from. Then give the following directions: One of you will be the ideal specimen from that planet, and the other will be the one who brings her to Earth and introduces her to the officer in charge at the entrance point. Each pair approaches the officer one at a time. The person who is introducing must convince the officer and the rest of the group that his partner is a worthwhile citizen and should be allowed to join Earth's society. He will explain what his partner can do. The "ideal specimen" demonstrates her abilities and tells how she will contribute to the Earth's civilization. The officer in charge asks the audience members how they vote—"Yes" or "No." The members of the audience are instructed to register their vote with thumbs up for "Yes" and thumbs down for "No." The officer then admits the visitors or sends them back to their home planet. (M, H)

The Big Whopper Exercise

Instruct members to encounter each other and speak only lies. Encourage them to make up an outlandish story about themselves, from name to occupation to life-style to hobbies. Discuss. (L, M, H)

Seasons Warm-Up

Depending on what season you're in, ask participants to tune in to the type of weather they hate most in that season. Instruct them to imagine they can see that weather in front of them. Ask them to walk into the weather and become it. Then they are to interact with others as the weather. They may use sounds or words as well as movement. (L, M, H)

Body Parts

Tell participants to take the role of the body part they feel most like today—for example, an aching back, clumsy feet. Tell them to walk around the room, accentuating that body part as they move; encounter someone else and speak to them as if they were that body part. This is a very silly exercise, so encourage people to be playful with it. (L, M, H)

Nasty/Nice

Instruct participants to take the role of the most obnoxious person they know and interact with the others in the group. After a while, ask them to think of the nicest person they know, take that role, and interact with the others. Discuss. (L, M, H)

Famous Person Empty Chair

Instruct participants to think of a prominent person whom they admire, past or present. Ask each person to put an empty chair in front of him. Ask him to imagine that the admired person is in the chair and to carry on a conversation with him or her, reversing roles back and forth. Discuss. (L, M, H)

Human Knot or Pretzel

One person goes out of the room. He will be the unwinder. The other people are in a line holding hands. The leader moves the group around in a series of twists and turns and winds them into a knot. The unwinder comes in and tries to unwind the knot without disconnecting anyone. (M, H).

Group Sculpture

Divide the group into two teams. One person from each group acts as sculptor/ observer. The Team One sculptor arranges the members in various positions to create some kind of interesting human sculpture. When the sculpture is complete, they freeze in their positions. The other team tries to create an exact replica of what they see. They mirror the positions of the frozen sculpture group. Their sculptor/observer helps them to correct their positions if necessary. After the process is complete, the second team creates its sculpture and is mirrored by the first team. (M, H)

Labels

The leader takes self-stick labels and writes a command on each label. Each one reads something different, such as the following:

Doubt me	Ridicule me
Agree with me	Adore me
Ignore me	Pamper me
Respect me	Listen carefully to me

The leader places the labels on participants' foreheads. They are not aware of what their label says. However, all participants can clearly read the labels of others. The director chooses a topic for discussion. All participants must react to a person according to what the label on the speaker's forehead reads. After the discussion, the director asks participants what they think their labels read. The people then discuss how they felt and what they learned about themselves through interaction based on labels. (M, H)

Back Talk

Divide the group into dyads with people of similar heights. Instruct them to have a conversation with their backs only, physically moving their back to communicate what they want to say. Discuss. (H)

Animals

Ask the group to brainstorm different kinds of animals. Then ask them to tune in to the animal that they feel most like right now. Ask them to see that animal standing in front of them, to walk into that animal and try it on, become that animal. Ask them to move around as the animal, interacting with others as they wish. After a few minutes, instruct them to shake the animal off and to tune in to an animal they would like to be more like and take that role. If both animals are the same, that is O.K. Discuss. (L, M, H)

Behind Your Back

Ask for a volunteer to stand with his back to the rest of the group. Ask the person and the group what this role relationship feels like and of what situations it reminds them. (H)

Some Dialogues to Use as Warm-ups

These warm-ups are suitable for all functioning levels. Divide the group into dyads. Each dyad says the lines as written as far as they go. Then they improvise what they feel comes next.

DIALOGUE #1

ONE: I'm not happy with the way things are.

TWO: What do you mean?

ONE: I feel hemmed in . . . confined.

TWO: What's confining you?

ONE: You are!

TWO: Me? How can you say that?

ONE: You don't give me any space.

TWO: Space? What kind of space?

DIALOGUE #2

ONE: Want to go out?

TWO: Yeah, that's a good idea.

ONE: We'll go down to Dinty's.

TWO: I don't like Dinty's.

ONE: I thought you wanted to go out.

TWO: I do, but not to that place.

ONE: Okay, forget it.

TWO: Why do you always do this to me?

DIALOGUE #3

ONE: I need help.

TWO: You're telling me.

ONE: I need your help.

TWO: I've given you all I can.

ONE: You can't leave me like this when I need you.

TWO: Oh, no? Watch me.

ONE: You can't do this.

TWO: I can't help you anymore. You'll have to find another way.

ONE: How?

DIALOGUE #4

ONE: You never listen to me.

TWO: You never say anything worth listening to.

ONE: That's some attitude.

TWO: I don't have an attitude. You do.

ONE: Me?

TWO: Yes, you. You always try to start an argument.

ONE: You're the one who's starting it.

TWO: Just shut up, will you?

DIALOGUE #5

ONE: It's your fault.

TWO: No, it isn't!

ONE: Then, who's fault is it?

TWO: I don't know.

ONE: You're lying.

TWO: No, I swear.

ONE: Tell the truth.

BIBLIOGRAPHY

Allen, John. *Drama in Schools: Its Theory and Practice.* London: Heinemann Educational Books, 1979.

Altschuler, C., and W. Picon. "The Social Living Class: A Model for the Use of Sociodrama in the School Classroom." *Group Psychotherapy* 33 (1980): 162–169.

Balinsky, B., and A. Dispenzieri. "An Evaluation of the Lecture and Role Playing Methods in the Development of Interviewing Skills." *Personnel and Guidance Journal,* March 1961: 583–585.

Balsham, J. "Humanistic Education and Sociodrama in the Context of a Social Living Class." Unpublished manuscript, 1974.

Barrett, M. Elizabeth. "Self-Image and Social Adjustment Change in Deaf Adolescents Participating in a Social Living Class." *Group Psychotherapy, Psychodrama and Sociometry* 39 (1986): 3–11.

Bartlett, John. *Familiar Quotations.* Boston: Little, Brown, 1939.

Baumgartner, Dena. "Sociodrama and the Vietnam Combat Veteran: A Therapeutic Release for a Wartime Experience." *Group Psychotherapy, Psychodrama and Sociometry* 39 (1986): 31–39.

Bell, S., and T. Ledford. "The Effects of Sociodrama on the Behavior and Attitudes of Elementary School Boys." *Group Psychotherapy, Psychodrama and Sociometry* 31 (1978): 117–135.

Bell, Steven. "Sociodrama as an Instructional Approach for Teaching about Exceptional Children and Youth." *Journal for Special Educators* 17, no. 4 (Summer 1981): 371–375.

Benson, C. S., and J. M. Gottman. "Children's Popularity and Peer Social Interaction." Unpublished manuscript, Indiana University, 1975.

Bion, W. R. *Experiences in Groups.* London: Tavistock, 1961.

Bischoff, Ledford J. *Interpreting Personality Theories.* New York: Harper & Row, 1964.

Bjerstedt, Ake. *Definitions of Sociometry: An Expert Vote.* New York: Beacon House, 1958.

Blatner, H. A. *Acting-In: Practical Application of Psychodramatic Methods.* New York: Springer, 1973.

Blatner, Adam, and Allee Blatner. *The Art of Play: An Adult's Guide to Reclaiming Imagination and Spontaneity.* New York: Human Sciences Press, 1988.

Bohart, A. "Role Playing and Interpersonal Conflict Reduction." *Journal of Counseling Psychology* 24, no. 1 (1977): 15–24.

Boltin, Gavin. *Towards a Theory of Drama in Education.* London: Longman, 1979.

———. *Drama in Education.* London: Langman, 1984.

———. "Some Issues Involved in the Use of Role-Play with Psychiatric Patients." *Dramatherapy* 2, no. 4 (Summer 1979): 11–13.

Braaten, L. J. "Developmental Phases of Encounter Groups and Related Intensive Groups." *Interpersonal Development* 5 (1974): 112–129.

Brown, P. "Legacies of a War: Treatment Considerations with Vietnam Veterans and Their Families." *Journal of Social Work* 29, no. 4 (1984): 372–379.

Buchanan, Dale Richard. "The Central Concern Model, A Framework for Structuring Psychodramatic Production." *Group Psychotherapy* 33 (1980): 47–62.

Burger, Isabel B. *Creative Drama in Religious Education.* Wilton, Conn.: Morehouse-Barlow, 1977.

Burnell, P. "Exploring Skills of Family Life at School." *Group Psychotherapy* 6, 304 (1954): 227–255.

Corsini, R. J., M. E. Shaw, and R. R. Blake. *Role Playing in Business and Industry.* New York: Free Press, 1961.

Cornyetz, P. "The Warming Up Process of an Audience." *Sociometry* 8, nos. 3–4 (1945): 218–225.

Courtney, Richard. *Play, Drama and Thought.* (3rd rev. ed.). New York: Drama Book Specialists, 1974.

Dyer, William G. *Team Building: Issues and Answers.* Reading, Mass.: Addison Wesley, 1977.

Fantel, E. "The Civilian and Army Social Atom Before and After." *Group Psychotherapy* 4, no. 2 (1951): 66–69.

Fink, Albert H., and Keith Brownsmith. "Training Teachers in Behavior Management through Simulations & Role-Playing." *Improving Human Performance Quarterly* 4 (April 1975): 157–164.

Foster, S. E. "The Possible Use of Sociodrama as a Training Technique for the Moderately Mentally Handicapped in School, Half-Way Training Centre, and Sheltered Workshop." *Slow Learning Child* 22 (1975): 38–44.

Fox, J., ed. *The Essential Moreno.* New York: Springer, 1987.

Furness, P. *Role-playing in the Elementary School.* New York: Hart, 1976.

Garcia, A. *Using Sociodrama for Training Actors in Audition and Interview Techniques.* Ann Arbor, Mich.: University Microfilms International, 1981.

Gendron, J. M. *Moreno: The Roots and Branches and Bibliography of Psychodrama, 1972–1980; and Sociometry, 1970–1980.* Beacon, N.Y.: Beacon House, 1980.

Gleick, James. *Chaos: Making a New Science.* New York: Viking Press, 1987.

Greenberg, I. A. *Psychodrama Theory and Practice.* New York: Behavioral Publications, 1974.

Haas, R. B., ed. *Psychodrama and Sociodrama in American Education.* Beacon, N.Y.: Beacon House, 1949.

Hagan, M., and M. Kentworthy. "The Use of Psychodrama as a Training Device for Professional Groups Working in the Field of Human Relations." *Group Psychotherapy* 4 (April–August 1951): 23–37.

Hale, A. *Conducting Clinical Sociometric Explorations* (rev. ed.). Roanoke, Va: Royal Publishing, 1986.

Hare, A. P. *Social Interaction as Drama.* Beverly Hills, Calif.: Sage, 1985.

Hart, J. W., and R. Nath. "Sociometry in Business and Industry: New Developments in Historical Perspective." *Journal of Group Psychotherapy, Psychodrama and Sociometry* 32 (1979): 128–149.

Hawley, Robert C. *Value Exploration through Role-Playing.* New York: Hart, 1975.

Heimbach, S. "Role-Playing as an Aid in Improving Reading Ability and Empathy." *Group Psychotherapy* 12, no. 1 (March 1959): 42–51.

Hollander, C., and S. Hollander. *The Warm-Up Box.* Denver: Snow Lion Press, 1978.

Jackson, Tony, ed. *Learning Through Theatre: Essays & Casebook on Theatre in Education.* Manchester, England: Manchester University Press, 1980.

Jennings, Sue, *Remedial Drama.* New York: Theatre Arts, 1974.

———. *Creative Drama in Groupwork.* London: Winslow Press, 1986.

———. *Drama Therapy, Theory and Practice for Teachers and Clinicians.* Cambridge, Mass.: Brookline Books, 1987.

Klepac, R. L. "Through the Looking Glass: Socio-Drama and Mentally Retarded Individuals." *Mental Retardation* 16 (1978): 343–345.

Kneist, C. R. "Increasing Interpersonal Understanding through Sociodrama." *Perspectives in Psychiatric Care* 6 (1968): 104–109.

Knepler, A. "Role Playing in Education: Some Problems in its Use." *Group Psychotherapy,* 12, no. 1 (March 1959): 32–41.

Ladd, G. W. "Social Networks of Popular, Average, and Rejected Children in School Settings." *Merrill Palmer Quarterly* 29 (1983): 283–307.

Landy, Robert J. *Handbook of Educational Drama and Theatre.* Westport, Conn.: Greenwood Press, 1982.

———. *Drama Therapy.* Springfield, Ill.: Chas. C. Thomas, 1986.

Leveton, E. *Psychodrama for the Timid Clinician.* New York: Springer, 1977.

Mc Caslin, Nellie. *Creative Drama in the Classroom.* New York: Longman, 1968.

Mendelson, P. D. "Sociometry as a Life Philosophy." *Group Psychotherapy* 30 (1977): 70–85.

Moore, Sonia. *The Stanislavski System.* New York: Viking Press, 1965.

Moreno, F. "The Learning Process in Nurses Training." In R. B. Haas, ed., *Psychodrama and Sociodrama in American Education.* Beacon, N.Y.: Beacon House, 1949.

Moreno, J. L. *The Words of the Father.* Beacon, N.Y.: Beacon House, 1941.

———. "Sociometry in Action." *Sociometry* 5 (August 1942): 298–315.

———. "The Concept of Sociodrama." *Sociometry* 6 (1943a): 434–449.

———. "Sociometry and the Cultural Order." *Sociometry Monograph* 2 (1943b).

———. "Organization of the Social Atom." *Sociometry* 10 no. 3 (1947): 287–293.

———. with Zerka T. Moreno. *Psychodrama–Second Volume.* Beacon, N.Y.: Beacon House, 1959.

———. with Zerka T. Moreno. *Psychodrama–Third Volume.* Beacon, N.Y.: Beacon House, 1969.

———. *The Theatre of Spontaneity* (2nd ed.). Beacon, N.Y.: Beacon House, 1973.

———. *Psychodrama–First Volume* (4th ed.). Beacon, N.Y.: Beacon House, 1977.

———. *Who Shall Survive?* (3rd ed.). Beacon, N.Y.: Beacon House, 1978.

Mouton, J. S., R. L. Bell, and R. P. Glake. "Role Playing Skill and Sociometric Peer Status." *Group Psychotherapy* 9, no. 1 (1956): 7–17.

Murray, E. "Sociodrama and Psychodrama in the College Basic Communication Class." In R. B. Haas, ed. *Psychodrama and Sociodrama in American Education.* Beacon, N.Y.: Beacon House, 1949.

Northway, M. S. *A Primer of Sociometry* (2nd ed.). Toronto: University of Toronto Press, 1967.

Otto, H. A. "Spontaneity Training with Teachers." In I. A. Greenberg, ed. *Psychodrama Theory and Practice.* New York: Behavioral Publications, 1974.

Peery, J. C. "Popular, Amiable, Isolated, Rejected: A Reconceptualization of Sociometric Status in Preschool Children." *Child Development* 50 (1979): 1231–1234.

Picon, W. J. "Self-Concept Change in Children Participating in a Social Living Sociodrama Class at Elementary School." Unpublished manuscript, Saint Elizabeths Hospital, Washington, D.C., 1975.

Putallaz, M. "Predicting Children's Sociometric Status from their Behavior." *Child Development* 54 (1983): 1417–1426.

Renshaw, P. D., and S. R. Asher. "Children's Goals and Strategies for Social Interaction." *Merrill Palmer Quarterly* 29 (1983): 353–374.

Rosen, C. E. "The Effects of Sociodramatic Play on Problem Solving Behavior Among Culturally Disadvantaged Preschool Children." *Child Development* 45 (1974): 920–927.

Rosenfeld, R., and S. Peltz. "Crisis Awareness Training for Helping Professionals: An Application Model." *Group Psychotherapy, Psychodrama and Sociometry* 31 (1978): 144–153.

Sarlin, M. D., and K. Z. Altschuler. "Group Psychotherapy with Deaf Adolescents in a Group Setting." *International Journal of Group Psychotherapy* 18 (1968): 337–344.

Seabourne, B. "An Action Sociogram." *Group Psychotherapy* 16, no. 3 (1963): 145–155.

Shattner, Gertrude, and Richard Courtney. *Drama in Therapy* (2 vols.). New York: Drama Book Specialists, 1979.

Shaw, Ann M., and C. J. Stevens. *Drama, Theatre and the Handicapped.* Washington, D.C.: American Theatre Association, 1981.

Simmons, Ronald Wynn. *Sociodrama in Education.* Ann Arbor, Mich.: University Microfilms International, 1972.

Siroka, R., E. Siroka, and G. Schloss. *Sensitivity Training and Group Encounter.* New York: Grosset & Dunlap, 1971.

Smilansky, S. *The Effects of Sociodramatic Play on Disadvantaged Schoolchildren.* New York: Wiley, 1968.

Spolin, Viola. *Improvisation for the Theatre.* Chicago: Northwestern University Press, 1963.

Stanford, G., and A. E. Roark. "Role Playing and Action Methods in the Classroo Group Psychotherapy and Psychodrama 28 (1975): 33–49.

Stanislavski, Konstantin. Creating a Role. New York: Theatre Arts Books, 1961.

———. An Actor's Handbook. New York: Theatre Arts Books, 1970.

Starr, A. Psychodrama: Rehearsal for Living. Chicago: Nelson-Hall, 1977.

Sternberg, Patricia. On Stage: How to Put on a Play. New York: Messner, 1982.

———. Be My Friend: The Art of Good Relationships. Philadelphia: Bridge Books, 19

Strain, P. "Increasing Social Play of Severely Retarded Preschoolers with Socio-D matic Activities." Mental Retardation 13 (1975): 7–9.

———, and R. Wiegerink. "The Effects of Sociodramatic Activities on Social In action among Behaviorally Disordered Preschool Children." Journal of Spe Education 10 (1976): 71–75.

Swink, D. F., and D. R. Buchanan. "The Effects of Sociodramatic Goal-Oriented R Play and Non-Goal-Oriented Role Play on Locus of Control." Journal of Clin Psychology 40, no. 5 (1984): 1178–1183.

Torrance, E. Paul, Encouraging Creativity in the Classroom. Dubuque, Ia.: Wm. C. Brow 1970.

———, and R. Myers. Creative Learning and Teaching. New York: Dodd, Mead, 197

———. "Sociodrama as a Creative Problem-Solving Approach to Studying the F ture." Journal of Creative Behavior, 3rd Quarter (1975): 182–195.

———. "Sociodrama in Career Education." Pre-Service Teacher Training in Career E ucation Project. Athens: University of Georgia, 1976.

Tschirgi, H., and J. Stinson. "Sociodrama—A Learning Experience." Improving Colle and University Teaching 25, no. 1 (Winter 1977): 27–28, 30.

Ward, Winifred. Playmaking with Children. New York: Appleton-Century-Crofts, 195

Warner, G. D. "Psychodrama Training Tips." Unpublished. Copies are available fro author, Maryland Psychodrama Institute, P.O. Box 1945, Hagerstown, MD 2174

Warren, Bernard. Creative Arts in Therapy. Cambridge, Mass.: Brookline Books, 1984

Way, Brian. Development Through Drama. New York: Humanities Press, 1972.

Weiner, H. "Psychodrama in Law Enforcement and Community Relations." In I. A Greenberg, ed. Psychodrama, Theory and Therapy. New York: Behavioral Publi cations, 1974.

Weiner, R. "Applying Crisis Theory and Sociodrama in Criminal Justice Education. Group Psychotherapy, Psychodrama, and Sociometry 26, nos. 1–2 (1973): 120 129.

Weisberg, Naida, and Rosilyn Wilder. Creative Arts with Older Adults. New York: Hu man Sciences Press, 1985.

Yalom, I. The Theory and Practice of Group Psychotherapy. New York: Basic Books, 1975.

Zeleny, L. "What is Sociodrama?" How to Do It Series No. 20 Washington, D.C.: National Council for Social Studies 1964.

INDEX

Act hungers, 5, 37, 39, 41, 42, 45, 52, 71
Action frame, 42
Action insight, 73
Action spectrogram, 115-16
Advice giving, 83
Aeschylus: *Oresteia*, 120
Alternatives, 85-86
Anger, 162
Aristotle: *Poetics*, 21
Aside, 8, 63, 69
Assertiveness, 134
Auxiliaries, 10

Balance, finding, 77
Behavior, new, 86, 161
Blatner, Adam, 23, 76
Buchanan, Dale Richard, 39
Business: sociodrama in, 137; administrators, 139; executives, 139; staff, 140

Canon of Creativity, 109-10
CAT (Creative Arts Team), 120, 126
Catharsis, 5, 21, 24, 40; facilitating, 57, 71, 141
Chekhov, Anton, 11

Children's Theatre Association of America, 7
Closing the action, 78
Closure, 20, 84
Cognitive frame, 85
Cohesion, 98
Coleridge, Samuel T., 45
Common denominators, 25
Community problems, 148
"Concept of Sociodrama," 147-48
Concretization, 66, 69, 76
Confidentiality, 26, 77, 138
Conflict resolution, 143
Conserve: cultural, 109; social, 109; technological, 109
Creative drama, 7-8, 120, 127
Creativity, 108-10, 144
Criticism, 96

De-role(ing), 84, 86
Directing, 89
Directorial contract, 96
Directorial function, 91
Directorial guiding, 95
Double (the), 59, 68; multiple, 60-61

Doubling, 8, 97
Dyer, William G., 142

Education: adult, 134; sociodrama in, 127; cultural issues, 129; foreign languages, 130; health and life skills, 131; history and social studies, 128; literature, 132; psychology and nursing skills, 133; religious, 135
Empty chair, 8, 61, 68
Enactment, 4, 18; periphery/center/periphery, 20
Enactors, 4, 43-45; enlisting, 43; interviewing, 44
Enneis, James, 41
Environment, 93, 100

Fantasy, 51, 104-05; exercise, 159
Freeze frame, 8, 65, 69
Freud, Sigmund, 50
Future projection, 8, 68, 69, 145

Givnish, Meg, 72
Goals. See Catharsis, Insight, Role training
Group action, 37
Group-centered sociodrama, 44-45

Haas, Robert Bartlett, 127
Hansen, Bert, 148
"Here and now," 15
Holistic benefits, 24

Ibsen, Henrik, 11
Ice breakers, 28; common denominator game, 30; getting to know you circle, 29-30; headline game, 30-31. See also Warm-ups
Impromptu Group Theatre, 10
Individual differences, 52, 54
Insight, 5, 22, 24, 40, 125, 129; facilitating, 59, 73, 86
Isolation, 157

Jackson, Tony, 120
Jennings, Helen Hall, 113

Letting go, 77, 80
Living Newspaper, 10, 29-31

"Magic If," 11-12
Magic screen, 72
Mendelssohn, Felix: A Midsummer Night's Dream, 109
Method, The, 11-12
Mirrione, James: Tower of Babble, 126
Mirror (mirroring), 8, 67, 69
Modeling, 94, 99
Moreno, Jacob L.: co-conscious and co-unconscious, 90; folklore, 159; foundations and origins, 8; Freud (with), 50; God, 55-56; historical background, 8; Living Newspaper, 10, 29-31; "Man is a role player," 47; Moreno, The Essential, 101-02; originator of sociodrama, 5; psychodrama, 5; role theory, 101; social activism, 147; sociodrama, 52; sociometry, theory of, 112; spontaneity theory, 107; surplus reality, 55; Theatre of Spontaneity, 161

Name games, 28
Networking, 142
Nonpersonal experience, 17

Open tension systems, 5, 38, 46

P.A.C.T. (Performing Arts for Crisis Training), 75
Periphery/center/periphery, 20
Personnel training, 138
Poe, Edgar Allan: "Annabel Lee," 133
Prejudice, 150
Problem Solving Theatre, 72
Protagonist-centered sociodrama, 45
Psychodrama, 5, 97
Psychotherapy, 6

Questions, director to group, 98

Rabelais, Francois: Words to the Reader, 160
Realism, 11
Refocusing, 82

Reframing, 98

Resistance, 75, 80

Role: aspects, 4, 102; collective aspects, 5-6, 102-03; private aspects, 5-6, 103; behavior, 161; components, 102; conflict, 48; confusion, 48; creating, 105; current, 47; defining, 101; expansion, 7, 47, 50; exploration, 7, 47; fantasy, 51; fatigue, 48; individual, 5; past, 47; playing (play), 105; psychodramatic, 104; psychosomatic, 103; rehearsal, 7, 50-51; relationships, 47; repertoire, 50, 53, 159; reversal, 55, 68; social, 104; taking, 105; theory, 101; therapeutic assignment, 160

Role training, 5, 21, 23, 125, 153; facilitating goal of, 74

Scene setting, 45

Sculpting, 8, 67, 69

Self-control, 77, 80

Self-esteem, 160

Shakespeare, William: A Midsummer Night's Dream, 109; As You Like It, 11; Hamlet, 53, 161; The Tempest, 122-123

Shared central issue, 5, 17, 25, 37, 40, 42, 115

Sharing, 4, 19, 81, 86, 92, 96; experiences, 82; modeling, 99

Social action, 148, 150

Social barometer, 116

Social skills, 156

Sociodrama: definition, 3; history of, 8, 147

Sociogram, 114

Sociometry, 98-111, 112

Soliloquy, 8, 62

Spectrogram, 115

Spontaneity, 92, 107; pathological, 108; restoring, 158; stereotyped, 108; training, 111; true, 108

Stanislavski, Konstantin, 11; The Method, 11

St. Elizabeth's Hospital, 41

Strindberg, August, 11

Structuring action, 55

surplus reality, 55, 124

Team building, 142

Techniques (of sociodrama), 8, 55; aside, 63; concretization, 66; doubling, 59; empty chair, 61; freeze frame, 65; future projection, 68; mirror, 67; role reversal, 55; sculpting, 67; soliloquy, 62; walk and talk, 64

Theatre, sociodrama in: actor training, 124; auditioning, 125; creating plays, 120; directing, 122; dramatic literature, 125; rehearsal process, 122; theatre arts, 119; theatre arts education, 119, 123; TIE (Theatre in Education), 119, 126

Theatre of Spontaneity, 10, 12, 147, 153

Theory of roles, 101

Theory of sociometry, 112

Theory of spontaneity, 107

Thurber, James, 104

Training: business and professions, 139; executives and administrators, 139; personnel, 138; staff, 140

Twain, Mark: The Prince and the Pauper, 132

Underpinnings, 101

Vallins, Gordon, 119

Walk and talk, 8, 64

Ward, Winifred, 7, 127

Warm-up, 4, 15

Warm-ups: affective, 16-17; balloons, 159; circle exclusion, 151; cognitive, 16-17; cohesive groups, 31; common denominator, 30; concretization, 159; designing, 25, 34-35; dialogue, 32; fantasy, 159; fill in the blanks, 161; getting-to-know-you, 29-30; headlines, 30-31; isolation, 157; masks, 145; name games, 28-29; pass the face, 145; please—no, 162; silent scream, 162; spin the bottle, 158; structured, 17, 25; terminating groups, 33; unstructured, 17, 25

Whodunit Mystery Weekend, 50

ABOUT THE AUTHORS AND CONTRIBUTORS

PATRICIA STERNBERG, Registered Drama Therapist (R.D.T.), is a Professor of Theatre and Film at Hunter College in New York City, where she heads the Developmental Drama program. She teaches courses in sociodrama, drama therapy, creative drama, children's theatre, and theatre in education, and also directs the Hunter College Mad Hatters—a group of college students who perform for young audiences. Professor Sternberg is an author and playwright with more than twenty-five plays produced and five published. *Sociodrama* is her seventh book. Others include *Be My Friend: The Art of Good Relationships, On Stage: How to Put on a Play,* and *Learning Through Drama in the Classroom.* She is also a practicing drama therapist and works with psychiatric patients, substance abuse groups, and emotionally disturbed children and adolescents.

ANTONINA GARCIA, a Registered Drama Therapist, is also certified as a Trainer, Educator, and Practitioner (T.E.P.) by the American Board of Examiners in Psychodrama, Sociometry and Group Psychotherapy and is Chairperson of that Board. She is a Fellow of the American Society of Group Psychotherapy and Psychodrama and is Past President of the New Jersey Chapter of that organization. Dr. Garcia is a Professor and the Coordinator of the Creative Arts in Therapeutic Settings Option at Brookdale Community College in Lincroft, New Jersey, where she teaches courses in sociodrama, psychodrama, creative arts therapy, and theatre. She also maintains a private practice and trains nationally and internationally.

ADAM BLATNER, M.D., T.E.P., and **ALLEE BLATNER** are coauthors of *The Art of Play: An Adult's Guide to Reclaiming Imagination and Spontaneity.* Adam is also author of *Acting In* and *Foundations of Psychodrama.* Adam Blatner is a child psychiatrist on the faculty of the University of Louisville School of Medicine.

DALE RICHARD BUCHANAN, M.S., is a T.E.P., certified by the American Board of Examiners in Psychodrama, Sociometry and Group Psychotherapy. He is Director, Clinical Therapy Branch, Commission on Mental Health for the District of Columbia, St. Elizabeth's Campus, Washington, D.C.

MADELEINE BYRNES, M.A., is a psychodrama director in private practice and a member of the Toronto Center for Psychodrama Collective. She is a founder of Sponte.

G. MAX CLAYTON, Th.D., T.E.P., is Director of the Australian College of Psychodrama; Director of Training in Psychodrama Institutes in Sydney, Australia, Auckland and Christchurch, New Zealand; Secretary, Board of Examiners, and distinguished member of the Australian and New Zealand Psychodrama Association.

LINDA GREGORIC COOK, R.D.T., is a Speech/Drama Coordinator, Arts in Education, New Orleans Public Schools and Drama Therapist, CPC Coliseum Medical Center, New Orleans, Louisiana.

ABEL K. FINK, Ed.D., T.E.P., is Professor of Educational Foundations, State University College of New York at Buffalo.

ANN E. HALE, M.A., T.E.P., is Founder and President, Northwest Action Methods Training Institute in Seattle, Washington, and Blue Ridge Human Relations Training Institute in Roanoke, Virginia.

MARCIA KARP and **KEN SPRAGUE** are Codirectors of the Holwell Center for Psychodrama and Sociodrama, East Down, Barnstaple, Devon, England.

ROSALIE MINKIN, M.S.W., A.T.R. (Art Therapist Registered), T.E.P., is a consultant at Temple University's Institute on Aging, Center for Intergenerational Learning. She is also an adjunct faculty member in the Social Work Department at California State University, Long Beach.

ZERKA T. MORENO, widow of J. L. Moreno, grew up with the Moreno Institute from its inception. She is Honorary President of the American Society of Group Psychotherapy and Psychodrama, and Honorary Member of the

Board of Directors of the International Association of Group Psychotherapy. Internationally known as a lecturer, teacher, and trainer, she coauthored *Psychodrama, Volumes II* and *III* with J. L. Moreno and *The First Psychodramatic Family* with J. L. Moreno and son Jonathan Moreno, and has authored numerous other articles.

WARREN PARRY is a T.E.P. in sociodrama and a psychodrama director in Australia. He was formerly the Director of Training at the Wasley Centre in Perth. He has specialized in the development of clinical, community, and organizational forms of sociodrama over the last twelve years. He is currently writing handbooks for trainees on this subject.

BARRY STEVENS is an actor and writer based in Toronto. He is a former mental health worker and a founding member of the Sponte theatre collective.

DAVID F. SWINK, M.A., T.E.P., is President of Action Training Institute. He has created hundreds of training programs for such organizations as the U.S. Senate, the State Department, the Secret Service, law enforcement agencies, universities, and corporations.